THE
SECOND COMING
OF JESUS THE
MESSIAH

THE
SECOND COMING
OF JESUS THE
MESSIAH

E. KEITH HOWICK

WindRiver Publishing
St. George, Utah

Queries, comments or correspondence concerning this work should be directed to the author and submitted to WindRiver Publishing at:

authors@windriverpublishing.com

Information regarding this work and other works published by WindRiver Publishing Inc., and instructions for submitting manuscripts for review for publication, can be found at:

www.windriverpublishing.com

Library of Congress Control Number: 2003102367
ISBN 1-886249-04-0

First Printing, 2003

Printed on acid-free paper by Malloy, Inc., Ann Arbor MI, the United States of America

Dedicated to the memory of:

Mahonri Carter Howick
Vera Martha Lythgoe Howick
Bonnie Howick Treglown
Carter Jay Howick

Robert Carlyle Braithwaite
Robert Glenn Braithwaite
J. Alden Braithwaite

and

Jeanne Braithwaite Finlinson

who have gone before and await His glorious return.

Key to Abbreviations

Abbreviation	Name of Work
AC	Lucien Carr, *American Commonwealths, Missouri, A Bone of Contention* (Boston and New York: Haughton, Mifflin and Company, 1896).
AGQ	Joseph Fielding Smith, *Answers To Gospel Questions,* Vol. 1 (Salt Lake City: Deseret Book Company, 1959).
AIC	*Arab-Israeli Conflict* (St. Paul, Minnesota: Greenhaven Press, Inc., 1979).
CC	Will Durant, *The Story of Civilization,* Vol. 3 *Ceasar and Christ* (New York: MJF Books, npd).
CE	*New Catholic Encyclopedia* Vol. IV (Washington D.C.: The Catholic University of America, 1967).
CHCC	Thomas Bokenkotter, *A Concise History of the Catholic Church,* rev. ed. (Garden City, New York: Image Books, 1979).
CL	Gerald N. Lund, *The Coming of the Lord* (Salt Lake City, Utah: Bookcraft, 1986).
DNTC	Bruce R. McConkie, *Doctrinal New Testament Commentary,* Vol. 1, *The Gospels* (Salt Lake City: Bookcraft, 1975).
DS	Joseph Fielding Smith, *Doctrines of Salvation* Comp. Bruce R. McConkie, 3 Vols. (Salt Lake City: Bookcraft, 1954).

Ed	Alfred Edersheim, *The Life and Times of Jesus the Messiah,* reprint ed. (Grand Rapids, Michigan: Wm. B. Eerdmans Publishing Company, 1981).
ER	John A. Widtsoe, *Evidences and Reconciliations* (Salt Lake City: Bookcraft, 1967).
Farrar	Frederic W. Farrar, *The Life of Christ,* 2 Vols. (New York: E. P. Dutton and Company, 1874).
FM	Thomas L. Snead, *The Fight For Missouri* (New York: Charles Scribner's Sons, 1888).
Geikie	Cunningham Geikie, *The Life and Words of Christ,* 2 Vols. (Vol 1, London: Cassell & Company, Limited, 1885)(Vol 2, London: Hodder and Stronghton, 1883).
GM	Golda Meir, *My Life by Golda Meir,* First American Edition (New York: G.P. Putnam's Sons, 1975).
GRF	Grant R. Jeffrey, *Armageddon Appointment with Destiny* (NY: Bantam Books, July 1990).
HC	Joseph Smith, Jr., *History of The Church of Jesus Christ of Latter-day Saints,* ed. B.H. Roberts, 7 Vols. (Salt Lake City: The Church of Jesus Christ of Latter-day Saints, 1955).
IDYK	LeGrand Richards, *Israel! Do You Know?* (Salt Lake City: Deseret Book Company, npd).

JD	*Journal of Discourses*, 26 Vols. (Liverpool: F.D. Richards, Latter-day Saints' Book Depot, 1855-1886).
Jerusalem	Jill & Leon Uris, *Jerusalem* (Garden City: Doubleday & Company, Inc., 1981).
Josephus	Flavius Josephus, *Josephus: Complete Works*, trans. William Whiston (Grand Rapids: Kregel Publications, 1971).
MD	Bruce R. McConkie, *Mormon Doctrine* (Salt Lake City: Bookcraft, 1966).
Mill M	Bruce R. McConkie, *The Millennial Messiah* (Salt Lake City: Deseret Book Company, 1982).
Miracles	E. Keith Howick, *The Miracles of Jesus the Messiah* (Salt Lake City: Bookcraft, 1985).
Mission	E. Keith Howick, *The Mission of Jesus the Messiah* (Salt Lake City: Bookcraft, 1990).
MM	Bruce R. McConkie, *The Mortal Messiah*, 4 Vols. (Salt Lake City: Deseret Book Company, 1979-81).
OJ	Larry Collins & Dominique LaPierre, *O Jerusalem!* (New York: Simon and Schuster, 1972).
Parables	E. Keith Howick, *The Parables of Jesus the Messiah* (Salt Lake City: Bookcraft, 1986).

Sermons   E. Keith Howick, *The Sermons of Jesus
                   the Messiah* (Salt Lake City: Bookcraft,
                   1987).

Smith's   William Smith, LLD, *Smith's Bible
                   Dictionary* Rev. F.N. & M.A. Peloubet
                   (Nashville: Thomas Nelson, 1962).

Torah   *The Torah A Modern Commentary,*
                   Edited by W. Gunther Plaut, (New
                   York: Union of American Hebrew
                   Congregations, 1981).

TPJS   Joseph Smith, Jr., *Teachings of the
                   Prophet Joseph Smith,* sel. Joseph
                   Fielding Smith (Salt Lake City: Deseret
                   Book Company, 1958).

WW   Matthias F. Cowley, *Wilford Woodruff*
                   (Salt Lake City: Bookcraft, 1986).

WTB   Rodney Barker, *And The Waters Turned
                   To Blood* (New York: Simon and
                   Schuster, 1997).

Contents

Introduction 1

Part One: The Signs Begin 7

   "All These Are the Beginning of Sorrows" 9

      The First Signs of the Second
      Coming: A.D. 33 to A.D. 70 9

   The Great Apostasy 16

      A.D. 70 to A.D. 325 16

   The Times of the Gentiles 23

      A.D. 325 to A.D. 1820 23

      The Covenant of Abraham 23

Part Two: The Latter Days 33

   The Restoration 35

   Judah 44

      Signs of the Second Coming
      Pertaining to Judah That Have
      Been Fulfilled 45

      Future Signs to Judah 50

   The Gathering 58

Part Three: Babylon 71

   The Devil and His Kingdom 73

      Who Is the Devil? 73

      The Devil's Past 74

      The Devil's Presence in the
      Latter Days 76

      The Devil's Future 79

      The Antichrist Beast 83

The Devil and His Kingdom–Continued 88

  The Second Beast 88

  The Woman. 95

  The End of the Devil's Kingdom 104

Part Four: Difficult Times 111

  Signs: Both General and Specific 113

    As in the Days of Noah. 115

    The Good-Times Sin 116

    The Effect of Signs on Mankind 121

    The Changing of the Times
    and Seasons 124

  Signs: The Earth's Three Phases 127

    The Earth. 127

    Phase One—Tumults That Will
    Occur to the Earth 128

    Phase Two—The Physical Cleansing
    of the Earth 129

    The Opening of the Seventh Seal 130

    Phase Three—The Earth Returns
    to Its Paradisiacal Glory 149

  Signs: Increased Devastations. 154

    The Desolating Scourge 154

    Wars and Rumors of War 157

    The Hailstorm 160

    The Nations 161

  Six Signs: Beginning with the Church 165

    Beginning with the Church 165

    The 144,000 170

The Last Laborers 172

The Heavens......................... 173

The Rainbow 175

Adam-ondi-Ahman................... 176

Part Five: The End Draweth Nigh.................... 179

The Three Cities 181

The City of Enoch 183

The City of Zion..................... 186

The City of Jerusalem 192

The Coming of the Lord 198

The Great and Terrible Day
of the Lord 198

The Lord Delayeth His Coming 201

When Will the Lord Come? 203

The Bridegroom Cometh 210

The Sign of the Son of Man 211

Dressed in Red 212

Judgment 216

Judgment in the Preexistence........... 216

Judgment on Earth 218

Judgment at Death................... 224

Judgment at the Second Coming........ 225

Delegated Judgment 226

Millennial Peace, War, and Resurrection........ 230

Millennial Judgment 230

The Little Season of Judgment and War.. 234

The Resurrection 238

The Final Judgment................... 240

Conclusion 243

Notes 249

Subject Index 259

Scripture Index................................. 267

Introduction

"And the glory of the Lord shall be revealed, and all flesh shall see it together: for the mouth of the Lord hath spoken it."

Isaiah 40:5

There are two major prophesied events in scripture: the Savior's First Coming to the house of Israel and his Second Coming to the world. All the prophecies of his First Coming were fulfilled in his birth, his ministry, his Atonement, his death on the cross, and his resurrection from the tomb. Just as those prophecies were fulfilled, so will the prophecies of his Second Coming be fulfilled. His First Coming is historical fact: his Second Coming a future reality. It only remains for us to know and recognize the signs of his coming and to be prepared to meet him when he comes.

One of the most interesting facts about the Lord's First Coming is that he came to the very people who were specifically looking for him—yet they missed him! Their writings contained numerous prophecies of his Advent and they knew of the great miracles he was expected to perform,[1] but when he came, fulfilled the prophecies, and performed the miracles, they still did

Jason Sperber

not acknowledge him as their Messiah. Why? Because they wanted a *different* Messiah than the one their prophets had foretold.[2]

> What they waited for, was a Kingdom of God— not in righteousness, joy, and peace in the Holy Ghost, but in meat and drink—a kingdom with miraculous wilderness-banquets to Israel, and coarse miraculous triumphs over the Gentiles. Not to speak of the fabulous Messianic banquet which a sensuous realism expected, or of the achievements for which it looked, every figure in which prophets had clothed the brightness of those days was first liberalized, and then exaggerated, till the most glorious poetic descriptions became the most repulsive incongruous caricatures of spiritual Messianic expectancy. The fruit-trees were every day, or at least every week or two, to yield their riches, the fields their harvest; the grain was to stand like palm trees, and to be reaped and winnowed without labour. Similar blessings were to visit the vine; ordinary trees would bear like fruit trees, and every produce, of every clime, would be found in Palestine in such abundance and luxuriance as only the wildest imagination could conceive.[3]

The Jews during Christ's ministry did not question his ability, but they constantly questioned his claim to the messiahship. "Show us a sign," they repeatedly demanded even though they had seen many signs. But the sign they wanted was the *messianic sign of the Son of Man*, a sign that would not be given until the Lord's Second Coming—and then not just to Israel, but to the world.

The messianic sign of the Son of Man is the sign we look for today. However, if we do not prepare ourselves any better than the Jews of old and learn to recognize the signs that will precede this final sign, we, like them, may also look beyond the mark and either miss his coming or be unprepared for it. "Pray always," the Lord cautions, "that you enter not into temptation, that you may abide the day of [my] coming, whether in life or in death" (D&C 61:39). This warning is clear, yet daily life seems to dull even the vigilant to the realities of prophecy. Somehow the devastating events that are prophesied are always in the future and will always happen to someone else, never us. Things that happen to us are explained away by science or by the inherent nature of things. At times we do not attribute them to God's authorship, at other times we attribute everything to him—either conclusion masking the recognition of the looked for signs. The Lord warned the Apostles that such would be the case as his Second Coming approached (see Matthew 24). He knew that the signs of his Coming would be treated as prophecy and as warnings were viewed in the days of Noah—people were "marrying and giving in marriage," just doing the normal, everyday things of life. Just as the antediluvians did not anticipate the Flood, the clear inference is that latter-day humankind will either not be looking for the Lord's Second Coming or they will be looking for the wrong things, and thus be unprepared when he comes.

Jesus himself prophesied that when he again comes, "two [will] be in the field; the one shall be taken, and the other left. Two women shall be grinding at the mill; the one shall be taken, and the other left. Watch therefore," he cautions, "for ye know not what hour your Lord doth come" (Matthew 24:40–42). To "watch" in this scriptural warning means to be prepared, spiritually prepared, to recognize and welcome the signs of the Second Coming.

Prophecies of the Lord's Second Coming are scattered throughout the scriptures: some are clear and easy to understand, others are couched in poetry or parabolic stories, and many are disguised with symbolic representations that make them difficult to identify. They were all recorded by prophets who were eagerly looking forward to the end of the world, to a time when all sin would cease and the Messiah would come and reign in peace and love.

The Second Coming of Jesus the Messiah is divided into five parts and sixteen chapters. The signs of the Second Coming are grouped into logical and descriptive categories and are presented topically and chronologically. Their classification and organization are mine. In any work describing prophecy (both fulfilled and unfulfilled), considerable interpretation is required. I therefore take full responsibility for the interpretation of the prophetic utterances reviewed in this book.

This text also contains material dealing with the Millennium, judgment, resurrection, the "little season," and the battles of Gog and Magog. While these topics do not deal specifically with the Second Coming (except for the first battle of Gog and Magog, called Armageddon), I felt they must be discussed in order to complete the Lord's involvement in his Father's plan of salvation.

The signs of the Second Coming began shortly after the Lord's resurrection. Some of them, such as the destruction of Jerusalem and the demolition of the temple, took place during the lifetime of some of his Apostles. The Lord himself prophesied of these momentous events and described them in words I have used as the title of chapter 1: "All These Are the Beginning of Sorrows" (Matthew 24:8). Thereafter, other signs of his future Advent occurred intermittently throughout the centuries, continuing through "The Great Apostasy" and "The Times of the Gentiles." These initial signs of Christ's Advent culminated in the Restoration of the gospel, which commenced the signs given for the latter days.

The initial signs of the latter days are dealt with in the chapters entitled "The Restoration," "Judah," and "The Gathering." Part 3 of my book, entitled "Babylon," deals specifically with such subjects as the devil's powerful influence over the people of the world throughout history, his evil latter-day kingdom, and his kingdom's final destruction. The cities of Enoch, Jerusalem, and Zion, and the roles they play in the signs of the Second Coming, are discussed in the chapter entitled "The Three Cities." Multiple signs, symbolically envisioned by John in the book of Revelation (some general and some specific), are dealt with throughout the text. The "great and dreadful day of the Lord" and the tribulations associated with the devastations that will occur prior to that day are discussed in Parts 4 and 5. The *time* of the Savior's coming will be examined and his actual Advent discussed; however, the exact *date* of his coming remains unknown.

Although this text deals almost exclusively with scriptural prophecies of the Second Coming, some quotations from other knowledgeable sources are used when it was determined that they added historical perspicacity. It is hoped that this work will give the reader insight into the signs, events, and scriptures that deal with the Lord's Advent. Its main purpose is to glorify and magnify the Savior and bring the signs of his Second Coming to our awareness so that we will be prepared to meet our God.

The fault of almost every generation in their eager anticipation of the Lord's Advent is that they try to force a current or historical event to fit a prophesied one. This is understandable, since it is often difficult to recognize a sign as it unfolds. But recognizing each and every sign when it occurs is not as important as being personally prepared to meet the Savior when he comes—"whether in life or in death" (D&C 50:5). Isaiah emphasized this message when he pled with Israel, "O house of Jacob, come ye, and let us walk in the light of the Lord" (Isaiah 2:5).

The many signs of the Lord's coming are clearly prophesied in scripture. These signs were given so that we will anticipate, understand, and recognize what will occur in the future, and they warn us to be prepared. They will help keep the righteous righteous and leave the wicked without excuse. May we heed Isaiah's cry and be vigilant, watching for the signs of Christ's coming, for as the Lord warns in Luke, "when ye see these things come to pass, know ye that the kingdom of God is nigh at hand" (Luke 21:31), even at the door!

Part One

The Signs Begin

"And Jesus left them, and went upon the Mount of Olives. And as he sat upon the Mount of Olives, the disciples came unto him privately, saying: Tell us when shall these things be which thou hast said concerning the destruction of the temple, and the Jews; and what is the sign of thy coming, and of the end of the world, or the destruction of the wicked, which is the end of the world?"

Joseph Smith–Matthew 1:4

"All These Are the Beginning of Sorrows"

> "For then, in those days, shall be great tribulation on the Jews, and upon the inhabitants of Jerusalem, such as was not before sent upon Israel, of God, since the beginning of their kingdom until this time."
>
> **Joseph Smith–Matthew 1:18**

The First Signs of the Second Coming: A.D. 33 to A.D. 70

The Lord's final public discourse was delivered in Jerusalem during the last week of his mortal ministry. It was a scathing denunciation of both the leaders and the people of Judah (see Matthew 23),[1] and he made it clear that he no longer claimed the great temple of Herod as *his* temple. He had withdrawn his approval of that magnificent edifice.[2]

At the completion of this powerful discourse a little party of disciples, with Jesus at their head, left the temple sanctuary and headed out of the city. When they were on the Mount of Olives, the Savior turned to the Apostles and made a stunning prophecy: the temple, the very symbol of Israel as the chosen people, would be destroyed! In fact, its destruction would be so complete that not one stone would be left standing on another (see Matthew 24:2). The Apostles were astonished: "Tell us, when shall these things be?" they asked, "and what shall be the sign of thy coming, and of the end of the world?" (Matthew 24:3.)

Instead of answering these questions directly, the Lord substituted a moral lesson (as was his habit). "Take heed," he cautioned, "that no man deceive you" (Matthew 24:4). He then prophesied of disturbing events that would occur before his Second Coming—in the immediate future (during the lifetime of the Apostles) and the latter days.

Almost every prophet that lived prior to the time of Jesus had prophesied of the Savior's First Coming so that each ensuing generation would anticipate it. They had also prophesied of his Second Coming, and the Lord, while yet in the flesh, further described some of the signs of his future Advent. The first of these signs would begin soon after his ascension (between the years of A.D. 33 and A.D. 70) so that every generation thereafter would anticipate his Second Coming just as prior generations had looked for his First. The Lord's prophecies were like those of other prophets: some were specific while others were general, some were personal while some were given to all Israel, some were intended to build faith and belief while some were meant as a warning. The Lord forewarned mankind that all of these prophecies and intense warnings of devastation and destruction would not mark the end—they were merely "the beginning of sorrows" (Matthew 24:8).

The Savior's initial prophecies can be divided into six categories:

1. *Prophecies Regarding the Apostles:*   Prior to his ascension, the Lord charged his Apostles to preach the gospel to the people of every nation, "baptizing them in the name of the Father, and of the Son, and of the Holy Ghost" (Matthew 28:19). He had previously warned these brethren that although their preaching would bring much individual joy and salvation, they would be scourged from synagogue to synagogue by the Jewish councils and would be delivered "up to be afflicted," killed, and "hated of all nations" for the Lord's name's sake (Matthew 24:9-10). The Savior further prophesied that "whosoever killeth you will think that he doeth God service" (John 16:2). Just as the Jewish leaders had perse-

cuted him, so too would they persecute the Apostles (see John 15:20).

But the Apostles still anticipated that the Lord would return in the immediate future and reign over his earthly kingdom—a conclusion that is unquestionably due to the tone of the Lord's instructions in Matthew. It was not to be so, however, as will be seen from the many signs and warnings that Jesus gave to teach them that his coming was far in the future (see Matthew 24:6).

2. *False Christs and False Prophets:* Jesus warned the Apostles that many false prophets and false Christs would arise after his death, and he cautioned them not to be deceived (see Matthew 24:4–5, 11,24). Israel had been led astray by such charlatans in the past; Jeremiah recounted such defection during his lifetime as one of the sins that caused the captivity of Israel. The false prophets had preached that Israel's sins and iniquitous ways were justified, and the wayward people had believed them (see Jeremiah 28).

The Savior prophesied that this situation would repeat itself, as later proven in several New Testament scriptures.[3] And the Jewish historian Josephus recorded that several of these seducers came before the destruction of Jerusalem.[4] But the Lord, through Jeremiah, declared: "I have not sent these [false] prophets, yet they ran: I have not spoken to them, yet they prophesied" (Jeremiah 23:21).

False Messiahs appeared before and after Christ. "Scores of rabbis, holy men, warriors, scholars and scribes stepped forth to claim they were the fulfillment" of the Messianic prophesies. Perhaps the most famous of these men was Simon Bar Kochba. He led the last revolt of organized Judaism against Rome between A.D. 132–35. He was declared to be the Messiah by Akiva, "the greatest rabbi of the era"[5] (see also Words of Mormon 1:15).

3. *Wars, Famines, and Pestilence:* Between A.D. 33 and A.D. 70, Israel was involved in multiple wars with Rome.[6] Nation did rise up against nation,[7] and famines, pestilence, and earthquakes have always been with us. However, the claims of false Messiahs, as well as violent political disturbances, would soon lead to the destruction of Jerusalem, Herod's amazing temple, and Israel as a nation.

4. Prophecies Regarding Jerusalem: Christ prophesied that the mighty city of Jerusalem would be destroyed. He wept over its fate (see Luke 19:41). "O Jerusalem, Jerusalem . . . how often would I have gathered thy children together, even as a hen gathereth her chickens under her wings, and ye would not! Behold, [as a result] your house is left unto you desolate" (Matthew 23:37–38).

The Savior warned the Jews that their enemies would "cast a trench about [them], and compass [them] round, and keep [them] in on every side" (Luke 19:43). They and their children would be killed and the temple would not have one stone left on another after the conflict (see Luke 19). This devastation would be in the lifetime of some of the Apostles. The Jews rebelled against Rome: Titus, a Roman general, laid siege to the city for seven months, keeping it "in on every side" until he finally conquered it.[8] The siege produced unbearable famine and overwhelming destruction. Josephus, an eyewitness inside Jerusalem during the siege, recorded that the relentless famine caused one woman to kill her own child, cook it, eat half herself, and offer the other half to some defending soldiers. They were appalled, refused the offer, and left her to her own destruction.[9] The Lord warned the Apostles and all who would listen to them to flee to the mountains for protection when they saw these things coming, for this great tribulation would be a fulfillment of the prophet Daniel's "abomination of desolation" (see Daniel 9:27; 11:31; 12:11; Matthew 24:15). The Israelites would be destroyed as a nation and dispersed out of God's sight because of their abominable sins, and the results would be the desolation of both Jerusalem and the kingdom of Judah.

5. Prophecies Regarding the Temple and Daily Sacrifice: Here the Lord was very specific. Herod's temple would be totally destroyed. The heathen army would desecrate it and sack its contents, and the once holy edifice would not have one stone left standing on another. This magnificent structure—requiring more than forty years to build, of which it was said, "He that has not seen the Temple of Herod, has never known what beauty is"[10]— would simply cease to exist (Matthew 24:2; Mark 13:2; Luke 21:6).[11]

The temple was the center of Judaism—the heart of the Law of Moses—and no ceremonies or sacrifices could be performed without it. Daniel foresaw the end of the daily sacrifice (the functional symbol of Israel's God and her anticipated Messiah) when he wrote, "And in the midst of the week he [the conquering prince of Rome] shall cause the sacrifice and the oblation to cease, and for the overspreading of abominations he shall make it desolate" (Daniel 9:27).

With the cessation of sacrifice came the end of all "oblations" (the religious symbols of Jewish worship). Israel had rejected her Messiah—he for whom they looked in all they did. Christ had fulfilled the law and it was no longer the correct method of worshiping God. Judah had rejected the Lord's covenant, anciently made with Abraham and renewed with Israel, by rejecting the God who gave it. It had given them a promised land and had made them custodians of the priesthood, with the responsibility to be "perfect" (see Genesis 17:1) and to help fulfill the Father's purpose of bringing "to pass the immortality and eternal life of man" (Moses 1:39), by taking the gospel, the plan of salvation, to all the world. But now, until the time of the Second Coming, Judah (the successor to the lost tribe of Levi) would not have the priesthood of God as her authority to act. There would be no promised land for Judah until prophecy regarding the latter days began to be fulfilled, and they would not have the blessing of taking salvation to the world. Yet they would remain the chosen people, for God would not break his covenant even though Israel had rejected him. And because of this rejection, Israel would receive the prophesied results—they would be scattered among all nations (Amos 9:8–9).

6. *The Scattering of Israel:* Solomon was the last king of united Israel. He was a great king, but had worshiped false gods. The Lord was angry with him and sent the prophet Ahijah to pronounce judgment upon his kingdom. Ten tribes of Israel would be taken from Solomon (and his successors) and given to Jeroboam an Ephraimite (see 1 Kings 11:31). These tribes formed the Kingdom of Israel, or the Northern Kingdom. They were: Reuben, Simeon, Levi (the majority of Levi lived in the Northern Kingdom), Dan, Naphtali, Gad, Asher, Issachar, Zebulun, and Joseph (Ephraim and Manasseh).

Solomon, who was near death when the kingdom was divided, was left with the single tribe of Judah (see 1 Kings 11:36); Benjamin, who was originally aligned with the ten tribes, soon shifted its allegiance to Solomon because of its close proximity to Jerusalem. There were also individual members of the other tribes (including Ephraim and Manasseh) living in Jerusalem at the time of the division (see 1 Kings 12:17, 21–23).[12]

The scattering of Israel began in approximately 721 B.C. with the destruction of the ten tribes. These tribes were conquered by Assyria, taken into captivity, and *lost*. The remnants of the lost tribes living in the kingdom of Judah eventually became known as Jews. It was from these remnants that Lehi (a Manassite [see Alma 10:3]) and Ishmael (an Ephraimite)[13] were called by the Lord and led to the Western Hemisphere. The next major scattering occurred around 570 B.C. when the Babylonians conquered the Kingdom of Judah and destroyed Jerusalem. From these two general scatterings of Israel, two tribes remained identifiable: Judah and Joseph (Ephraim and Manasseh). The other ten tribes—Reuben, Simeon, Levi, Dan, Naphtali, Gad, Asher, Issachar, Zebulun, and Benjamin—remained lost.

Moses foresaw the scattering of Israel and prophesied: "And the Lord shall scatter you among the nations, and ye shall be left few in number among the heathen, whither the Lord shall lead you" (Deuteronomy 4:27). The final scattering of Israel took place in A.D. 70 when the Roman general Titus conquered and destroyed Jerusalem. Jeremiah and Ezekiel described the first destruction of Jerusalem and scattering of Judah, but their words also have double reference to the scattering that occurred after Titus's successful campaign. Jeremiah recorded that the Lord would "scatter [Judah] . . . among the heathen, whom neither they nor their fathers have known" (Jeremiah 9:16). Ezekiel elaborated:

> And I [the Lord] will scatter toward every wind
> all that are about him [the tribe of Judah and any
> of the rest of Israel that are with it] to help him,
> and all his bands; and I will draw out the sword
> after them.

> And they shall know that I am the Lord, when I shall scatter them among the nations, and disperse them in the countries.
>
> But I will leave a few men of them from the sword, from the famine, and from the pestilence; that they may declare all their abominations among the heathen whither they come; and they shall know that I am the Lord (Ezekiel 12:14–16).

And Nephi prophesied that the people of Judah would be "scourged by all people . . . wander in the flesh . . . become a hiss and a by-word, and be hated among all nations" (1 Nephi 19:13–14), because they had crucified the God of Israel.

In the book of Zechariah, the Lord described *righteous* Israel as the "apple of his eye" (Zechariah 2:8), but her subsequent wickedness provoked the Lord, and in the book of 1 Nephi he compared her to "an olive-tree, whose branches [would] be broken off and scattered upon all the face of the earth" (1 Nephi 10:12).

The remnants of the tribe of Joseph on the Western Hemisphere was never further scattered because its existence was unknown to the tribe of Judah and the Gentiles. Nevertheless, in time, these people also fell into total apostasy. The righteous among them were destroyed and the wicked remnant completely rejected the covenant of Abraham. The priesthood was also withdrawn along with their right to a promised land.

With the scattering of Israel complete, the first prophesied signs of the Second Coming (between A.D. 33 and A.D. 70) were fulfilled. Jerusalem was no longer the center of God's law, for with remarkable clarity the prophet Zechariah prophesied: "Behold, I will make Jerusalem a cup of trembling unto all the people round about . . . and in that day [the latter days] will I make Jerusalem a burdensome stone for all people" (Zechariah 12:2–3). Jerusalem today is one of the most volatile spots in the world, and thus it will remain until the Lord's Second Coming.

The Great Apostasy

"And he gave some, apostles; and some, prophets. For the perfecting of the saints, for the work of the ministry, for the edifying of the body of Christ."

Ephesians 4:11-12

A.D. 70 to A.D. 325

"Go ye therefore, and teach all nations, baptizing them in the name of the Father, and of the Son, and of the Holy Ghost: Teaching them to observe all things whatsoever I have commanded you: and, lo, I am with you alway, even unto the end of the world. Amen" (Matthew 28:19–20; see also Mark 16:15–16). With this commission to his Apostles given prior to his ascension, Christ called for the establishment of his church upon the earth. Bolstered by their witness of the Lord's resurrection, the Apostles enthusiastically began their ministry by preaching salvation "at Jerusalem" (Luke 24:47). Because Jesus had declared that he had been sent to "the lost sheep of the house of Israel" and not to the world at large (Matthew 15:24),[1] the Apostles primarily taught the Jews in their synagogues and in their public places[2]—and their initial labors were rewarded by about three thousand souls being added to the Church (see Acts 2:41).

"For a time the Church remained completely Jewish, a sect within Israel of those who believed in the resurrection of Jesus and regarded him as the promised Messiah who was about to come again to definitively establish the reign of God."[3] But with the conversion of Cornelius, a Gentile (see Acts 10), Peter recognized that the gospel was to be expanded far beyond those of Judah's linage. And when Paul was aggressively rejected by the Jews in Corinth, he "shook his raiment, and said unto them, Your blood be upon your own heads; I am clean: from henceforth I will go unto the Gentiles" (Acts 18:6).

The early Church spread rapidly, but with growth came dissension, disagreement, and division. The Apostles knew from the Lord's teachings that his Advent would not be soon, and they prophesied that the fledgling church would not survive until he came again. Peter was the first to make this prophecy as he and John spoke to the Jews in the temple at Jerusalem. He chastised them for rejecting Christ and called them to repentance, declaring that although Jesus had preached to them in the flesh, he had now been received into heaven "until the times of *restitution* of all things" (Acts 3:21; emphasis added). But to have a "restitution of all things" requires that a falling away must take place first.

The anticipation of Christ's immediate return grew as the gospel spread throughout the people. Without dampening the spirit generated by the desire to again receive the Lord, Paul wrote to the Thessalonians and with firm resolve instructed them concerning Christ's Second Coming. "Be not soon shaken in mind . . ." he cautioned, "for that day shall not come, except there come a falling away first, and that man of sin [the devil] be revealed" (2 Thessalonians 2:2–3). Paul was making it clear to the Thessalonians that the day of Christ's coming was *not* near: on this point they should not be deceived by "any means." The Second Coming would not take place until after the devil had caused an apostasy from the truth. He continued to explain that this was a time when Satan, with all his delusions, would show great "power and signs and lying wonders" (2 Thessalonians 2:9) and would deceive those who did not love the truth (see 2 Thessalonians 2:10–11).

The falling away started early in the Apostles' ministry. Dissension over doctrine and procedure began almost as rapidly as new converts accepted the gospel. As Gentile converts were brought into the Church, the requirements of the Law of Moses and the practice of circumcision became problems. The Jews *knew* they were the chosen people; therefore, they believed that the covenants extended under the Law of Moses could not be given to the Gentiles unless the Gentiles also accepted that Law. But Paul saw the gospel as a liberation from the Law, and so argued (see Acts 13:38–39; Galatians 2:16, 21; 5:1; Philippians 3:8–9).

This was not the only problem, however. Some converts falsely claimed to be Apostles, and they presented a threat to the authority of the Church (see Revelation 2:2). Some Jews thought they had authority over the Christian converts because of their leadership in the Jewish synagogue, but they were condemned by John the Revelator as being of the "synagogue of Satan" (Revelation 2:9). Some even claimed that the eagerly anticipated resurrection of the righteous had already occurred (see 2 Timothy 2:18). Moreover, the purpose of the sacrament (remembrance of the atonement of Christ) was soon distorted (see 1 Corinthians 11:19–22).

The last problem that precipitated the Apostasy was the disappearance of the Apostles. The prophesied persecution of the Twelve began to take its toll early, first with James, who was beheaded by Herod Agrippa I (see Acts 12:2), and then with the rest of the Apostles as they were pursued, persecuted, captured, and killed. The need for the continued presence of the Apostles is best exemplified by Paul, who, after years of absence while preaching the gospel, returned to Jerusalem and met with his fellow brethren to make sure that his teachings were still correct (Galatians 2:2).

As the Apostles proselyted throughout the world, they called local authorities to oversee the newly formed branches of the Church. Since they were able to return to these local branches less and less often before their deaths, it was left to the local leaders to maintain the activity of the members and the doctrinal integrity of the gospel. By approximately A.D. 101, all of the Apostles had either been killed or, in the case of John, taken by the Lord. With no central authority to govern the branches, they were now left to their own devices.

By the middle of the second century, a bishop had been established over each of the surviving church branches;[4] by the end of the second century, without apostolic authority to guide them, the churches had progressed through what has been described as the "development approach" (a system of authority based on the system's developing creed; its hierarchy of bishop, priest, and deacon; and the scriptures).[5] They had rejected the necessity of apostolic authority on the argument that if they (meaning the Apostles) were in charge, why had they disappeared?[6] The bishops rationalized that since they had initially been appointed by the Apostles, they "stood in legitimate succession in a line reaching back to the Apostles themselves"[7] (as well as the protectors of the oral traditions and a developing canon of scripture).

Without central authority, the doctrinal divisions which the Apostles had rectified during their ministry continued to escalate in the fledgling church until even the position of Christ's relationship with the Father was challenged.[8] This internal spiritual conflagration became extensive, but the church had an even greater disruptive influence being generated from without. Rome was the center of the world and had powerful legions to enforce its authority; although the early Christians had experienced short periods of relative peace, almost from the time of the Apostles until the reign of Constantine, Rome persecuted them relentlessly.

One of several stories about Constantine's conversion states that he received a vision of Christ and was told in the vision to ornament his soldiers' shields with the Savior's monogram—the Greek letters *chi* and *rho*. He obliged and then won the battle that made him emperor of all Rome. Another version of his conversion stated that both he and his entire army saw a luminous cross appear in the afternoon sky bearing the message, "in this conquer."[9] According to this account, the vision inspired him to adopt Christ and have a symbolic cross painted on the shields of his troops. In reality, Constantine used both the Christian and pagan religions to solidify his political power, and he did not personally adopt Christianity until his final illness in A.D. 337.[10] Nonetheless, he made Christianity the state religion after his purported conversion, and had a powerful influence on the Christian church. His influence and assistance in resolving doctrinal conflicts within the church completed the apostasy from the truth.

Constantine's determination to unify Christianity resulted in the calling of the Council of Nicaea,[11] where on May 20, A.D. 325

approximately 220 bishops met to resolve their doctrinal differences, regulate authority, and develop a religious creed. The council of Nicaea and the councils that followed after Constantine's death culminated in the Constantinople Council of A.D. 381. Prior to the meeting of these ecumenical councils, however, political factions had elevated the authority of the churches of Rome, Antioch, and Alexandria over that of the other churches. The fourth Canon of the Council of Nicaea declared that these three churches were now the supreme ruling entities of the Christian church. Rome soon became the most prominent among these three because it was (1) the capital of the empire; (2) the possessor of great wealth (and had assisted many of the other churches financially); and (3) reputed historically as the last place Peter and Paul had taught—as well as the place of their martyrdom and burial.[12]

This centralization of authority in Rome eventually developed into the supreme papal authority of Western Christendom. "These powerful papal monarchs . . . controlled a vast ecclesiastical machinery that regulated in minute detail the moral and social behavior of medieval men—kings and princes as well as peasants and townspeople."[13]

After the Constantinople Council of A.D. 381, the remains of the original church vanished and the apostate church "erected a durable structure of authority, a framework of steel that has enabled it to meet every conceivable crises."[14] The controversies over the relationship of God, the Son of God, and the Holy Ghost were resolved into what has become know as the Nicaean Creed.[15] This creed was eventually formalized and adopted into what became known as the Creed of Constantinople.[16]

Paul had prophesied to Timothy that the time would come when "sound doctrine" would not be endured and the truth would be turned into "fables" (see 2 Timothy 4:3–4). By A.D. 381 that time had arrived. Christianity did not succeed in destroying paganism, it simply adopted it![17] Thus, the falling away prophesied by Paul was complete, but the premise upon which the "development approach" of church authority was based was erroneous. The early Church had been organized with Apostles because they were called and ordained by the Lord and given a specific witness of his divinity and his resurrection, with the commission to bear witness of these truths throughout the world. Therefore, the true Church must be founded on an apostolic ministry that has received a personal witness of the divinity of Jesus Christ and a commission to share this witness with the world (see 1 Corinthians 15:5–8; Ephesians 2:20).

That the apostolic call was not to be restricted to the original Twelve was attested to when Matthias was chosen to fill the vacancy in the twelve created by the death of Judas Iscariot (see Acts 1:23–26). Also, the personal witness that Paul received of Christ's divinity and resurrection as he traveled to Damascus prepared him for his apostleship. This same commission has been given in the latter days to the Apostles of the Restoration, thus maintaining the structure of the original Christ-established gospel.[18]

Early in the fourth century, the apostasy of Christianity on the Eastern Hemisphere was progressing toward its apex while the apostasy of the tribes of Joseph on the Western Hemisphere was not far behind. After the Savior appeared to the Western Hemisphere following his resurrection (all of the wicked having been killed during the destruction that occurred when he was crucified [see 3 Nephi 8]), the Church enjoyed two hundred years of peace and righteousness. But by the time those with a personal witness of the Savior had died (with the exception of the three special witnesses), the seeds of apostasy had begun to grow again.

The Saints of the Western Hemisphere did not have the fundamental problems faced by Church members in the East—there were no Gentiles with pagan ways to spread their influence. Instead, sins connected with worldliness opened a chasm that eventually lead to rejection of the gospel, apostasy from the truth, and the total destruction of the righteous. The Book of Mormon testifies that there began to be "pride . . . the wearing of costly apparel . . . [and a desire for] the fine things of the world." The people "began to be divided into classes; and they began to build up churches unto themselves to get gain, and began to deny the true church of Christ" (4 Nephi 1:24, 26). They "wilfully [rebelled] against the gospel of Christ" (4 Nephi 1:38), and became "exceeding wicked" (4 Nephi 1:45). After this it would only take about one hundred years more until the people of the Western Hemisphere would be in total apostasy.

The Old Testament prophet Isaiah foresaw the total apostasy of all the tribes of Israel (see Isaiah 5:3–19). He declared that this apostasy would occur because the people had "transgressed the laws, changed the ordinance, [and] broken the everlasting covenant" (Isaiah 24:5). Thus, the "famine" spoken of by Amos occurred to all Israel and by adoption to the Gentiles: "not a famine of bread, nor a thirst for water, but of hearing the words of the Lord" (Amos 8:11). Amos prophesied that the people of Israel would "wander from sea to sea, and from the north even to the east, they shall run to and fro to seek the word of the Lord, and shall not find it" (Amos 8:12). The devil's fight for dominion over the people of the earth, as prophesied by John the Revelator, had begun anew (Revelation 12:12–17); and the prophecy of Isaiah, which stated that the people would want their seers and prophets to "prophesy *not* unto [them] right things, [but] speak . . . smooth things, [and] prophesy deceits," was being fulfilled (Isaiah 30:10; emphasis added).

The Times of   3
the Gentiles

"How long shall it be to the end of these wonders? It shall be for a time, times, and an half;
and when he shall have accomplished to scatter
the power of the holy people, all these things
shall be finished."

Daniel 12:6–7

"Jerusalem shall be trodden down of the Gentiles, until the times of the Gentiles be fulfilled."

Luke 21:24

A.D. 325 to A.D. 1820

The next sign of the Second Coming was the prophesied times
of the Gentiles. The times of the Gentiles began in approximately
A.D. 325 as a result of the complete apostasy from the gospel and
withdrawal from the covenant of Abraham by the house of Israel
and the original Church. Before we discuss these times in detail,
however, it would be helpful to first understand exactly what the
covenant of Abraham was, and *is* yet today.

The Covenant of Abraham

When Abraham was 99 years old, God made a covenant with
him (see Genesis 17:1). It was an everlasting covenant which the
Lord promised he would never revoke nor break. This irrevocable covenant consisted of three parts: *part one* is absolute and
unconditional, but *parts two* and *three*, though absolute, are con-

ditionally based on the righteousness of God's chosen people. If his people sin and become unworthy, they will remain the chosen people, but the right to the blessings of the covenant will be rescinded until the Lord restores it to them again.

Part One: Abraham was promised he would have seed, and his seed would forever be designated as the Lord's *chosen* people. God chose them, and he will never reject them.

Part Two: The chosen people will be blessed with a *promised land*. For Abraham, the promised land was Canaan (see Genesis 17:8), and Canaan remained the promised land for the generations of Isaac and Jacob (Israel). When Moses led the children of Israel out of Egypt, they returned to this promised land and divided it among the twelve tribes. After the ten tribes were lost, Judah (the Southern Kingdom) retained the general area of Canaan, including Jerusalem. This area later became generally known as Palestine. When the tribe of Joseph (Ephraim and Manasseh) was later scattered, a remnant of the tribe was led out of Jerusalem and given the Western Hemisphere as its promised land (see 1 Nephi 2:20; 3 Nephi 20:13–14).

Part Three: The chosen people will be given the *priesthood* (see Abraham 1:4; 2:11). This priesthood was originally given to Adam by God. That priesthood lineage then descended from Adam to Abraham (see Abraham 1:3), and through Abraham it became part of the Abrahamic covenant. All of the blessings of the gospel of salvation, "even of life eternal" come through the priesthood (Abraham 2:11). Without the priesthood, eternal life (i.e., living in the presence of God) cannot be realized.

These three parts comprise the irrevocable covenant that God made with Abraham. All Abraham had to do to receive the blessings of this covenant was to accept it and comply with its conditions. His acceptance, and the acceptance of all those who will follow the covenant in the future, bestows two responsibilities:

    a.   The recipient must walk uprightly before God and be "perfect" (Genesis 17:1). God clearly stated his intentions regarding what was expected from his chosen people: "And we [the Creators] will prove them herewith, to see if they will do all things whatsoever the Lord their God shall command them" (Abraham 3:25). In other words, "walk before me, and be thou perfect" (Genesis 17:1). This same requirement was reiterated by the Savior when he gave the Sermon on the Mount during his ministry (see Matthew 5:48).

    b.   The recipient must offer the gospel of salvation to the world (see Abraham 2:11). Those under the covenant are required to "testify and warn the people" (D&C 88:81). This responsibility is required because the gospel, the plan of salvation, is the plan that must be followed if mankind is to regain God's presence. Once the covenant has been accepted, "it becometh every man who has been warned to warn his neighbor" (D&C 88:81). The Lord's chosen people have the responsibility to take the gospel to "all nations, kindreds, tongues, and people" (D&C 42:58) with the result that "he that believeth and is baptized shall be saved; but he that believeth not shall be damned" (Mark 16:16) and shall be "left without excuse" (D&C 88:82). The sins of those individuals will then be "upon their own heads" (D&C 88:82).

From Abraham, the covenant passed first to Isaac (see Genesis 17:21) and then to Jacob, whose name was changed to Israel (see Genesis 32:28). Thereafter, it went to the twelve sons of Jacob, collectively known as the twelve tribes (or house) of Israel (see Exodus 6:7–8; Deuteronomy 4:20).[1] However, *anyone* can become one of God's "chosen" people and share in the blessings of the covenant of Abraham if he or she is willing to accept the gospel (see 2 Nephi 30:1–2). Acceptance of the gospel—evidenced by baptism, confirmation, and obedience to God's commandments—automatically makes an individual part of Israel's lineage (see Romans 8:14–17; Galatians 4:4–7.) But Israel (and those who had been adopted into Israel by membership in the original Church) apostatized from the gospel of the New Testament when they "transgressed the laws, changed the ordinance, [and broke] the everlasting covenant" (Isaiah 24:5). As a result, the Abrahamic covenant was withdrawn from them and the times of the Gentiles began.

An intellectual and spiritual darkness settled upon all earth's inhabitants as the times of the Gentiles were ushered in. The light of the gospel was gone, and when the Roman Empire finally fell, the "torch of learning in the West flickered and nearly died out."[2] Lay education was rare, and "intellectual life—of the most rudimentary kind indeed—was practically confined to the monasteries."[3]

The Holy Roman Empire rose from the ashes of Rome like the mythical phoenix. It soon became powerful enough to control and regulate all within its sphere of influence—from kings to paupers.[4] It controlled spirituality by threat of excommunication (expulsion from God's kingdom to endless torment) and by controlling the availability of the scriptures, including the canonization or authorization of texts. In addition, it alone was allowed to interpret the scriptures.

These times of intellectual and spiritual darkness were prophesied by both Isaiah and Micah. Isaiah warned, "Woe unto them that call evil good, and good evil; that put darkness for light, and light for darkness; that put bitter for sweet, and sweet for bitter!" (Isaiah 5:20.) For "darkness shall cover the earth, and gross darkness the people" (Isaiah 60:2). Isaiah's contemporary, Micah, similarly prophesied, "Therefore night shall be unto you, that ye shall not have a vision; and it shall be dark unto you, that ye shall not divine; and the sun shall go down over the prophets, and the day shall be dark over them" (Micah 3:6).

Just as God's prophets foretold of this time of vast darkness, so also did they prophesy of the light that would eventually return: "And the Gentiles shall come to thy light, and kings to the brightness of thy rising" (Isaiah 60:3). Bringing people out of the dark ages, however, was no easy task. They had gone so far astray that in A.D. 1343 the "cult of indulgences" was officially sanctioned. This "cult" maintained that the virtues of Jesus and the early saints "had left a treasury of merits" that others could draw upon to obtain a "remission of the temporal punishment due to their sins." Access to these merits was given by "Church indulgence . . . often a donation of money."[5]

With the rise of universities and the expansion of knowledge in the 11th century, light slowly started invading the Dark Ages. Spiritual enlightenment also increased following Martin Luther's revolt against the authority of the Holy Roman Empire in the 16th century. John Calvin, usually referred to as the "architect of Protestantism," further energized Luther's revolt. His biblical commentaries formulated the doctrine from which would spring the Protestant churches; while most non-Lutheran churches of the time were Calvinists, they eventually split into a host of separate churches.[6]

Protestantism loosened the grip of the Dark Ages in two ways: (1) it caused the universal church to release its grasp on the people as a whole, and (2) it laid the groundwork for the struggle for freedom of religion that made the restoration of the gospel possible. On the other hand, these reformations offered people alternative faiths to believe in, which made the work of Luther, Calvin, and other reformers a mixed blessing when the gospel was finally restored. A like situation existed at the time of Christ. When the Lord and his Apostles implemented the gospel, it became for many simply another alternative to the existing apostate beliefs. In an effort to dissuade the people from believing in Jesus, the Jewish leadership claimed that his teachings were from the devil (a contention known as the Beelzebub Argument).[7]

As time went by, Protestantism became further divided in its doctrinal beliefs, resulting in the proliferation of Protestant churches, thus providing even more alternatives to the Lord's gospel. Nonetheless, with the rise of Protestantism came the Age of Enlightenment. Mankind began looking for new frontiers to conquer. Many ancient prophecies were fulfilled as men began to venture into the unknown. Columbus discovered the New World (see 1 Nephi 13:12); the Puritans and others seeking religious freedom began to migrate (see 1 Nephi 13:13,16); and a new and powerful nation—the United States of America—was born of war to ensure religious freedom for all its citizens (see 1 Nephi 13:17–19). All of these events would in time help make the restoration of the gospel possible. The Lord prophetically warned the Gentiles, however, that even though they had discovered and populated the Americas, if they did not repent of their evil ways he would "come out in justice against [them]" (Mormon 5:24).

The migration from Europe to the Western Hemisphere also fulfilled a prophecy that the Lord gave to the Nephites. He told them that the Gentiles would eventually scatter the Lamanite remnants on the Western Hemisphere and that the Gentiles would then "be a scourge unto the people of [that] land" (3 Nephi 20:28).

Many prophets have described what the times of the Gentiles after the Dark Ages would be like. Nephi tells us that "in the days of the Gentiles" on the Western Hemisphere and on all other lands, the people will be "drunken with iniquity and all manner of abominations" (2 Nephi 27:1). Isaiah describes the spiritual state of the people as "drunken, but not with wine; they stagger, but not with strong drink. For the Lord hath poured out upon [them] the spirit of deep sleep, and hath closed [their] eyes" (Isaiah 29:9–10). And Nephi, referencing the words of Isaiah, continues: "Ye have rejected the prophets; and your rulers, and the seers hath he covered because of your iniquity" (in other words, because of their apostasy, the Lord had withdrawn his prophets from them) (2 Nephi 27:5).

The people in this apostate era participated continually in the "good times" sin as described by Isaiah: "And behold joy and gladness, slaying oxen, killing sheep, eating flesh, and drinking wine: let us eat and drink; for tomorrow we shall die" (Isaiah 22:13). Jeremiah expands this theme by declaring: "And they [the false prophets and teachers during the times of the Gentiles] [will] say unto every one that walketh after the imagination of his own heart, No evil shall come upon you" (Jeremiah 23:17).

Nephi provides the following detailed description of the apostasy and of the "good times" sin:

> Yea, and there shall be many which shall say: Eat, drink, and be merry, for tomorrow we die; and it shall be well with us.

And there shall also be many which shall say: Eat, drink, and be merry; nevertheless, fear God—he will justify in committing a little sin; yea, lie a little, take the advantage of one because of his words, dig a pit for thy neighbor; there is no harm in this; and do all these things, for tomorrow we die; and if it so be that we are guilty, God will beat us with a few stripes, and at last we shall be saved in the kingdom of God.

Yea, and there shall be many which shall teach after this manner, false and vain and foolish doctrines, and shall be puffed up in their hearts, and shall seek deep to hide their counsels from the Lord; and their works shall be in the dark.

And the blood of the saints shall cry from the ground against them.

Yea, they have all gone out of the way; they have become corrupted.

Because of pride, and because of false teachers, and false doctrine, their churches have become corrupted, and their churches are lifted up; because of pride they are puffed up.

They rob the poor because of their fine sanctuaries; they rob the poor because of their fine clothing; and they persecute the meek and the poor in heart, because in their pride they are puffed up.

They wear stiff necks and high heads; yea, and because of pride, and wickedness, and abominations, and whoredoms, they have all gone astray save it be a few, who are the humble followers of Christ; nevertheless, they are led, that in many instances they do err because they are taught by the precepts of men.

O the wise, and the learned, and the rich, that are puffed up in the pride of their hearts, and all those who preach false doctrines, and all those who commit whoredoms, and pervert the right way of the Lord, wo, wo, wo be unto them, saith the Lord God Almighty, for they shall be thrust down to hell! (2 Nephi 28:7–15.)

Although the Gentiles would be "a scourge" to the descendants of Joseph on the Western Hemisphere (see 3 Nephi 20:28) and Jerusalem on the Eastern Hemisphere would be "trodden down" (Luke 21:24), the promises the Lord made through his prophets indicate that these abominable conditions would not continue forever. Paul gave the following instructions to the Roman Gentiles who had accepted the gospel: "For I would not, brethren, that ye should be ignorant of this mystery [of why the Gentiles should be allowed into the covenant], lest ye should be wise in your own conceits [think yourselves better than Israel]; that blindness in part is happened to Israel, until the fulness of the Gentiles be come in" (Romans 11:25). The Lord rejected and scattered Israel, including those Gentiles on the Eastern Hemisphere that had come into the covenant through baptism, until the fulness of the Gentiles was complete.

Concerning the end of the "times of the Gentiles," the Lord declared through Isaiah that he would "proceed to do a marvellous work among this people [the Gentiles], even a marvellous work and a wonder" (Isaiah 29:14; see also 2 Nephi 27:26). This marvelous work would commence with a vision and with the restoration of a book that would provide a second witness to the divinity of Jesus Christ. Isaiah acknowledged that the "words of a book" would come forth; Nephi elaborated on this when he said that the book would contain the revelation of God "from the beginning of the world to the ending thereof"—revelation that would turn the things of the Gentiles upside down (see Isaiah 29; 2 Nephi 27:6–35). The restoration of this work was to consummate only after the "light" burst forth "among them that sit in darkness." That light is "the fulness" of the Lord's gospel (D&C 45:28), and in the generation that it was restored, *"the times of the Gentiles [were] fulfilled"* (D&C 45:30; emphasis added).

The times of the Gentiles began because of the apostasy and rejection of the gospel and the covenant of Abraham. The times of the Gentiles ended with the restoration of the gospel (which commenced in 1820) and the restoration of the covenant of Abraham. The Lord's chosen people again had access to the priesthood (see D&C 13, 107), and the promised lands of Judah and Joseph (Jerusalem and Zion) became available to them for their habitation. The "times of the Gentiles" were over and the sign fulfilled, because the light of the gospel was once again on the earth.

Part Two

The Latter Days

"Arise, shine; for thy light is come, and the glory of the Lord is risen upon thee."

"Therefore, behold, I will proceed to do a marvellous work among this people, even a marvellous work and a wonder."

Isaiah 60:1; 29:14

The Restoration 4

"That in the dispensation of the fulness of times he might gather together in one all things in Christ, both which are in heaven, and which are on earth; even in him."

Ephesians 1:10

Fifteen hundred years passed between the time the early Church apostatized from the truth and the time the gospel was restored. The Savior had ascended into heaven, his Apostles (with the exception of John) were all dead, and apostasy had totally destroyed his Church on both the Eastern and the Western Hemispheres. As the apostate "times of the Gentiles" drew to a close, however, the foreappointed time of the restoration arrived (see D&C 45:24–30). It was time for the covenant of Abraham to be reestablished, and the dispensation of the fulness of times, a time "made up of all the dispensations that ever [had] been given since the world began," would now be ushered in.[1]

The restoration of the gospel was foreseen by the Old Testament prophet Daniel in approximately 600 B.C. He received this vision in Babylon while he was a captive of King Nebuchadnezzar. The circumstances were as follows: Nebuchadnezzar had had a distressing dream and "his spirit was troubled" to know what the dream meant—even though he could not remember what it had been about! (see Daniel 2:1–9.) When the king's wise men could not recall and interpret the dream for him, he sent out a decree ordering all of them to be slain. Since Daniel and his fellows were prophets and visionary men, they also fell under the king's decree. But Daniel had not heard about the king's problem, so when he was told that his life was in jeopardy, he went to Arioch, the captain of Nebuchadnezzar's guard, to find out why the decree had been issued. Arioch told him about the king's dream and the inability of his wise men to recall it. Daniel then went to Nebuchadnezzar and told him that, given a little time, he could tell him what his dream was and what it meant. The king granted his petition and Daniel returned to his house.

That night, the Lord revealed the secret of Nebuchadnezzar's dream to Daniel in a vision, so the next day he went back to Arioch and said, "Destroy not the wise men of Babylon: [but] bring me in before the king, and I will shew unto [him] the interpretation" of his dream (Daniel 2:24). Daniel was again admitted to the king's presence, where he proceeded to recount and interpret Nebuchadnezzar's dream: "Thou, O king, [saw] a great image [of a man] . . . whose brightness was excellent, [and it] stood before thee; and the form thereof was terrible. This image's head was of fine gold, his breast and his arms of silver, his belly and his thighs of brass, his legs of iron, his feet part of iron and part of clay" (Daniel 2:31–33).

The man-image that Nebuchadnezzar saw represented the kingdoms of the earth. The head of gold depicted Babylon, the greatest of all the kingdoms (see Daniel 2:38). The rest of the image is commonly assumed to comprise the empires of Persia-Medes (breast and arms of silver), Greece (belly and thighs of brass), and Rome (legs of iron). Eventually, the Roman Empire would break into ten kingdoms described as the "feet and toes" of the man-image: ten kingdoms that would be partly strong yet partly broken—a mixture of iron and "miry clay" (Daniel 2:41). These kingdoms (and the nations that descended from them during the Dark Ages) are historically described as the Holy Roman Empire, an empire that was held together by a religious power (the "seed of men")[2] based in Rome, which had derived its strength from the political prowess of the old "iron" empire (see Daniel

2:43). But the dream revealed that the nations of iron and clay would not "cleave" one to another. Eventually, the religious yoke that bound them together would be broken, and they would become individual, secular nations.

Daniel's interpretation continued: "Thou sawest . . . that a stone was cut out without hands, which smote the image upon his feet that were of iron and clay, and brake them to pieces. Then was the iron, the clay, the brass, the silver, and the gold, broken to pieces together, and became like the chaff of the summer threshingfloors; and the wind carried them away, that no place was found for them: and the stone that smote the image became a great mountain, and filled the whole earth" (see Daniel 2:34–35).

The small stone "cut out without hands" represents God's kingdom, a kingdom that will never be destroyed (Daniel 2:44). And when it smites the image and breaks all of the kingdoms of the man-image apart—becoming a "great mountain" that fills "the whole earth—it is interpreted to mean that God's kingdom will eventually supersede or infiltrate all national boundaries; that through the restoration of the gospel, God's power will grow until it will eventually consume all the kingdoms of the world (see Daniel 2). Thus, long before Paul prophesied that the Second Coming would not occur until after a falling away (see 2 Thessalonians 2:1–3) and before Peter prophesied that all things would be restored after the apostasy (see Acts 3:19–21), Daniel envisioned the restoration and the establishment of God's work in the latter days.

In symbolic vision, John the Revelator actually saw the restoration of the gospel taking place. He saw the devil successfully overcome the church that Christ and his Apostles had established while they were upon the earth. Then, following the passage of a long period of time (see Revelation 12:5–6), he saw "another angel fly in the midst of heaven, having the everlasting gospel to preach unto them that dwell on the earth," and he saw the gospel taken "to every nation, and kindred, and tongue, and people" (Revelation 14:6).

The prophets of the Western Hemisphere recorded a much clearer vision of the great events presaging the Second Coming. Nephi saw the establishment of America upon the Western Hemisphere and the scattering of the seed of Lehi (Native Americans) by Gentile settlers (see 1 Nephi 22:7). After that, he saw the Lord "proceed to do a marvelous work among the Gentiles," even the restoration of the gospel (see 1 Nephi 22:8). A descendant of Nephi, also named Nephi, recorded the Savior's words as he visited the descendants of Lehi following his resurrection. The Lord spoke of the future gathering of Israel (his chosen people) and then said, "I give unto you a sign, that ye may know the time when these things shall be about to take place" (3 Nephi 21:1). That sign was the coming forth of the Book of Mormon, signaling the beginning of the restoration of the gospel. The Lord declared that the sign (the Book of Mormon) would "be made known unto the Gentiles" (3 Nephi 21:2), so that they, and the seed of Lehi might "know that the work of the Father hath already commenced unto the fulfilling of the covenant which he hath made unto the people who are of the house of Israel" (3 Nephi 21:2,7; see also verses 1–9).

One might say that the work of the restoration began in 1805 when a boy by the name of Joseph Smith was born—a boy raised up to fulfill the prophecies of the restoration given by the Book of Mormon prophet Lehi almost twenty-four hundred years earlier. Prior to his death, Lehi gave a blessing to his youngest son, who was also named Joseph. In this blessing, Lehi cited the brass plates and indicated that Joseph of Egypt had prophesied that God would raise up a seer in the last days and that he would be of his (Joseph of Egypt's) tribal lineage. This seer was compared to Moses[3] in that he would "bring forth [God's] word unto the seed of [Joseph of Egypt's] loins." His name would be called Joseph (after both his own father and after Joseph of Egypt), and he would bring to "pass much restoration unto the house of Israel, and unto the seed of [Lehi's] brethren." (See 2 Nephi 3.)

Joseph Smith's first vision took place in 1820. In this astounding revelation he was privileged to see God the Father and his Son, Jesus Christ. While the first vision revealed many truths which are not the purview of this discussion, it is important to note that this vision called Joseph to do the work of the Lord, ended the times of the Gentiles, commenced the restoration of the gospel, and opened the dispensation of the fulness of times (see Joseph Smith–History 1).

Joseph's second vision occurred on September 21, 1823. The angel Moroni, whom John the Revelator had seen in his great vision (see Revelation 14:6), appeared to Joseph to commence the restoration of all things. Under the direction of the Lord, Moroni gave Joseph the instructions and teachings that would lead to the discovery and translation of the Book of Mormon. With the restoration of the Book of Mormon, the gospel was then restored in its fulness (see Joseph Smith–History 1:30–54).[4] The Lord later confirmed that the gospel had been restored by an heavenly angel (see D&C 133:36–37) and that it would serve as an ensign for all the nations of the earth (see Isaiah 5:26; 11:12).

The Bible is the first witness of the Savior's divinity, but many plain and precious things have been lost from its pages through centuries of retranslation and interpretation. Still, it is Judah's record, preserved as a witness to the Gentiles of the chronicle of God's chosen people, and it includes the covenants and blessings he originally gave the children of Israel (see 1 Nephi 13:20–29). The Book of Mormon corrects many of the false doctrines that have arisen from incorrect interpretations or misunderstood verses found in the Bible (see 2 Nephi 3:12), and it confirms the truths found therein (see 1 Nephi 13:34–41). It also contains the history of part of the remnant of Ephraim and Manasseh (commonly known as the Nephites and the Lamanites). However, the Bible and the Book of Mormon together provide a *complete* witness of the divinity of the Lord Jesus Christ in the sense that out of the mouth of two or more witnesses shall the truth of all things be established (see Deuteronomy 17:6; D&C 6:28).

Initially, the Book of Mormon was not warmly received by most communities in mid-nineteenth century America. The unusual way it was discovered and translated caused a considerable amount of controversy, controversy that was foretold by the prophecies contained within its pages. For example, when people first heard about the Book of Mormon, their frequent response was that they had already received the "word of God" and that they had received "enough" (2 Nephi 28:29). Some would cry, "A Bible! A Bible! We have got a Bible, and there cannot be any more Bible" (2 Nephi 29:3). The Book of Mormon itself confounded these arguments by testifying that although the Bible was indeed a divine witness from the Jews, God had "more nations than one" capable of producing a sacred record (see 2 Nephi 29:1–7).

The Book of Mormon is not a figment of someone's imagination. Isaiah saw it coming forth out of the "dust . . . of them which have slumbered," a book that would be delivered to "him that is not learned." He further stated that a "sealed" portion of the book would be delivered in a day when "wickedness and abominations" would abound, but that the "sealed" portion would "be kept" from the wicked. (see Isaiah 29:4–12; JST, Isaiah 29:11–20; IV, Isaiah 29:4–13; 2 Nephi 27:6–29.)

Moroni echoed Isaiah's simile when he described the book as coming forth "out of the dust" (Moroni 10:27), and other Book of Mormon prophets recorded that the book would rest until it should come forth, "even as it were out of the ground," in the latter days (2 Nephi 26:15–16). But as the Lord promised Enos and Mormon, the book *would come forth*—to the Lamanites, the Gentiles, the Jews, and all the house of Israel "in his own due time"(see Enos 1:13–16; Mormon 5:12–15).

None of these ancient prophets knew *exactly when* the Book of Mormon would be restored. Moroni described the day of its restoration as one when the people would believe that "miracles [had been] done away" (Mormon 8:26). He said that the "blood of saints [would] cry unto the Lord, because of secret combinations and the works of darkness" (Mormon 8:27). There would be "wars," "rumors of wars," "earthquakes," "tempests," "fires," "vapors of smoke in foreign lands," "great pollutions upon the face of the earth," "murders," "robbing," "lying," "deceivings," and "whoredoms," and "all manner of abominations," and there would be churches established to get gain and forgive sins for money (Mormon 8:29–31). Of that time Moroni said, "There shall be many who will say, Do this, or do that, and it mattereth not, for the Lord will uphold such at the last day" (Mormon 8:31). He further prophesied, "The power of God shall be denied, and churches [shall] become defiled and be lifted up in the pride of their hearts; yea . . . leaders of churches and teachers shall rise in the pride of their hearts, even to the envying of them who belong to their churches" (Mormon 8:28).

Nevertheless, Moroni knew that regardless of when the book came forth, it would come forth because of its "great worth," and with an "eye single to [God's] glory" (Mormon 8:14–15). Nephi supported this when he recorded Jesus' statement that the book would come in accordance with "the time and the will of the Father" (3 Nephi 23:4) and that it would evidence the fact that the Father had commenced his work on the earth for the last time (See 3 Nephi 21).

The restoration of the Book of Mormon heralded the beginning of many extraordinary events:

1. The Savior's ancient church was "called forth out of the wilderness" (Revelation 12:6; D&C 33:5) and restored as an organized entity on April 6, 1830, in Fayette, New York.[5] John the Revelator had seen the church driven into the wilderness ·by Satan because of the "tares" the devil had sown among the wheat (see Matthew 13:24–30, 37–43; D&C 86:1–7),[6] but it would now function in the latter days "for the restoration of his people" (D&C 84:2).

2. The covenant of Abraham (so long withheld from the children of men) was reestablished, and the chosen people were again recognized by God (see Jeremiah 31:31–33; Hosea 2:18–23; D&C 52:2; 86:9; 110:12). With the restoration of the covenant came the restoration of its blessings and requirements:

   a. *The Promised Land*: Latter-day revelations established Zion as the promised land on the Western Hemisphere for all of Israel who would accept it (see D&C 38:18–20; 48:5; 52:5,42; 57:1–3). Jerusalem on the Eastern Hemisphere would once more be inhabited by Judah until the Second Coming of Christ (Chapter 5).

   b. *The Priesthood*: The Aaronic Priesthood was restored by John the Baptist on May 15, 1829, and the Melchizedek Priesthood was restored by Peter, James, and John sometime before the end of June 1829 (see D&C 13; Joseph Smith–History 1:72). The priesthood is an integral part of the gospel. Without it no missionary work can be done and none of the saving ordinances can be performed. When the priesthood was restored, the Lord made it clear that it would continue uninterrupted until the time of his Second Coming—and beyond (see D&C 13).

c.   *The Gospel*: This is the "little stone" that Daniel saw in his vision. It will eventually roll forth and fill the whole earth (see Daniel 2; D&C 65:2; 133:37–74). This work heralds the gathering of the covenant people (see Isaiah 18) and will overcome error and apostasy (see Isaiah 29:13–14). The gospel, with all of its saving principles and ordinances, will "be preached in all the world, for a witness" of the divinity of Jesus Christ (Matthew 24:14; Joseph Smith–Matthew 1:31), and it will invite all that desire righteousness to share in the covenant of Abraham (see Isaiah 55). Finally, the gospel will specifically testify of Jesus Christ to the people of Judah so they might recognize their errors and eliminate their false gods (see Zechariah 13:1–5).

3.   Crucial keys from the prior dispensations were gathered into this, the last dispensation (the dispensation of the fulness of times) in a vision received by Joseph Smith in the Kirkland Temple on April 3, 1836. In that vision:

a.   Moses returned to restore the keys for the gathering of Israel.

b.   Elias reinstated the covenant of Abraham.

c.   Elijah appeared to restore the sealing power, which will "turn the hearts of the fathers to the children, and the heart of the children to their fathers, lest [the Lord] come and smite the earth with a curse" (D&C 110:15; see also Malachi 4:5–6.)[7]

The sealing power of Elijah gives man the ability to use God's power to perform the ordinances of salvation that are required to return to his kingdom. Without this sealing power, the plan of salvation would become ineffective and no one would be able to return to God's kingdom.

With the covenant of Abraham once more upon the earth, it becomes the responsibility of those who share in the covenant to take the gospel of salvation to all the world—to teach the Gentiles, to gather Israel, and to restore Judah.

Judah

"Because I knew that thou art obstinate, and thy neck is an iron sinew, and thy brow brass; I have even from the beginning declared it to thee; before it came to pass I shewed it thee: lest thou shouldest say, Mine idol hath done them, and my graven image, and my molten image, hath commanded them."

Isaiah 48:4–5

"O Jerusalem, Jerusalem, thou that killest the prophets, and stonest them which are sent unto thee, how often would I have gathered thy children together, even as a hen gathereth her chickens under her wings, and ye would not!"

Matthew 23:37

The "abomination of desolation" is a double-reference prophecy given by the Old Testament prophet Daniel (see Daniel 9:27). It was later reiterated by the Lord in the New Testament (see Matthew 24:15). It was fulfilled for the first time in A.D. 70 when the Romans conquered Jerusalem and scattered Judah, and it will be fulfilled for the second time after Judah has been gathered just prior to the Second Coming. The dispersion of Judah started much earlier than A.D. 70, however. It began when the Southern Kingdom was taken into captivity by Babylon in approximately 600 B.C. (see Ezekiel 12:11–16). A remnant of Judah's people returned to Jerusalem around 530 B.C., but approximately 600 years later the Roman conquest completed her destruction and initiated her long diaspora. The diaspora of Judah (along with the rest of Israel) continued throughout the dark ages of apostasy and did not come to an end until early in the nineteenth century when the "times of the Gentiles" concluded with the restoration of the gospel (and the covenant of Abraham) to Joseph Smith.

Signs of the Second Coming Pertaining to Judah That Have Been Fulfilled

Once the Lord had reestablished his Church in the latter days as an ensign to the world, it was time to "assemble the outcasts of Israel, and gather together the dispersed of Judah from the four corners of the earth" (Isaiah 11:12). In a vision granted to Joseph Smith in 1823, the angel Moroni quoted this same scripture and declared that it was about to be fulfilled, meaning that the gathering of both Israel and Judah would now begin (see Joseph Smith–History 1:40). Moses, who had gathered Israel from Egypt and led them to the promised land of Canaan centuries before, restored the keys of the gathering of Israel to Joseph Smith in the Kirkland Temple on April 3, 1836 (see D&C 110:11). A few years later, Joseph dispatched Orson Hyde (a man of Jewish descent and one of the first latter-day Apostles) to Palestine to specifically dedicate that land for the gathering of the tribe of Judah. On October 24, 1841, Elder Hyde delivered the following in his dedicatory prayer as he stood on the Mount of Olives in Jerusalem:

> Now, O Lord! Thy servant has been obedient to the heavenly vision which Thou gavest him in his native land; and under the shadow of Thine outstretched arm, he has safely arrived in this place to dedicate and consecrate this land unto Thee, for the gathering together of Judah's scattered remnants, according to the predictions of the holy Prophets—for the building up of Jerusalem again after it has been trodden down by the Gentiles so long, and for rearing a Temple in honor of Thy name . . .
>
> Grant, therefore, O Lord, in the name of Thy well-beloved Son, Jesus Christ, to remove the barrenness and sterility of this land, and let springs of living water break forth to water its

> thirsty soil. Let the vine and olive produce in their
> strength, and the fig-tree bloom and flourish. Let
> the land become abundantly fruitful when
> possessed by its rightful heirs; let it again flow
> with plenty to feed the returning prodigals who
> come home with a spirit of grace and
> supplication.[1]

Elder Hyde's prayer thus initiated the long-predicted gathering of the tribe of Judah.

The spirit of gathering is interesting in that it moves on those to be gathered without direction from any earthly source. In one of Elder Hyde's reports he stated that "the idea of the Jews being restored to Palestine is gaining ground in Europe almost every day . . . the great wheel is unquestionably in motion, and the word of the Almighty has declared that it shall roll."[2]

Perhaps even more interesting than Elder Hyde's comment is the report Golda Meir made in her autobiography regarding the spirit of gathering:

> A great deal has already been written—and much
> more will certainly be written in the future—about
> the Zionist movement, and most people by now
> have at least some notion of what the word
> 'Zionism' means and that it has to do with the
> return of the Jewish people to the land of their
> forefathers—the Land of Israel, as it is called in
> Hebrew. But perhaps even today not everyone
> realizes that *this remarkable movement sprang up
> spontaneously, and more or less simultaneously, in
> various parts of Europe toward the end of the
> nineteenth century.* It was like a drama that was
> being enacted in different ways on different stages
> in different languages but that dealt with the same
> theme everywhere: that the so-called Jewish
> problem (of course, it was really a Christian
> problem) was basically the result of Jewish
> homelessness and that it could not, and would
> not, be solved unless and until the Jews had a land
> of their own again. Obviously, this land could

only be Zion, the land from which the Jews had
been exiled 2,000 years before but which had
remained the spiritual center of Jewry throughout
the centuries and which, when I was a little girl
in Pinsk and up to the end of World War I, was a
desolate and neglected province of the Ottoman
Empire called Palestine (emphasis added).[3]

Although Golda Meir probably did not understand the ori-
gins of the movement she described and had undoubtedly never
heard of Orson Hyde, her description of the results of Elder Hyde's
prayer and the movement of the spirit of gathering on the descendants of Judah could not have been more eloquent.

Isaiah foresaw this gathering and the process by which it
would occur. In the 49th chapter of his book, he declared in beautiful prose that the Lord was the means by which salvation would
be extended to both the Gentiles and to Israel (see Isaiah 49:4–6).
In verses 7 through 13 of the same chapter, he prophesied of the
gathering's commencement, declaring that the covenant of
Abraham would be made available to the Gentiles and to Israel
and that those so long in captivity would "go forth" and be free:
they would be gathered "from far," "from the north and from the
west," from the "land of Sinim," (whereabouts specifically unknown but assumed to be the most distant lands of the earth)
from wherever they had been scattered. Isaiah exulted in the
Lord's promise: "Sing, O heavens; and be joyful, O earth; and
break forth into singing, O mountains: for the Lord hath comforted his people, and will have mercy upon his afflicted" (Isaiah
49:7–13).

Isaiah's prophecy notes that Israel complained bitterly during her long period of dispersion, claiming that the Lord had forgotten his chosen people. But, as the scripture states, "can a
woman forget her sucking child, that she should not have com-
passion on the son of her womb?" "Yea," the Savior said, "they
may forget [their Lord], yet will I not forget [Israel]" (Isaiah 49:14–
16).

Isaiah continues to describe the gathering process by declaring that the gathering will be so great that the land will be "too
narrow by reason of the inhabitants"—too small to contain those

who want to gather to the Holy Land (see Isaiah 49:17–20). Under the Lord's direction the Spirit will move upon all, even kings and queens, to assist in the gathering process: "even the captives of the mighty shall be taken away, and the prey of the terrible" delivered from oppression, for the Savior declared, "I will contend with him that contendeth with thee, and I will save thy children" (Isaiah 49:22–25). "I will feed them that oppress thee with their own flesh; and they shall be drunken with their own blood, as with sweet wine: and all flesh shall know that I the Lord am thy Saviour and thy Redeemer, the mighty One of Jacob" (Isaiah 49:26).

The prophesied assistance from kings and queens had at least a partial fulfillment with the *Balfour Declaration*. The *Balfour Declaration*, named for Arthur James Balfour, Britain's foreign secretary under King George V, was published on November 2, 1917. Couched in the form of a letter from Lord Balfour to Lord Rothschild, the British government committed itself to "the establishment in Palestine of a National Home for the Jewish People." The British government declared that it would use "its best endeavors to facilitate the achievement of this objective."[4] Although progress was delayed by the First and Second World Wars, on November 29, 1947, the United Nations finally voted for the partition of Palestine and the end of the British Mandate. Thirty-three nations voted in favor, 10 abstained, and 13 were against the partition.[5] May 14, 1948, was the day the United Nations established as the deadline for the termination of the British Mandate in Palestine. On this day, the Jewish National Council assembled and resolved that "by virtue of our natural and historic right and of the resolution of the General Assembly of the United Nations, [we] do hereby proclaim the establishment of a Jewish state in the Land of Israel—the State of Israel."[6]

The creation of the State of Israel fulfilled Isaiah's prophecy concerning the restoration of Judah. Nephi cited this prophecy from Isaiah 40:9 and stated that "after they were restored they should no more be confounded, neither should they be scattered again" (1 Nephi 15:20). The establishment of Israel was also a fulfillment of the 1841 prayer of Elder Hyde and the words that Zechariah uttered 500 years before Christ: "And the Lord shall inherit Judah his portion in the holy land, and shall choose Jerusalem again" (Zechariah 2:12).[7]

Zechariah's prophecy, however, was not completely fulfilled with the establishment of the State of Israel in 1948. The city of Jerusalem was divided between the Jews and the Palestinians at the time the State was created, and continued to be divided until the Six Day War of 1967 when Israel captured the old city.[8] At the conclusion of the Six Day War, the Holy City was once again under the control of Judah. Zechariah prophesied: "The Lord shall inherit Judah his portion in the holy land, and shall choose Jerusalem again . . . In that day will I make the governors of Judah like an hearth of fire among the wood, and like a torch of fire in a sheaf; and they shall devour all the people round about, on the right hand and on the left: and Jerusalem shall be inhabited again in her own place, even in Jerusalem" (Zechariah 2:12; 12:6). This same prophecy was also made by Isaiah (see Isaiah 62:5–12); by the Lord (see 3 Nephi 20:29, 33–34); and by Orson Hyde.[9]

The balance of Isaiah's prophecy regarding the "captives of the mighty" being taken away and the "prey of the terrible" being delivered from captivity may have had its fulfillment in many individual stories of miraculous deliverances, but it also appears to have been fulfilled in at least two major instances. The condition of the Jews under Hitler's Third Reich fits Isaiah's description of Judah as the "prey" of the mighty, and while millions of Jews were killed in the Holocaust, there were many survivors from countries all over Europe who finally made their way back to Israel. Another example was the USSR, one of the last modern strongholds of Jewish captivity. When the Russian empire disintegrated, many Jewish citizens were free to return to the Holy Land. Both of these dictatorial regimes seem to fit into Isaiah's prophetic description wherein he foresaw that the Lord would cause those who oppress Judah to "feed" upon their own flesh and become drunken with their own "blood"—a poetic description of their self-destructive activities and policies (see Isaiah 49:26).

When Elder Hyde gave his dedicatory prayer in Jerusalem, he blessed Palestine that it would rise from the "desolate and neglected" state Golda Meir described[10] to a highly productive state. This too was in fulfillment of ancient prophecy. Ezekiel described the dispersion and restoration of Judah and declared that in the latter days "the desolate land shall be tilled . . . And [the people] shall say, This land that was desolate is become like the garden of Eden; and the waste and desolate and ruined cities are become fenced, and are inhabited" (Ezekiel 36:34–35). Amos, also speaking of the latter days, declared that Israel would "build the waste cities, and inhabit them," and "plant vineyards, and drink the wine thereof," and "also make gardens, and eat the fruit of them." He prophesied that the Lord would "plant them upon their land." "No more" would they be "pulled up" out of the land the Lord had given them (Amos 9:14–15; see also Isaiah 29:17; 35:1–2). One need only look at modern-day Israel to see the literal fulfillment of these prophesies. Through their ingenuity and hard work, Israel has tilled and planted to make the desolate land blossom and become as the Garden of Eden.

Another of Isaiah's prophecies was fulfilled while Israel was in its birth pangs. He foresaw Judah receiving "sons from far [away]" bringing "silver" and "gold" during her restoration (Isaiah 60:9). Wilford Woodruff made a similar prophecy when he said, "They [Judah] will go and rebuild Jerusalem and their temple. They will take their gold and silver from the nations and will gather to the Holy Land."[11] In literal fulfillment of these gathering prophecies Golda Meir was sent to the United States in January of 1948 on a nationwide speaking engagement; she returned to Israel with $50,000,000 to be used in building the nation's defenses.[12] Many nations (principally the United States) have given foreign aid to Israel since that time, and many Jewish individuals and groups from around the world have made private contributions to the building up of the Holy Land.

Today, with the land of their inheritance restored, the Jews once again have a "promised land"—a place to call home.

Future Signs to Judah

Although the establishment of Israel and the gathering of the tribe of Judah has produced a strong nation, many great signs pertaining to the Jews have yet to occur before the Lord comes again.

Spiritual Enlightenment: The Lord will "pardon" the sins of the tribe of Judah (see Isaiah 40:1–2). After suffering through centuries of the diaspora, they will yet be sanctified by their God (see Hosea 1:7; see also D&C 109:64; 133:35) and will again become a "delightsome people" (2 Nephi 30:7). The truths of the Book of Mormon will be taught to them and to all the "remnant of the house of Israel," and will serve as a witness to them that their long-awaited Messiah came in the meridian of time and will come again in the latter days (see 3 Nephi 29:8; Mormon 5:12–15).

Zechariah prophesied that as Judah again begins to believe in God as their deliverer and in Jesus as their Savior, their centuries of spiritual darkness will be replaced by the light of truth. He declared that "in those days it shall come to pass, that ten men shall take hold out of all languages of the nations, even shall take hold of the skirt of him that is a Jew, saying, We will go with you: for we have heard that God is with you" (Zechariah 8:23). There are great spiritual blessings yet in store for Judah as her people begin to believe in the God who has restored and gathered them. In time they will come to recognize him as their Messiah.[13]

The Temple and the Daily Sacrifice: The first temple in Jerusalem was built by Solomon approximately 3,000 years ago. It was destroyed when Babylon captured Judah around 600–560 B.C. A second temple was built by the returning Babylonian exiles and was later greatly enlarged and refurbished by Herod the Great. It was destroyed by Rome in A.D. 70. A third temple is yet to be built in Jerusalem, and it will be built upon the same temple mount as the temples of antiquity. Many prophets have seen this temple in visions from the Lord. Ezekiel described its size and layout (see Ezekiel 40). Isaiah described its beauty: "The glory of Lebanon shall come unto thee, the fir tree, the pine tree, and the box together, to beautify the place of my sanctuary; and I will make the place of my feet glorious" (Isaiah 60:13). Zechariah was told that the Lord's house would again be built in Jerusalem (see Zechariah 1:16), and he saw in vision the day when "the foundation of the house of the Lord of Hosts was laid" (Zechariah 8:9). He also saw those who would build and occupy it (see Zechariah 6:13–15; 8:7–9). Finally, the prophet Wilford Woodruff was also shown by the Lord that the temple in Jerusalem would be built in the latter days.[14]

Once the temple in Israel is completed, sacrifice will again be offered by the sons of Levi "unto the Lord in righteousness" (D&C 13:1).[15]

Wars and the Fall of Jerusalem: It is possible that the construction of the temple (or the attempted construction) in Jerusalem and the offering of sacrifice therein may be the catalyst that will bring the fulfillment of other prophecies to Judah. Prior to the Second Coming, Jerusalem will again be engulfed by her enemies. The Holy City will be encircled by what John described as an army of 200,000,000 men (see Revelation 9:16). This may be literal, but more likely it is symbolically describing an army of enormous size that will rise up against Israel in the last days.[16] Nonetheless, after a siege that will last for three and one-half years and following the great battle of Armageddon, the ancient city of Jerusalem will fall to her enemies (see Joel 3:1–8; Revelation 11:2).

In verses twelve through sixteen of the 16th chapter of Revelation, John symbolically described how the devil will exercise his power and influence in the latter days so that nations will rise up to destroy Jerusalem (the symbol of God). This period of destruction will occur at the culmination of the devil's power on the earth just prior to the Second Coming, and it is described by John as the great "plague" of the "sixth angel."

Two Prophets to Judah:

Revelation 11:1–12

1. And there was given me a reed like unto a rod: and the angel stood, saying, Rise, and measure the temple of God, and the altar, and them that worship therein.

2. But the court which is without the temple leave out, and measure it not; for it is given unto the Gentiles: and the holy city shall they tread under foot forty and two months.

3. And I will give power unto my two witnesses, and they shall prophesy a thousand two hundred and threescore days, clothed in sackcloth.

4. These are the two olive trees, and the two candlesticks standing before the God of the

earth.

5.   And if any man will hurt them, fire proceedeth out of their mouth, and devoureth their enemies: and if any man will hurt them, he must in this manner be killed.

6.   These have power to shut heaven, that it rain not in the days of their prophecy: and have power over waters to turn them to blood, and to smite the earth with all plagues, as often as they will.

7.   And when they shall have finished their testimony, the beast that ascendeth out of the bottomless pit shall make war against them, and shall overcome them, and kill them.

8.   And their dead bodies shall lie in the street of the great city, which spiritually is called Sodom and Egypt, where also our Lord was crucified.

9.   And they of the people and kindreds and tongues and nations shall see their dead bodies three days and an half, and shall not suffer their dead bodies to be put in graves.

10. And they that dwell upon the earth shall rejoice over them, and make merry, and shall send gifts one to another; because these two prophets tormented them that dwelt on the earth.

11. And after three days and an half the Spirit of life from God entered into them, and they stood upon their feet; and great fear fell upon them which saw them.

12. And they heard a great voice from heaven saying unto them, Come up hither. And they ascended up to heaven in a cloud; and their enemies beheld them.

Sometime during the last great battles that will occur near Jerusalem prior to the Second Coming, two prophets will be raised up to Judah. Their arrival will be a specific sign of the Lord's imminent Advent. Some have speculated that they will be

Apostles of The Church of Jesus Christ of Latter-day Saints;[17] others feel that they will either be Apostles or members of the First Presidency.[18] There is also the possibility that they will come from Judah herself, raised up independent of the Church as prophets to that branch of God's chosen people.

God has often raised up multiple prophets to different parts of Israel. In the eighth century B.C. he raised up Amos to the Southern Kingdom and Hosea to the Northern Kingdom of Israel, and Micah and Isaiah to the Southern Kingdom of Judah.[19] There is no record that these prophets knew of or communicated with each other. Lehi was raised up during the time of Jeremiah to warn Jerusalem of God's pending judgments. Later, he and his followers were led to the Western Hemisphere while Jeremiah remained on the Eastern Hemisphere to prophesy to Judah. During his ministry, Christ described Lehi's descendants as "other sheep" who were not of the tribe of Judah. After his resurrection, the Apostles on the Eastern Hemisphere established the Lord's Church and preached his gospel while his disciples on the Western Hemisphere did the same thing. Although the disciples of the Western Hemisphere knew of Judah in the East, Judah knew nothing of the descendants of Lehi in the West (see 3 Nephi 16:4).

God clearly states that he will bring forth his word to "the children of men, yea, even upon all the nations of the earth" (2 Nephi 29:7). "I shall speak unto the Jews and they shall write it; and I shall also speak unto the Nephites and they shall write it; and I shall also speak unto the other [lost] tribes of the house of Israel, which I have led away, and they shall write it . . . the Jews shall have the words of the Nephites, and the Nephites shall have the words of the Jews; and the Nephites and the Jews shall have the words of the lost tribes of Israel; and the lost tribes of Israel shall have the words of the Nephites and the Jews" (2 Nephi 29:12–13). Nephi confirms in these scriptures that the Lord speaks to his chosen people and can obviously raise up prophets from any of them.

The two unique prophets who will preach to Judah in the last days were seen in vision by John the Revelator (see Revelation 11), Isaiah (see Isaiah 51:18–20), and Zechariah (see Zechariah 4:11–14). The scriptures state that they will prophesy to Judah and the

Gentiles with great power for three and one-half years prior to the Lord's coming while the last terrible siege of Jerusalem rages around them (see Revelation 11:2–3).[20] God will protect them from harm during this period (see Revelation 11:5). He will give them the power to shut the heavens "that it rain not," and they will have "power over waters" to pollute them, and "to smite the earth with all plagues, as often as they will" (Revelation 11:6). Finally, when the Second Coming draws nigh, they will be killed by the conquering armies entering Jerusalem. Their bodies will lie in the streets for three and one-half days (see Revelation 11:9) while the enemies of Israel throughout the world rejoice at their deaths and revel in their victory over the Jews (see Revelation 11:10).

But their revelry will be short lived, for at the end of the three and one-half days, "the Spirit of life from God" will enter into the two prophets and they will stand "upon their feet," which will cause "great fear" to fall upon Judah's adversaries. The two prophets will then hear "a great voice from heaven saying unto them, Come up hither." And they will ascend "up to heaven in a cloud," and their enemies will watch them disappear (see Revelation 11:11–12). It is at this time that the Savior will deliver Judah from her enemies and lead her to victory[21] in a campaign so devastating that Ezekiel metaphorically declares that the implements of war taken from the enemy will provide fuel for the fires of Judah's people for the next seven years (see Ezekiel 39:8–10).

Another David to lead Judah in the latter days: Orson Hyde petitioned the Lord in his dedicatory prayer to "constitute [Judah's] people a distinct nation and government, with David Thy servant, even a descendant from the loins of ancient David to be their king."[22] While some scriptures indicate that this great leader will be like David of old (raised up to assist in Israel's final delivery), and other scriptures seem to anticipate a strong political leader whose name will be David (see Ezekiel 34:23–24; Jeremiah 30:9), some feel it would be more logical to interpret these references as symbolically referring to Christ, who is a descendant of David and who is the true King of the Jews.

Isaiah described this great deliverer as coming forth from the "stem of Jesse . . . out of his roots" (Isaiah 11:1). The "stem of Jesse" *is* Jesus Christ (D&C 113:1–2), the same deity who gave the vision in Revelation to John the Revelator and who stated therein that he was "the root and the offspring of David" (Revelation 5:5; 22:16). The Savior will stand as the ensign for the Gentiles and the gathering of Judah (see Isaiah 11:10; D&C 113:6) and will defend "the inhabitants of Jerusalem" (Zechariah 12:8) when the children of Israel turn again and seek the Lord their God. Jacob's original blessing on Judah foreshadowed this interpretation. *The Torah* states: "The scepter shall not depart from Judah, nor the ruler's staff from between his feet; So that *tribute* shall come to him" (emphasis added). Then, in defining the word *tribute*, *The Torah* states that it means "literally, 'until he comes to Shiloh,' or 'until Shiloh comes'... One Jewish tradition, taking Jacob's blessing to be a prophecy for the *end of time* ... interpreted 'Shiloh' to mean the Messiah, a new David who would come out of the house of Judah."[23] It thus seems clear from the scriptures that the "other David" will be the same individual whom David acknowledged as his King (see Psalm 44:4); the leader who entered Jerusalem at the conclusion of his ministry as its King (see Zechariah 9:9; John 12:14–15); and the deity who declared to Isaiah, "I am the Lord, your Holy One, the creator of Israel, your King" (Isaiah 43:15).[24]

Earthquakes and the Mount of Olives: After the two unique prophets seen by John the Revelator ascend into heaven (as described in chapter 11 of Revelation), a great and devastating earthquake will occur which John symbolically states will destroy a tenth part of the city of Jerusalem and will kill seven thousand men—not to mention women and children (see Revelation 11:13).[25] There will be "voices, and thunders, and lightnings; and there was a great earthquake, such as was not since men were upon the earth" (Revelation 16:18). The Mount of Olives will cleave in two from east to west, "and there shall be a very great valley [formed]; and half of the mountain shall remove toward the north, and half of it toward the south" (Zechariah 14:4).

The Lord appears to Judah: Terrified by the enormous earthquake, many of the Jews will run into the newly formed "valley of the mountains" where the Lord will appear to them (see Zechariah 14:5; Revelation 1:7). He will bear the wounds of his crucifixion on him, and one will say, "What are these wounds in thine hands?" He will answer, "Those with which I was wounded in the house of my friends" (Zechariah 13:6; 12:10; John 19:37).

Then will the Jews recognize their Messiah, and weep and lament and worship him (see D&C 45:52–53)—and the Savior will deliver Judah and rule thereafter in Jerusalem.[26]

As the Lord ushers in his reign, Jerusalem will become the "mountain of the Lord's house" (Isaiah 2:2–3; see also Psalm 122:1–9; D&C 133:13) and will become one of two great earthly capitals from which he will reign for a thousand years.[27]

The Promised Land: When the Second Coming occurs, the land of Jerusalem (the promised land) will revert back to its "own place"—perhaps physically as well as spiritually (see D&C 133:24). The land will be restored to the twelve tribes of Israel (see Ezekiel 45:4–8) for their inheritance (see 3 Nephi 20:29). And all former enemies of Israel will be overcome, the ancient animosity between Judah and Ephraim eliminated, the way provided for the other tribes to join them (Isaiah 11:13–15) and Jerusalem and Zion will be established together (see Isaiah 2:2–3; 3 Nephi 20:34–46; Ether 13:4–11); "for out of Zion shall go forth the law, and the word of the Lord [shall go forth] from Jerusalem" (Isaiah 2:3).

The Gathering

> "Thus saith the Lord God; Behold, I will take
> the children of Israel from among the heathen,
> whither they be gone, and will gather them
> on every side, and bring them into their own
> land."

> Ezekiel 37:21

Jacob, whose name was changed to Israel by the Lord, had twelve sons: Reuben, Simeon, Levi, Judah, Zebulun, Issachar, Dan, Gad, Asher, Naphtali, Joseph, and Benjamin. These twelve sons became known as the house of Israel, the twelve tribes of Israel, or just Israel. God chose these tribes to be his people. He declared to Moses, "Ye shall be a peculiar treasure unto me above all people" (Exodus 19:5; in *The Torah* translation of the same verse reads: "You shall be My treasured possession among all the peoples").[1] Isaiah confirmed this unique selection when he declared, "Thus saith the Lord that created thee, O Jacob, and he that formed thee, O Israel . . . I am the Lord, your Holy One, the creator of Israel" (Isaiah 43:1, 15).

Israel was a united nation for the most part until the death of Solomon. After his death, the nation was divided and became known as the Northern Kingdom and the Southern Kingdom. The Northern Kingdom was also called the Kingdom of Israel, and it was inhabited by the tribes of Reuben, Simeon, Zebulun, Issachar, Dan, Gad, Asher, Naphtali, and large parts of Benjamin, Joseph, and Levi. This kingdom was conquered by Assyria in approximately 721 B.C. The tribes living therein, having been rejected by the Lord due to their wickedness, were carried off by the Assyrians and became *lost* (see 2 Kings 17:6; 18:11–12). They have since been described as the *lost ten tribes* or *the lost tribes of Israel* (see 2 Nephi 29:13; 3 Nephi 17:4; 21:26).

After the destruction of the Northern Kingdom, the Southern Kingdom eventually became known as Israel. It was also known as the Kingdom of Judah because Judah was the only whole tribe to inhabit it (although parts of the tribes of Benjamin, Levi, Joseph, and individual members of other tribes also resided there). Because of the predominance of the tribe of Judah, those of the populace who belonged to other tribes also became known politically as Jews. An example of this is the prophet Lehi. He records that he was a descendant of Joseph (see 1 Nephi 5:14), yet his son Nephi records that the remnants of his seed were Jews (see 2 Nephi 30:4). A second example is found in the book of Esther. Mordecai, who raised Esther, was introduced in the text as "a certain Jew," yet he was of the tribe of Benjamin (see Esther 2:5). Eventually (and especially today) the terms *Jews* and *Israel* have become synonymous. This amalgamation of terminology is the predominant reason for the apostate belief that the doctrine of the gathering concerns only the Jews. The Jews themselves have adopted this amalgamation of their name to the extent that they project it not only forward but also backward, at least as far as the Exodus, where one commentary on *The Torah* states that the purpose of the Passover Seder is to "[rehearse] the Exodus and the birth of the Jewish people."[2] In this quotation they clearly use the term *Jewish* rather than *Israelite*.

As the Lord told Nephi, however, "Know ye not that there are more nations than one?" (2 Nephi 29:7.) Twelve tribes were scattered, and twelve tribes must be gathered.

No church can claim to be God's true church without teaching the doctrine of the gathering correctly and claiming that God is the source of its authority to gather the people. The gathering is one of the greatest signs the people of the earth will receive to confirm the fact that the Savior's ancient gospel has been restored and that his Second Coming is at hand. It is also one of the doctrines that creates the most confusion in the Christian and Jewish worlds. While the gathering is defined as the physical accumulation of the people of Israel to their promised lands, it also denotes the gathering of all the people of the world—Jew and Gentile—to the Lord and his gospel (see Isaiah 49:6).

In the strict sense, a Gentile is someone who has descended from Japheth, the oldest (see Moses 8:12; IV, Genesis 7:85) son of Noah (see Genesis 10:1–5). However, the term *Gentile* is used in multiple ways throughout the scriptures to describe (1) those nations into which Israel was scattered, (2) the heathen, (3) the unrighteous, (4) those not of Israel, and (5) non-Jews.[3] For the purpose of gathering the people of the earth to the gospel, the term *Gentile* would include all of the above, as well as those who are neither Israelite nor Gentile: i.e., those of the seed of Abraham who are descendants of Ishmael and Abraham's other children, and those who descended from Noah's son Ham. Even though these races are not classified as Gentiles in other situations and are not specifically referred to in the gathering scriptures, Isaiah 49:6 makes it clear that the Lord's gospel is to be offered to *all* the people of the earth. Therefore, this general gathering of the repentant to the gospel is inclusive of all peoples (see 2 Nephi 30:1–2).

The story of the scattering and gathering of Israel (including all who repent and come into the kingdom of God) is told by Zenos in his familiar allegory of the vineyard. The allegory compares Israel and the Gentiles to trees and branches in a vineyard. The vineyard represents the world, God the Father is the master of the vineyard, Jesus is the servant, and the others are the Savior's prophets, missionaries or representatives (see Jacob 5). Israel is likened to a tame olive tree planted in the vineyard. The olive tree flourishes for a time, but eventually the master sees that it is beginning to decay, so he prunes and digs around it (allegorically calling Israel to repentance). After the pruning, the vineyard begins to bring forth tender new branches. These branches represent the Moses period where, through repentance and recommitment, Israel returns to the covenant (see Jacob 5:4–6) and, after the generation of unbelievers die in the wilderness, is led into the promised land (see Jacob 5:7–9). But in the allegory, the main top of the tree begins to perish (see Jacob 5:6), so the master of the vineyard instructs the servant to "pluck the branches from a wild olive-tree" and replace the "main branches which are beginning to wither away" (Jacob 5:7). The wild branches represent the Gentiles who were either conquered by or assimilated into the tribes of Israel while Israel occupied the promised land (see Jacob 5:10).

The servant continues to work in the vineyard and eventually transplants many of the "natural branches of the tree" into the "nethermost" part of the vineyard (the lost ten tribes) (see Jacob 5:11–15; Nehemiah 1:9). He then continues to prune (via the Babylonian conquest and captivity) the better parts of the vineyard where the "wild branches" have been grafted in until the tree (Judah) again produces good fruit, "like unto the natural fruit" (Jacob 5:16–18). When he goes to view the natural branches that he hid in the nethermost part of the vineyard (the ten tribes), he finds that they too have produced "much fruit" (Jacob 5:19–22).

Then the master of the vineyard directs the servant to "look hither and behold the last [tree]." The master had planted this tree in a "good spot of ground," and nourished it for a long time. But only part of the tree brought forth "tame fruit," while the rest of the tree brought forth "wild fruit," even though he had nourished this tree the same as the others. This tree allegorically represents the branch of Joseph (the Nephites and the Lamanites), which was led from Jerusalem and transplanted into the best part of the vineyard (the Western Hemisphere) at the time of Jeremiah. The branches that are "part tame" represent the Nephites, and those that are "part wild" depict the Lamanites. The master wants the servant to "pluck off the branches" that have not produced good fruit and "cast them into the fire." But the servant petitions the master to have patience and "nourish" the tree a little longer (see Jacob 5:25–28). The master agrees to do this, and for a time he and the servant continue to nourish *all* the trees in the vineyard.

A long time passes (see Jacob 5:29). The master and the servant again go to labor in the vineyard. They find that the tame olive tree into which they grafted the wild branches (representing Judah after her return from Babylon up to the time of Christ) has produced much wild fruit, none of it good.   The allegory then makes specific mention of the "natural branches" that were planted in the best part of the vineyard (the Nephites and the Lamanites who replaced the Jaredites, who were an earlier planting by the Lord) (Jacob 5:38–51). The "natural branches" have also produced wild fruit, and have totally overcome that part of the tree "which brought forth good fruit, even that the branch had withered away and died" (the destruction of the Nephites by the Lamanites) (Jacob 5:40–43). All the trees in the vineyard have become corrupt (from the time of the Savior's earthly ministry until the Apostasy) and are producing only wild fruit. They have all overcome their roots (the covenant of Abraham) (see Jacob 5:38–39). And although with much work the vineyard will again produce good fruit for a short period of time (after the Lord's resurrection), eventually all parts of the vineyard will become corrupt (go into total apostasy) (see Jacob 5:38–51).

It grieves the master to lose his trees. "Who is it," he asks, "that has corrupted my vineyard?" (Jacob 5:46–47, 49.) And the servant explains that it is the loftiness of the vineyard (the self-righteousness of the leaders and the people) which has overcome the strong, righteous roots of the trees (see Jacob 5:48).

The master again wants to destroy the vineyard, but the servant convinces him to withdraw the wild branches and restore the natural branches back to the tame olive tree (preparing the people for the restoration of the gospel and the gathering of the righteous) (see Jacob 5:51–60). The master agrees, and new servants are called to labor in the vineyard. The master gives them the covenant and instructs them to clean out the wild branches and again bring back the natural branches to the tame tree (the gathering of Israel). He then causes them to prune the vineyard for the last time (see Jacob 5:61–69). (Laborers will be called to spread the gospel in the latter-days, and the fruits of their labors [the righteous] will be gathered to God in preparation for the Lord's Second Coming) (see Jacob 5:70–74).

After the Lord's final Advent, a "long time" will be spent "gathering the good fruit from his vineyard" (gleaning the righteous from the world during the millennial period). But eventually, the vineyard will again be infested with evil, and the master will cause both the good fruit and the bad fruit to be gathered: the good he will preserve unto himself, and the bad he will "cast away into its own place in preparation for the final judgment. "And then," the Lord concludes, "cometh the [little] season and the end; and my vineyard [the world] will I cause to be burned with fire" (Jacob 5:75–77; Matthew 13:24–30; see also D&C 101:44–62).

Five distinct groups of people must be gathered in preparation for the Second Coming of the Lord: Judah, the ten lost tribes, the Lamanites (Manasseh), Ephraim, and the Gentiles (which would include the Arabs and the those of African descent).

1. *Judah*: Judah is to be gathered to Jerusalem, a scriptural synonym for the promised land, which is now encompassed within the State of Israel (Chapter 5).

2. *The Ten Lost Tribes:* Since the ten tribes are *lost*, any reference to their location is speculative. And while individual members of any given tribe may be located and brought within the gospel covenant, the unit of Israel known as the lost tribes will not be *found* until the Second Coming. The following information is all we know about them:

a. Joseph Smith stated that John the Revelator was preaching among them.[4]

b. They are described as being located in the "north" countries (see Jeremiah 16:14–15; D&C 110:11; 133:26). (We know from these scriptures, however, that the Lord remembers them.)

c. The Savior went to the lost tribes after his resurrection and ministered to them (see 3 Nephi 17:4).

d. In the last days, the "work of the Father" will commence among them (albeit this work will be independent of the Church, because they are lost) (see 3 Nephi 21:26).

e. Their scriptural records will eventually be available to the other tribes (see 2 Nephi 29:13).

f. They will be gathered out from the wicked at the destruction of the devil's kingdom (see Isaiah 13:5).

g. They will be gathered from the north country[5] to join the other tribes of Israel (Judah and Joseph) (see Jeremiah 3:18; Zechariah 2:6; Articles of Faith 1:10).

h. At their return a great highway will be cast up (probably not an actual highway, but the symbolical means by which the Lord will gather them) (Isaiah 11:16; 35:8–10; D&C 133:27).

i. Their former enemies "will become a prey unto them" (D&C 133:28).

j. They will eventually receive all of the blessings of the covenant of Abraham in Zion: the gospel will be preached to them, and they will receive their glory (see Isaiah 35:8–10; 3 Nephi 21:26; D&C 133:28).

k. They will bring their treasures to the tribe of Ephraim in Zion, "And there shall they fall down and be crowned with glory, even in Zion, by the hands of the servants of the Lord, even the children of Ephraim" (D&C 133:32; see also Isaiah 60:8–12).

l. Songs of everlasting joy will be sung at their return (see D&C 133:33).[6]

3. *The Lamanites*: Even though the Lamanites are described in the allegory of the vineyard as an unrighteous and wild branch of the tame olive tree, the Book of Mormon promises that they will be preserved and their days prolonged until the time that they are gathered (see Helaman 15:11–16) and grafted back into the olive tree as a natural branch (see 1 Nephi 15:16). The desire to gather the Lamanites to the restored gospel of Jesus Christ commenced soon after the organization of the Church in April of 1830. During a conference of the Church on September 26, 1830, several brethren expressed the desire to serve a mission to the Lamanites. Joseph inquired of the Lord concerning this, and what

is now section 32 of the Doctrine and Covenants was received in response. The Lord's revelation in this section commenced missionary work among the Lamanites.

One purpose of the Book of Mormon is to convince the Lamanites of the truth of the gospel (see Mormon 5:12–15). In addition, through this book they will come to realize that they are of the house of Israel (see 2 Nephi 30:3–6) and that it was prophesied that the gospel would be taken to them (see 1 Nephi 15:14; Alma 9:16–17; 3 Nephi 20–21).

Because of this opportunity, many Lamanites will be called to repentance, will receive the Bible and the Book of Mormon, will accept Christ, and will once again come under the covenant of Abraham (see Mormon 7:1–10). When they accept these blessings, their civilization will flourish in the wilderness and "blossom as the rose" (D&C 49:24; see also 3 Nephi 5:21–26).[7]

4. *Ephraim*: The Lord's ancient prophets prophesied that almost immediately after the restoration of the gospel, missionaries would be sent to the world to declare its glad tidings (see Isaiah 18; Jeremiah 16:14–16). They would be sent to the nations of the world and the isles of the sea to gather Israel home (see D&C 133:7–8).[8] They would gather a scattered Ephraim (see Zechariah 10:6–12) and all Israel from the four quarters of the earth (see Matthew 24:31; 1 Nephi 22:25; D&C 133:7).

Just as the spirit of gathering moved on the tribe of Judah after Orson Hyde's dedicatory prayer (Chapter 5), so also did it move on those who heard the gospel of salvation preached in Great Britain during the early years of the Church (even though Joseph Smith instructed those leaving for the British mission *not* to teach the gathering until the gospel had been established there and the Spirit clearly manifested otherwise).[9] However, the keys of the gathering had been restored (see D&C 110:11), and the gathering spirit moved upon mankind regardless of whether the missionaries taught it or not.

> No sooner were the people baptized than they were seized with a desire to gather with the main body of the Church. 'I find it is difficult to keep anything from the Saints,' writes Elder Taylor in his journal of this period, 'for the Spirit of God

reveals it to them.' '. . . Some time ago Sister Mitchell dreamed that she, her husband and a number of others were on board a vessel, and that there were other vessels, loaded with Saints, going somewhere. She felt very happy and was rejoicing in the Lord.' Another sister, Elder Taylor informs us, had a similar dream, and was informed that all the Saints were going. Neither of these sisters nor any of the Saints at that time, knew anything about the principle of gathering, yet all were anxious to leave their homes, their kindred and the associations of a lifetime, to join the main body of the Church in a distant land, the members of which were total strangers to them. The same spirit has rested upon the people in every nation where the Gospel has been received. There has been little need of preaching the gathering, the people as a rule have had to be restrained rather than encouraged to the matter of gathering to Zion and her stakes.[10]

The Spirit had spoken clearly and the gathering from the British Mission moved forward rapidly.

In compliance with the covenant of Abraham, the Lord commanded that the converts of The Church of Jesus Christ of Latter-day Saints be gathered to a promised land (see D&C 29:7–8; September 1830). In preparation for fulfilling of this commandment, the Lord told the Saints in the East to assemble in Ohio. This was the first commandment to gather in this dispensation (see D&C 37:3). From there the Saints were to go westward until the Lord revealed where the city of the New Jerusalem would be located (see D&C 42:9; February 9, 1831). The Lord then moved rapidly to reveal the exact location of Zion, for "the Spirit of the Lord Jesus Christ is a gathering spirit."[11]

In March of 1831 he commanded:

Wherefore I, the Lord, have said, gather ye out from the eastern lands, assemble ye yourselves together ye elders of my church; go ye forth into the western countries, call upon the inhabitants to repent, and inasmuch as they do repent, build up churches unto me.

And with one heart and with one mind, gather up your riches that ye may purchase an inheritance which shall hereafter be appointed unto you.

And it shall be called the New Jerusalem, a land of peace, a city of refuge, a place of safety for the saints of the Most High God (D&C 45:64–66).

In June 1831, the Lord told Joseph Smith and Sidney Rigdon to leave their houses and go to the land of Missouri (see D&C 52:3). They were instructed to hold a conference on "the land, which I will consecrate unto my people, which are a remnant of Jacob, and those who are heirs according to the covenant" (D&C 52:2). However, the land which was declared to be the land of their inheritance was then in the hands of their "enemies" (see D&C 52:42). Finally, on July 20, 1831, Joseph recounted that the "very spot upon which He [the Lord] designed to commence the work of the gathering, and the up building of an 'holy city,' which shall be called Zion,"[12] was revealed to be in Missouri:

Hearken, O ye elders of my church, saith the Lord your God, who have assembled yourselves together, according to my commandments, in this land, which is the land of Missouri, which is the land which I have appointed and consecrated for the gathering of the saints.

Wherefore, this is the land of promise, and the place for the city of Zion.

And thus saith the Lord your God, if you will receive wisdom here is wisdom. Behold, the place which is now called Independence is the center place; and a spot for the temple is lying westward, upon a lot which is not far from the courthouse (D&C 57:1–3).

The sacred location of the city of Zion "spoken of by David, in the one hundred and second Psalm, [would] be built upon the land of America,"[13] where the "ransomed of the Lord" could "return and come to Zion with songs and everlasting joy upon their heads" (Isaiah 35:10).

Although Zion was *not* redeemed at that time because of the transgressions of the early Saints (see D&C 105:9), it will yet be redeemed in the Lord's due time (see D&C 136:18).

Missionaries are now sent to gather Ephraim (along with the remnants of the other tribes of Israel) from among the wicked in "all the lands whither [the Lord has] driven them" (Jeremiah 16:14–16; see also Isaiah 18) so that they may receive the word of God and come to the ensign (gospel) that God has established in the latter-days (see Isaiah 11:11; Daniel 2). Obstacles will be removed to allow the gathering to take place, for as the Lord said in Ezekiel, "I will bring you out from the people, and will gather you out of the countries wherein ye are scattered, with a mighty hand, and with a stretched out arm, and with fury poured out . . . . I will cause you to pass under the rod [of judgment], and I will bring you into the bond of the covenant" (Ezekiel 20:34, 37).

Until the Lord redeems Zion and gathers the Saints for his return to the New Jerusalem, converts are to be gathered where "the Lord shall locate a stake of Zion" (D&C 109:39; 136:10). These stakes are to be appointed in "regions round about" as "they shall be manifested" unto the Lord's servants and will be created as "curtains or the strength" for Zion (D&C 101:21; 115:18).

5. *The Gentiles (including the Arabs and Those of African Descent)*: There are nowhere near the number of scriptural references concerning the gathering of the Gentiles (and none specifically relating to the Arabs and those of African descent) as there are concerning the gathering of Israel, but there is a sufficient number to make two things clear:

a.   The Gentiles (definition page 71) will have the gospel declared unto them and will have the opportunity to gather and become heirs according to the covenant.

b.   Once they repent and become heirs according to the covenant, they are included in all of the general gathering scriptures.

The title page of the Book of Mormon states that the message of the book (the gospel) is brought forth not only for the remnants of the house of Israel, but also for the "convincing of the Jew and Gentile that Jesus is the Christ." During his visit to the Western Hemisphere, the Lord stated that there were many "not of this land" who had not yet heard his voice, and he declared that his words would "be manifested unto the Gentiles" (3 Nephi 16:1–4). He prophesied that in the latter days the truth would "come unto the Gentiles" (3 Nephi 16:7), but that many would reject it (see 3 Nephi 16:10). He reaffirmed this teaching in Doctrine and Covenants 18:26, stating that the gospel would be declared both to the Gentiles and to the Jews, and that missionaries would be prepared to extend the gospel to them—"as many as will believe" (D&C 90:8). Finally, Paul wrote to the Romans describing the Gentiles as a "wild olive tree" that, when grafted in among the branches of the good olive tree, could partake of the "root and fatness of the [natural] tree" (see Romans 11:16–26) and become heirs to the covenant of Abraham.

The sign of the gathering, both the specific gathering and the general gathering, has been preached by almost all of God's prophets from earliest times. Enoch rejoiced in the knowledge of Zion (the New Jerusalem) and those who would gather to it (see Moses 7:62), and Moses, after prophesying of the diaspora, declared:

> But if from thence thou shalt seek the Lord thy God, thou shalt find him, if thou seek him with all thy heart and with all thy soul.
>
> When thou art in tribulation, and all these things are come upon thee, *even in the latter days*, if thou turn to the Lord thy God, and shalt be obedient unto his voice;
>
> (For the Lord thy God is a merciful God;) he will not forsake thee, neither destroy thee, nor forget the covenant of thy fathers which he sware unto them. (Deuteronomy 4:29–31; emphasis added).

Isaiah spoke of the gathering in many chapters of his book,[14] Jeremiah spoke of it in five of his chapters,[15] and Ezekiel in five of his.[16] It is also mentioned in Hosea (see 1:10–11), Amos (see 9:11–15), Micah,[17] Zephaniah, Zechariah, and Joel.[18] Book of Mormon prophets also spoke of it,[19] and once the restoration was complete, the Lord spoke of it repeatedly in the Doctrine and Covenants.[20]

John the Revelator was given a vision of a "little book," which symbolically represented the gathering. The Lord commanded John to eat the little book, but although it was sweet to his taste, it was bitter in his belly (see Revelation 10:9–10; D&C 77:14). The book was bitter to John when he saw those who would not repent and come unto Christ. It was sweet when he saw the culmination of the gathering and the reuniting of the great cities of Jerusalem, Enoch, and the New Jerusalem at the Lord's Second Coming (see Revelation 21).

The sign of the gathering is ongoing. It commenced with the restoration of the gospel and will accelerate as the Lord's Advent becomes imminent. It is recorded that angels will assist men in the final gathering (Joseph Smith–Matthew 1:37), and it will not be completed until all the righteous have been gathered into the Savior's kingdom.

> Therefore, behold, the days come, saith the Lord, that they shall no more say, The Lord liveth, which brought up the children of Israel out of the land of Egypt;
>
> But, The Lord liveth, which brought up and which led the seed of the house of Israel out of the north country, and from all countries whither I had driven them; and they shall dwell in their own land" (Jeremiah 23:7–8; see also 16:14–16).

Part Three

Babylon

"And there followed another angel, saying, Babylon is fallen, is fallen, that great city, because she made all nations drink of the wine of the wrath of her fornication."

Revelation 14:8

"And Babylon, the glory of kingdoms . . . shall be as when God overthrew Sodom and Gomorrah."

Isaiah 13:19

The Devil and 7
His Kingdom

> "And no marvel; for Satan himself is transformed into an angel of light. Therefore it is no great thing if his ministers also be transformed as the ministers of righteousness."
>
> 2 Corinthians 11:14–15

Who Is the Devil?

Satan, Lucifer, Beelzebub, leviathan, son of the morning, prince of this world, the serpent, prince of the power of the air, the beast, the great red dragon—all these titles are names of the devil, the source of all evil. He is described in the book of Moroni as an entity that "persuadeth no man to do good, no, not one" (Moroni 7:17). Who is the devil? He is the antithesis of Jesus Christ!

John the Revelator refers to the devil's kingdom as "Babylon" or the "great and abominable church" as he defines the consummate power of the evil one's empire: "Babylon" because of the great biblical city that was the center of the devil's ancient power and sorceries; the "great and abominable church" because Satan's latter-day organization, while it may not be an actual church, is the antithesis of Christ's church upon the earth. John tells us that written on the crown of the woman who symbolically represents the city of Babylon is the phrase, "the mother of harlots and abominations of the earth" (Revelation 17:5). All her evils are "the midst of wickedness [the center of all evil things], which is spiritual Babylon" (D&C 133:14).

The Devil's Past

In the beginning, Lucifer was with God the Father in the pre-existence. He was a choice son of our Heavenly Father. Before he was cast down to the earth for disobedience, he was known as the "son of the morning" (Isaiah 14:12). But evil was found in this once noble spirit, because he rejected the Father and sought to exalt his "throne above the stars of God" (Isaiah 14:13).

While citing God's condemnation of the prince of Tyrus, Ezekiel gives us a double-reference description of the devil. Ezekiel makes it clear that while there may have been an actual prince of Tyrus, it is really Lucifer that is being described. And while Ezekiel portrays him as "full of wisdom" and "perfect in beauty," God is condemning him:

> Thou hast been in Eden the garden of God . . .
> thou wast upon the holy mountain of god . . . Thou
> wast perfect in thy ways from the day that thou
> wast created, till iniquity was found in thee. By
> the multitude of thy merchandise they have filled
> the midst of thee with violence, and thou hast
> sinned . . . Thine heart was lifted up because of
> thy beauty, thou hast corrupted thy wisdom by
> reason of thy brightness: I will cast thee to the
> ground, I will lay thee before kings . . . I will bring
> thee to ashes upon the earth in the sight of all them
> that behold thee. All they that know thee among
> the people shall be astonished at thee: thou shalt
> be a terror, and never shalt thou be any more
> (Ezekiel 28:13–19; see also Isaiah 14:12–16).

Isaiah concurs with Ezekiel's lament: "How art thou fallen from heaven, O Lucifer, son of the morning! how art thou cut down to the ground" (Isaiah 14:12).

Jesus, like Satan, was also with the Father in the pre-existence, as were all of the Father's children who would come to this earth. As spirits we did not have physical bodies. We assume that our spirits appeared much as they do now, except that they resided as spiritual tabernacles; however, all of the Father's spirit children were designated to come to this earth and acquire a physical body under the plan of salvation. Among these spirits were "noble and great ones" (see Abraham 3:22–23) who would eventually occupy positions of authority and power on the earth in their temporal manifestations.

At a certain point in our progression in the pre-existence, the Father called a great council. He presented his plan for mortality—the plan of salvation. But Lucifer objected and presented a plan of his own. In his heart he wanted to have God's glory: "I will ascend into heaven . . ." he declared. "I will ascend above the heights of the clouds; I will be like the most High" (Isaiah 14:13–14).

God rejected Satan's plan, but the evil one's power and influence were so great that while yet in the presence of the Father, he convinced "the third part of the stars of heaven [the spirit children of God]" to rebel and follow him in his fight against the plan of salvation (Revelation 12:4; see also 12:3–9). Because of his rebellion and disobedience, Satan failed his "first estate" (the premortal existence; see Abraham 3:26), and he, as well as those who followed him, were punished by being cast out of the Father's presence: "cast . . . into the earth" (Revelation 12:9), never to receive a tabernacle of flesh. The "son of the morning" became "Satan, yea, even the devil, the father of all lies" (Moses 4:4), forever exiled from the Father's presence, for where God is, the devil and his angels can never come (see D&C 29:29). Thereafter, Lucifer had but one purpose: "to deceive and to blind men, and to lead them captive at his will, even as many as would not hearken unto [God's] voice" (Moses 4:4).

Several of Satan's exploits on the earth are described in the scriptures.[1] He has always had the power to tempt men and women and lead them spiritually captive—*if* they subject themselves to him. John the Revelator saw Satan's past and future activities in a vision and described him as "a great red dragon" (Revelation 12:3), the source of all evil and all evil power. And, as the "star" that fell from heaven to earth, he held the "key" to the "bottomless pit" (Revelation 9:1). When he opened that pit, a black smoke (representing evil in all its forms) issued forth and darkened the "sun and the air" (the light of the gospel being overcome by the devil's evil; i.e., the great apostasy) (Revelation 9:2). Out of the smoke came "locusts upon the earth"—wicked men who were given evil power, "as the scorpions of the earth," which allowed them to inflict harm on and control humanity. But these evil men were not as powerful as Elijah or Nephi! They could not "hurt" the earth. They could not cause famines and earthly catastrophes or seal the heavens from rain as Elijah and Nephi, the Lord's true prophets, had done, nor could they kill people. But just as Job was tormented by the devil, these wicked men were also able to afflict mankind (described as the sting of the scorpion) for a symbolic "five months" (an indeterminate period of time). They were allowed to do this because the men and women they tormented had succumbed to their evil power. As a result of their torment, people "[sought] death" but could not find it (see Revelation 9:3–10).

John attempts to describe the strange, symbolic locusts of torment he is seeing by *comparing* them to things he knows. But the limits on his vocabulary make it difficult for us to identify them. Finally, he defines the source of evil as a king (the devil) who rules the wicked of mankind. He is not a king in the literal sense, however; this is a symbolical representation of his reign over the evil in the hearts of mankind (see Revelation 9:1–11).

The Devil's Presence in the Latter Days

After John had envisioned the great power of the devil throughout the millennia prior to Christ and up through time to the Dark Ages, his vision expanded to show him Satan's extraordinary powers in the latter days, particularly just prior to the Lord's Second Coming. The devil's initial major offensive against righteousness in the last days began with the first vision received by Joseph Smith, the prophet of the Restoration. As Joseph began to pray for spiritual enlightenment, he was "seized upon" by the devil's power, a power which entirely overcame him and bound his tongue so that he "could not speak." "Thick darkness" closed around him, and he felt he was "doomed to sudden destruction."[2] Praying with all his strength, he was finally released from Satan's grasp and thereafter enjoyed the brilliant presence of both the Father and the Son (Joseph Smith–History 1:15–17).

Lucifer has expressed his power in many ways. In the latter days he has possessed some men[3] and attacked others.[4] It is recorded in the *History of the Church* that he fought against the first Lamanite mission.[5] He was the principal cause of the Missouri persecutions,[6] an achievement which earned him the dubious title of "father" of the Missouri mobs.[7] He has deceived some individuals with revelations supposedly given through "magic" stones.[8] He influenced Sister Sally Crandall, an early member of the Church in the Hulet Branch, to think that she could "know and see men's hearts." Because of this "gift," Sally Crandall and Sylvester Hulet, the head of the Hulet Branch, would not receive even the teachings of Joseph Smith himself unless his teachings agreed with the gifts these branch members felt they possessed.[9] The Hulet Branch also believed that they "received the word of the Lord by the gift of tongues," but the Church brethren of the time determined that the devil had deceived them, "as the gift of tongues is so often made use of by Satan to deceive the Saints."[10] The devil also created secret combinations, as in days of old, to attack the Church from within.[11] "In open vision by daylight," Brother W. W. Phelps "saw the destroyer in his most horrible power, ride upon the face of the waters."[12] The *History of the Church* also tells us that an enraged devil will become the cause of much destruction and war in the latter days.[13]

Lucifer has the ability to deceive and mislead mankind by appearing as "an angel of light."[14] He was even the cause of a division in Joseph Smith's own family, and the instigator of a "division among the Twelve, also among the Seventy, and bickering and jealousies between the Elders and the official members of the Church." But Joseph was determined to "amicably dispose of and settle all family difficulties," as well as the conflicts between the Brethren. He knew that the cloud would burst and that "Satan's kingdom" would eventually be "laid in ruins."[15] Finally, Joseph said, "there are signs in heaven, earth and hell . . . The devil knows many signs, but [he] does not know the sign of the Son of Man, or Jesus."[16]

While Satan may or may not have known all the requirements and revelations surrounding the restoration of the gospel, he has always been a great anticipator of the restoration of some of the gospel's principal doctrines. Prior to the restoration of the doctrine of consecration and stewardship, he inspired a counterfeit united order to be developed in Kirtland called "common stock."[17] On another occasion, he designed a counterfeit polygamy scheme which was practiced by John C. Bennett in Nauvoo before polygamy was practiced by the Church. Dr. Bennett "seduced an innocent female by his lying, and subjected her character to public disgrace . . . But his depraved heart would not suffer him to stop [there]. Not being contented with having disgraced one female, he made an attempt upon others; and . . . overcame them also, evidently not caring whose character was ruined, so that his wicked, lustful appetites might be gratified." Not only did he indulge in these practices himself, he convinced others to do the same—falsely claiming that the prophet and other authorities of the Church had sanctioned his practices. When his evil ways were discovered he attempted suicide, but he was unsuccessful. He later lost his membership in the Church and supposedly affiliated himself with some Missourians who were plotting destruction against members of the Church.[18]

Joseph rarely taught on the subject of Satan, but he did admonish the members to be aware of the devil's flattering deception of self-righteousness when he declared, "We are full of selfishness; the devil flatters us that we are very righteous, when we are feeding on the faults of others."[19] Joseph denounced self-justification for transgression, stating that if "Satan [was] generally blamed for the evils which we did . . . [and] . . . was the cause of all our wickedness, men could not be condemned. The devil could not compel mankind to do evil; all was voluntary. God *would* not exert any compulsory means, and the devil *could* not [emphasis added]."[20]

The devil can also ensconce his power in a church or a religion. Paul, after enumerating a litany of Satan's evils among the people of the earth, describes the devil's influence among the religions of the latter days: religions that have "a form of godliness, but [deny] the power thereof." The members of these religions are "ever learning," he states, yet "never able to come to the knowledge of the truth." He writes Timothy and warns him (as he warns us all) to "turn away" from such religions (see 2 Timothy 3:1–7). Nephi declared, "Behold there are save two churches only; the one is the church of the Lamb of God, and the other is the church of the devil" (1 Nephi 14:10). In another chapter Nephi describes Satan's church as the "great and abominable church," and states that the devil is "the founder of it" (1 Nephi 13:6). The "abominable church" that Nephi speaks of is not any *particular* church but is inclusive of all religions that are opposed to the "church of the Lamb of God." These "forms of godliness" symbolically describe Satan's deceptive counterfeit doctrines of salvation, which *cause* men to "ever learn," but never "come to the knowledge of the truth."

John the Revelator was describing the devil's power and the enormity of his success through deception when he symbolically referred to Satan's "church" as the "great whore that sitteth upon many waters . . . the mother of . . . abominations" (Revelation 17:1, 5); this power caused John to wonder "with great admiration" (Revelation 17:6).

Satan's deceptions can take many forms besides churches or religions. Paul warns the Colossians that men will also be spoiled "through philosophy and vain deceit, after the tradition of men, after the rudiments of the world" (Colossians 2:8), and through "profane and vain babblings, and oppositions of science falsely so called" (1 Timothy 6:20).

The Devil's Future

Revelation 13:1–10

1. And I stood upon the sand of the sea, and saw a beast rise up out of the sea, having seven heads and ten horns, and upon his horns ten crowns, and upon his heads the name of blasphemy.

2. And the beast which I saw was like unto a leopard, and his feet were as the feet of a bear, and his mouth as the mouth of a lion: and the dragon gave him his power, and his seat, and great authority.

3. And I saw one of his heads as it were wounded to death; and his deadly wound was healed: and all the world wondered after the beast.

4. And they worshipped the dragon which gave power unto the beast: and they worshipped the beast, saying, Who is like unto the beast? who is able to make war with him?

5. And there was given unto him a mouth speaking great things and blasphemies; and power was given unto him to continue forty and two months.

6. And he opened his mouth in blasphemy against God, to blaspheme his name, and his tabernacle, and them that dwell in heaven.

7. And it was given unto him to make war with the saints, and to overcome them: and power was given him over all kindreds, and tongues, and nations.

8. And all that dwell upon the earth shall worship him, whose names are not written in the book of life of the Lamb slain from the foundation of the world.

9. If any man have an ear, let him hear.

10. He that leadeth into captivity shall go into captivity: he that killeth with the sword must be killed with the sword. Here is the patience and the faith of the saints.

John the Revelator saw many elements of the devil's kingdom as they would appear in the days prior to the Second Coming, and he depicted these elements symbolically in the book of Revelation. These symbols are linked with many thing—elements of the gospel, historical visions, revelations given by the Lord, miracles, even the existence of the Savior himself—and they are infused with descriptions of Satan's false doctrines through imitation, substitution, and counterfeiting in his attempt to deceive the hearts of men. Other prophets—such as Daniel, Zechariah,

Isaiah, and Ezekiel—also saw adaptations or portions of John's vision, and their descriptions help us to understand the words of Revelation.[21]

The following are definitions and explanations of the principal symbols found in John's vision of the devil's latter-day kingdom:

The Dragon: The term *dragon* always refers to the devil; however, he may also be referred to by one of his other names or by other symbols. Normally it is not difficult to determine whether these names or symbols are referring to Satan, even when they are used to describe other elements of the vision.

The Beast: This is the beast of Revelation 13:1. It appears out of the sea and has seven heads and ten horns. It represents the symbolic Antichrist leader of the devil's kingdom.

Another Beast: This beast comes out of the earth. It has two horns like a lamb and speaks like a dragon. It is the symbolic false prophet of the Antichrist beast.

The Woman: There are two women in John's vision. The woman of Revelation, chapter 12, represents Christ's Church (see JST, Revelation 12:7). The woman of Revelation, chapter 17, represents the devil's kingdom.

The Great and Abominable Church: This phrase is used to symbolically refer to the devil's latter-day kingdom, in whatever form it takes. It is not an actual church.

The waters: The waters represent people: individuals, multitudes, kings, nations, tongues, or any other general term that would designate mankind.

Time: When this term is used (as well as other symbols or terms that relate to time), it may or may not have any relevance to *actual time.* Like the term "months" in Revelation 9:5, it might represent an *undefined* period of time. An undefined short period may be designated as "hours" by John, while a longer period may be represented by "days," or a large number of "hours." Usually the sequence of the verses identifies the general time period intended. There are, however, a few specific references to time which may be literal that are identified later in the chapter.

War: John may actually be depicting a literal war when he uses this term, but it can also be used to represent other methods of destroying Christ-oriented belief.

The Lamb: "The Lamb" always refers to Jesus Christ.

Worship: This is not the type of *worship* normally associated with religion. In the context of John's vision, the term is generally symbolic. It means belonging to, in adherence with, or in agreement with the devil's kingdom.

Mark: There are two marks referred to in Revelation. One mark is described as a "seal" placed by God on the forehead of the righteous. The other mark is the "mark of the beast." It is represented by the number 666 and is described as being located on the right hand and the forehead. Both of these marks symbolically represent those who have had their calling and election made sure—either with God or with the devil. They are not actual marks on the body.

Buy and Sell: These terms are used to represent economic power or the material goods of the world.

Locusts: "Locusts" represent wicked men.

Scorpion's Sting: This is a symbol of torment, destruction, discomfort, or restriction.

Mystery Babylon: This phrase represents the use of sorcery and other religious or mystical deceptions which were used in the Babylonian Kingdom. It can also represent anything used by the devil to deceive mankind.

The Great Whore: This phrase refers to the devil's kingdom in whatever form it takes. Satan's kingdom is also referred to as "the woman," "the great and abominable church," and "the great city."

The Bottomless Pit, or Perdition: These phrases refer to God's final punishment of the devil and his followers.

The Great City: This phrase refers to the devil's earthly kingdom in the latter days. His kingdom is also referred to as "the woman," "the great and abominable church," and "the great whore."

Merchandise: This term depicts the things of the earth and represents worldly wealth and power in whatever forms they may take.

All of the above symbols and terms will be used in the following discussion of John's vision.

The Antichrist Beast

Paul introduced the latter-day Antichrist to the Thessalonians when he told them about the apostasy that would take place before the Lord's Second Coming. He told them that the "man of sin . . . the son of perdition" would be revealed to the world. He would oppose the Lord and exalt himself "above all that is called God, or that is worshipped." He would make himself a substitute for God by sitting "in the temple of God, showing himself that he is God." Further, Paul stated that the Antichrist would come with Satan's power and be able to create "signs and lying wonders" to deceive mankind (see 2 Thessalonians 2:3–11).

John saw this same Antichrist in his vision, and while his vision is symbolic, it is more informative and graphic than Paul's statement to the Thessalonians. His vision of the Antichrist beast began while he "stood upon the sand of the sea." As he gazed out from the shore he saw a beast rise up out of the water. The beast was unlike anything John had ever seen. It had seven heads and ten horns: upon each horn was a crown, and written upon each of the seven heads was the word *blasphemy* (see Revelation 13:1).

The description of the beast lends insight into John's problem. He is seeing things in his vision that are symbolic—things representative of other *objects, people, events,* and *information*—and he does not have the words to adequately describe them. Therefore, he draws analogies to the things with which he is familiar—and this is a key to understanding the vision! John compares the symbolic images he sees to the things he knows and for which he has a vocabulary, but due to the strange complexity of the images, his descriptions do not accurately depict what he is seeing. The beast rising out of the sea is a perfect example of this problem.

John continues to describe his vision: the beast he sees is also like a leopard, except that its feet are more like those of a bear and its mouth like that of a lion. (In the Joseph Smith Translation of the Bible, the following sentence is inserted just before John's description of the beast: "And I saw another sign, in the likeness of the kingdoms of the earth" [JST, Revelation 13:1].)

When the prophet Daniel saw this vision he described four great beasts: the first was like a lion with eagle's wings, the second like a bear, another like a leopard with four heads, and a fourth with iron teeth and ten horns (see Daniel 7). Remember, however, that it is not the image but the information that the image is conveying that is important.

Thus we see that both John and Daniel are viewing the history of nations, the influence of the devil upon them, and both the rise of and the diversity of the devil's kingdom in the latter days. And while it is interesting to attempt to envision in the mind's eye what the beast actually looks like, its appearance is unimportant. We may *wrest* the scriptures to say that the beast is cunning like a leopard, powerful like a bear, and supreme or exalted like the king of beasts (the lion), but it is inconsequential to the information conveyed in the vision.

After describing the beast, John rapidly moves to the substance of the vision. "The dragon gave [the beast] his power, and his seat, and great authority" (see Revelation 13:2). The dragon is Satan, the source of power for the historical, worldly kingdoms of the earth portrayed in the vision, and the one who gives the beast (the Antichrist) his seat (position) and his authority (power) to rule in the devil's latter-day kingdom.

As the vision progresses, John observes that one of the seven heads of the beast receives a deadly wound—a death wound! But the beast is miraculously healed, and the world wonders and worships the dragon who gave the beast power, saying, "Who is like unto him, and who is able to make war with him." This element of the vision has long caused mankind to look for a leader who would receive a terrible head wound and then miraculously recover, but John's vision is symbolic; therefore, this probably does not represent the unprecedented healing of an actual man. Certainly the beast with seven heads does not! What it probably means is that whatever form the devil's kingdom takes in the latter days, it will initially have a severe problem that will threaten its survival. But it will survive.

And the world will wonder "after the beast," meaning that they will be astonished or amazed that the entity survived its injury. Thereafter, they will worship the dragon which gave "power unto the beast," the literal interpretation of which would be that the *whole world* worshipped the devil, which of course is foolishness. The use of the term *worship* in this instance means *adherence*. Therefore, the world adheres to, follows, is influenced by, or belongs to whatever form the devil's kingdom will take in the latter days, and perhaps the world will even be deceived into thinking that it was the miraculous intervention by God that saved the entity from destruction.

It is possible that the devil's kingdom may be an organization, a cartel, a board of directors, a company, or even a system like the Internet. The statements of the people who are so astonished by the seemingly miraculous recovery of the entity in John's vision (i.e., "Who is like unto the beast? who is able to make war with him?") are merely window dressing. They are used to describe the tremendous success of Satan's organization and serve as examples of the powerful influence the devil's kingdom will have over people in the latter days.

In the visions of both John and Daniel, the beast is given a mouth and the ability to speak "great things" (Daniel 7:8). And what "great things" will it speak? "Blasphemy against God . . . his name . . . his tabernacle, and them that dwell in heaven" (see Revelation 13:5–6). Although this verse may be literal, in view of the success Satan's kingdom will enjoy in the latter days (after its miraculous recovery from near destruction), the "blasphemy against God" could represent an unrighteous form of *pride*. The beast might be using the power of communication to convince mankind of its own greatness and accomplishments, thus taking the place of God in their praise and adoration.

John's vision further relates that "power was given unto [the beast] to continue [speaking] forty and two months" (Revelation 13:5). This means that Satan's kingdom will enjoy the pinnacle of its great latter-day success for a period of time equal to that specified in Revelation 11, wherein it states that God's two prophets will prophesy to Jerusalem for a period of three and one-half years (see chapter 5; see also Revelation 11:3). Both the Lord's prophets and the Antichrist beast will have an equivalent period of time in which to function during the apex of their existence: forty-two months or three and one-half years. While most references to time in John's vision are symbolic and difficult to define, this period seems to have two possible meanings: one, that God's prophets and the Antichrist will each literally function for a period of three and one-half years; or two, that their work coincides in length of time, but that period of time, though lengthy, is undefined.

John's vision now gets specific about the activities of the Antichrist beast. He will make war against the saints by attacking their beliefs and their credibility. He will make them appear offensive to the world, and he will exclude them from his organization, whatever it is. During this period his power and dominion will expand, for John declares that he will have power over all "kindreds, and tongues, and nations" (Revelation 13:7). Taken literally, this would mean a world dictator: but again the words are symbolic and describe the effects of the beast's influence, not the influence of a single individual. It is therefore apparent that the influence of the devil's kingdom in the latter days will have such an enormous effect on mankind that almost everyone in the world will either succumb to or be affected by its evil authority. This is what John means when he says, "All that dwell upon the earth [in the latter days] shall worship him [the beast]" (Revelation 13:8), except those who are true believers, whose names are written in the Lamb's book of life and who will be warred against or excluded from the beast's organization.

Revelation 13:1–10 teaches us five specific things concerning the devil and his kingdom:

1.   The devil has exerted great influence over all the kingdoms of the world throughout history.

2.   The devil will firmly establish his kingdom in the latter days, regardless of the organizational form it takes.

3.   The devil will be the source of the power and authority held by the Antichrist beast.

4.   Satan will use anyone who will submit to him to accomplish his ends.

5.   The majority of the world's people will follow, adhere to, be influenced by, or belong to whatever organization it is that the devil establishes in the latter days.

John concludes this initial description of the Antichrist beast with a familiar scripture—"If any man have an ear, let him hear" (Revelation 13:9), a phrase he used in almost identical form as he closed his admonitions to each of the seven churches in the book of Revelation, chapters 2 and 3. This phrase means the same in all instances: John has given us the information and it is up to us (through the Spirit) to understand it.

Finally, John issues a warning: "He that leadeth into captivity shall go into captivity: he that killeth with the sword must be killed with the sword. Here is the patience and the faith of the saints" (Revelation 13:10). The Saints must be patient in tribulation, for they will be subject to the inversion of the Golden Rule if they are not: i.e., people will get what they give!

The Devil and His Kingdom— Continued

The Second Beast

Revelation 13:11-18

11. And I beheld another beast coming up out of the earth; and he had two horns like a lamb, and he spake as a dragon.

12. And he exerciseth all the power of the first beast before him, and causeth the earth and them which dwell therein to worship the first beast, whose deadly wound was healed.

13. And he doeth great wonders, so that he maketh fire come down from heaven on the earth in the sight of men,

14. And deceiveth them that dwell on the earth by the means of those miracles which he had power to do in

the sight of the beast; saying to them that dwell on the earth, that they should make an image to the beast, which had the wound by a sword, and did live.

15. And he had power to give life unto the image of the beast, that the image of the beast should both speak, and cause that as many as would not worship the image of the beast should be killed.

16. And he causeth all, both small and great, rich and poor, free and bond, to receive a mark in their right hand, or in their foreheads:

17. And that no man might buy or sell, save he that had the mark, or the name of the beast, or the number of his name.

18. Here is wisdom. Let him that hath understanding count the number of the beast: for it is the number of a man; and his number is Six hundred threescore and six.

"And I beheld another beast coming up out of the earth; and he had two horns like a lamb, and he spake as a dragon. And he exerciseth all the power of the first beast [the Antichrist] before him, and [he] causeth the earth and them which dwell therein to worship the first beast, whose deadly wound was healed" (Revelation 13:11-12). This second beast (be it man or entity) is the symbolic false prophet of the Antichrist beast—and an important figure in John's vision since he serves as a vanguard in the devil's kingdom. The fact that he has horns like a lamb and speaks like a dragon conjures up visions of a wolf in sheep's clothing, an individual or an organization that appears benign, but is in fact terribly dangerous. John specifically notes that this beast exercises "all the power of the first beast." This would indicate that the purpose of this beast is the same as that of the Antichrist—to deceive the people of the earth and lead them captive away from righteousness.

John's vision reveals that the beast will attempt to accomplish this goal in several ways:

1. *Worship of the Beast:* The Antichrist beast "causes" people to *worship* (belong to or be influenced by) him, and economic greed is the cause that the devil uses to entice people to participate in his organization in the latter days.

2. *The Wonders of the False Prophet:* The second beast is apparently capable of doing "great wonders," even making "fire come down from heaven." If this were a literal description of his powers, he would be capable of duplicating the power Moses exercised before Pharaoh (see Exodus 9:23), of matching the destructive judgment God pronounced upon Sodom and Gomorrah (see Genesis 19:24), or even using the power Elijah exercised when he called down fire from heaven to consume the sacrifice at the challenge of the wicked priests of Baal (see 1 Kings 18:38). But because John's vision is symbolic, the description of the second beast's power is probably not literal. John could be symbolically representing the fact that the *influence* of the false prophet may, to the astonishment of mankind, produce an effect *equivalent* to that produced by Moses and the Lord in the examples cited. The scriptures further state that the second beast will deceive mankind by "the means" (or way) he does his miracles. The conclusion that can be drawn from John's writing is that the false prophet is capable of accomplishing something so extraordinary that it is perceived by mankind to be miraculous. Moreover, since he has the power to perform his miracles "in the sight of the [first] beast," it seems obvious that his activities have the sanction not only of the Antichrist but of the devil as well. Through his miraculous deceptions he will be able to convince people that the "devil's kingdom" is the source of their blessings, thus substituting Satan and his organization for the Father and his kingdom.

Again, the "wound that was healed" is mentioned in these verses to emphasize the miraculous power of the evil Antichrist beast and his prophet. It would appear that Satan's organization makes such a miraculous recovery and becomes so successful after nearly being destroyed, that with the help of the second beast, it is able to convince mankind to join its organization by deceiving them as to its real intent.

3. *The Image of the Beast:* John next sees the second beast direct "them that dwell on the earth" to make an image (or statue) of the Antichrist beast (see Revelation 13:14). This is probably

not the statue of a man (such as King Darius had created of himself and imposed upon his subjects and the prophet Daniel); more likely it is like the image Nebuchadnezzar saw in his dream. That image represented, among other things, the greatness of Nebuchadnezzar's kingdom. In like manner, the "image to the beast" that the false prophet causes to be constructed symbolically represents the greatness of the Antichrist's evil kingdom. This is not difficult to imagine since images of organizations and individuals are all around us today. Successful people often create an emblem or logo that expresses their purpose or accomplishments, for in the words of a popular television advertisement, "Image is everything!" Thus, in John's vision, the false prophet beast creates an image of the devil's organization that will be known and marveled at worldwide.

4. *The Image Comes to Life:* The organization represented by the image of the beast assumes a life of its own through its influence. It wields great power. People will belong to it, they will adhere to its requirements, they will desire its association, and they will relish the rewards it provides. By these means it is brought to *life*, or has a *presence* of its own.

5. *The Image Speaks:* The second beast gives the power of speech to the image of the Antichrist. This is not a statue talking: more likely this is an entity or organization communicating with its adherents through directives, bulletins, or e-mails. In this manner, it disseminates and implements the requirements and policies instituted by Satan's organization. Regardless of the method used to spread this information, however, the *speech* will deceive, captivate, and confuse men and women so thoroughly that they will "call evil good, and good evil" (Isaiah 5:20).

Paul calls this method of speaking the "working of Satan with all power and signs and lying wonders" (2 Thessalonians 2:9). He states that it is designed "with all deceivableness of unrighteousness" (2 Thessalonians 2:10) so that those who are deluded by it might be "damned . . . believe not the truth, [and take] pleasure in unrighteousness" (2 Thessalonians 2:12). Men and women may be sufficiently beguiled that they will consider themselves "wise in their own eyes, and prudent in their own sight!" (Isaiah 2:21.) They may degenerate to the point that they will "justify the wicked for *reward*, and take away the righteousness of the righteous from him!" (Isaiah 2:23; emphasis added.)

Regardless of the method Satan uses to achieve his goal, his objective will remain the same: he wants to exalt himself "above all that is called God, or that is worshipped" (2 Thessalonians 2:4). By putting his evil "beasts" in control of all temporal blessings, he will strive to make himself a substitute for God. By deceiving and conquering the hearts and souls of mankind with worldly wealth, he will attempt to steal the "glory" of God: his children.

Nephi graphically describes the magnitude of these efforts in the last days: "For behold, at that day shall [Satan] rage in the hearts of the children of men, and stir them up to anger against that which is good. And others will he pacify, and lull them away into carnal security . . . and thus [he] cheateth their souls, and leadeth them away carefully down to hell" (2 Nephi 28:20-21).

6. *Worship or Be Killed:* The false prophet causes all those who will not "worship the image of the beast" to be "killed." Remember, *worship* in this sense means everyone must belong to, be influenced by, or participate in whatever entity the Antichrist beast has established in order to gain the perceived blessings that membership in his organization might entail. Therefore, the word *killed* is also considered symbolic. If an actor tries out for a part in a play but does not get the part, his chances to be in the play are *dead*. In this sense, if the righteous of the earth will not join the beast's organization or are ostracized from it, their opportunity to share in its rewards and compensations have been "killed." Although this process may cause the righteous some temporal hardships, the scriptures indicate that they will triumph in the end by inheriting God's kingdom.

7. *The Mark of the Beast:* The beast will identify those who join his organization by giving them a mark on "their right hand, or in [their] forehead." Some may feel that the beast is forcing his adherents to accept this mark, but judging from the way the word *causeth* is used in John's vision, that is not the case. The word *causeth* seems to be used when a reward is implied for those who have done all that Satan's forces require of them. This mark duplicates the seal that the Lord will place in the foreheads of the

righteous. According to John, those who bear the Lord's seal cannot be harmed by the evil servants of the devil (see Revelation 9:4-5).

It is not coincidental that the seal of God and the mark of the devil symbolically represent similar conclusions. The recipient of either mark knows that he or she has qualified or been sealed to the kingdom of the grantor. The symbolism makes each mark a reward of the grantor, God or the devil; however in reality, both marks are received from God, one a reward for obedience and the other a punishment for evil.

The "mark of the beast" is symbolically represented in the book of Revelation as "the number of a man." That number is 666. This does not represent a *man* in the singular sense, however, nor is it the name of a man converted to its numerical equivalent. It means that those who are members of the devil's kingdom (or organization) in the latter days will have something required of them that will cause them to become specifically identified with it in some way. In this manner the devil will know his own. This identification will not literally be engraved upon the forehead or the right hand of those who belong to his kingdom, but his disciples will acknowledge those who represent the Antichrist and his false prophet and will be given exclusive membership in his organization.

This process of *marking* a people is another example of the devil mimicking the gospel. From the very beginning, God has symbolically or literally *marked* his people. In Exodus and Deuteronomy, the dedication of the first born son (symbolized with a mark "upon [his] hand, and for a memorial between [his] eyes") commemorated the deliverance of Israel from Egypt (see Exodus 13:9; Deuteronomy 6:8). This mark was given so that the Israelites would remember the covenant and the laws God had given them. For centuries, many Jewish men have taken this to literally mean the "wearing of the law," and consequently they wear two sets of *tefillin* (phylacteries worn on forehead and sideburns) to this day.[1]

The prophet Ezekiel records that God marked the righteous and destroyed those without the mark for idolatry: "And the Lord said . . . Go through the midst of the city, through the midst of

Jerusalem, and set a mark upon the foreheads of the men that sigh and that cry for all the abominations that be done in the midst thereof . . . let not your eye spare, neither have ye pity" for those who are guilty of idolatry and who do not have the mark, "but come not near any man upon whom . . . the mark [is placed]" (Ezekiel 9:4-6).

Finally, those living in the latter days who adhere to the gospel are baptized as a sign that they believe. When John states that the Lord *marks* his covenant people, he is referring to baptism into the Savior's Church. Baptism is the *mark or sign* of the covenant. However, John's reference to the devil's mark does not specifically identify what that mark is. It could be referring to a loyalty oath, a membership card, or any other means which would identify those who voluntarily belong to Satan's latter-day kingdom.

The fact that both the devil's followers and the Lord's chosen people will receive symbolical marks in their foreheads could signify that in each instance the recipient understands his or her commitment and is willing to accept the requirements of the one they choose to follow. The mark in the hand may symbolize their willingness to perform the requisite tasks that pertain to their kingdom of choice. John's vision does not reveal how the devil's mark will be realized, but in all probability it will come into being during the normal course of events.

8. The Devil's Kingdom Is Economic: Revelation 13:17 clearly identifies economics as the source of power that the devil will use against the righteous in the last days. He will make the wealth of the world appear more desirable than eternal life, which is the wealth of God (see D&C 6:7). Those who belong to his organization will need the mark of identification signifying membership in his kingdom if they are to manipulate and multiply their wealth, for without the "mark of the beast," men and women will not be able to "buy or sell" their goods (whatever they may be). We are told in the scriptures that his organization (often referred to as "the great and abominable church") will exercise such great power over the hearts and minds of men in the latter days that if possible, even the very elect may be deceived into joining it (Joseph Smith–Matthew 1:22).

The Woman

Revelation 17

1. And there came one of the seven angels which had the seven vials, and talked with me, saying unto me, Come hither; I will shew unto thee the judgment of the great whore that sitteth upon many waters:

2. With whom the kings of the earth have committed fornication, and the inhabitants of the earth have been made drunk with the wine of her fornication.

3. So he carried me away in the spirit into the wilderness: and I saw a woman sit upon a scarlet coloured beast, full of names of blasphemy, having seven heads and ten horns.

4. And the woman was arrayed in purple and scarlet colour, and decked with gold and precious stones and pearls, having a golden cup in her hand full of abominations and filthiness of her fornication:

5. And upon her forehead was a name written, MYSTERY, BABYLON THE GREAT, THE MOTHER OF HARLOTS AND ABOMINATIONS OF THE EARTH.

6. And I saw the woman drunken with the blood of the saints, and with the blood of the martyrs of Jesus: and when I saw her, I wondered with great admiration.

7. And the angel said unto me, Wherefore didst thou marvel? I will tell thee the mystery of the woman, and of the beast that carrieth her, which hath the seven heads and ten horns.

8. The beast that thou sawest was, and is not; and shall ascend out of the bottomless pit, and go into perdition: and

they that dwell on the earth shall wonder, whose names were not written in the book of life from the foundation of the world, when they behold the beast that was, and is not, and yet is.

9. And here is the mind which hath wisdom. The seven heads are seven mountains, on which the woman sitteth.

10. And there are seven kings: five are fallen, and one is, and the other is not yet come; and when he cometh, he must continue a short space.

11. And the beast that was, and is not, even he is the eighth, and is of the seven, and goeth into perdition.

12. And the ten horns which thou sawest are ten kings, which have received no kingdom as yet; but receive power as kings one hour with the beast.

13. These have one mind, and shall give their power and strength unto the beast.

14. These shall make war with the Lamb, and the Lamb shall overcome them: for he is Lord of lords, and King of kings: and they that are with him are called, and chosen, and faithful.

15. And he saith unto me, The waters which thou sawest, where the whore sitteth, are peoples, and multitudes, and nations, and tongues.

16. And the ten horns which thou sawest upon the beast, these shall hate the whore, and shall make her desolate and naked, and shall eat her flesh, and burn her with fire.

17. For God hath put in their hearts to fulfil his will, and to agree, and give their kingdom unto the beast, until the words of God shall be fulfilled.

18. And the woman which thou sawest is that great city, which reigneth over the kings of the earth.

The last major participant in John's vision of Satan's latter-day kingdom is a woman. The scriptures also describe her as the "dragon" or the "great and abdominal church," terms that put her on an equal footing with the evil beasts of the devil. Her persona parallels that of the woman who represents the Lord's Church described in Revelation 12:1—another example from John's vision of the devil imitating elements of the gospel.

This woman, symbolically described as "the great whore," is representative of absolute evil in all its forms (see Revelation 17:1). Her ability to deceive and control mankind is described as "fornication." Through her powerful economic hold over the nations of the earth, she has caused whole civilizations to become "drunk with the wine of her fornication" (in essence causing them to worship a false god—the greatest of all sins), for she has successfully caused the pursuit of earthly wealth and power to be substituted for the desire to know God and to obey his commandments.

John is next carried away into the wilderness where he sees this evil woman sitting on the great beast with seven heads and ten horns. This scene interlocks all of the prior elements John has seen in his vision: the Antichrist beast, the false prophet beast, the devil's influence on the nations (historically and in the latter days), and the means by which Satan's control is exercised: i.e., worldly wealth and power. However, the beasts and the evil woman are all representative of the devil's kingdom with a common goal—to cause the downfall of mankind.

John vividly describes the woman's exotic economic wealth: she wears garments of purple and scarlet "decked with gold and precious stones and pearls," and she holds "a golden cup in her hand" (Revelation 17:4). She is most exquisite and powerful and full of lustful promise. Through her cunning she has deceived nations into willingly giving her their economic power and sovereignty. She has caused mankind to disregard both the first and second great commandments, to completely adulterate the truths of the gospel, and to negate their covenant with God (see Revelation 17:12-13). Her "golden cup" is a symbol of her tremendous success, overflowing with "abominations and filthiness." She is given a title: "Mystery Babylon the Great, the Mother of Harlots, and Abominations of the Earth" (Revelation 17:5). These names make it clear that the devil's latter-day kingdom—regardless of the wealth it bestows on its adherents—is the epitome of all evil.

Using the negative attributes of selfishness and greed, mankind has historically been deceived into believing that Satan is their god and king; through the avarice of this woman, the devil and his beasts will continue to deceive men and nations and subject them to Satan's power and authority.

Mystery Babylon: Mystery Babylon was an occult religion based on astronomy that was practiced in Nebuchadnezzar's kingdom. When Nebuchadnezzar had his famous dream, his first reaction was to call all the "magicians . . . astrologers . . . sorcerers, and . . . Chaldeans" (Daniel 2:2) in Babylon and charge them to help him (1) recall the dream (for he had forgotten it), and (2) interpret it. The Israelites also learned the wicked and idolatrous ways of this mystical religion while they were under Babylonian captivity, and were actively worshiping its false gods when King Josiah commanded them to "put down the idolatrous priests . . . [who burned] . . . incense in the high places . . . unto Baal, to the sun, and to the moon, and to the planets, and to all of the host of heaven" (2 Kings 23:5).

The occult Mystery Babylon religion was initially assimilated by the Babylonians from the Chaldeans and was subsequently passed down through all the kingdoms envisioned in Nebuchadnezzar's dream to Rome. Rome was still actively practicing it during John's time, along with the worship of various ancient gods by several associations of priests. ("The most influential of the priestly colleges was that of the nine *augurs* who studied the intent or will of the gods." Their "art went back through Etruria to Chaldea and beyond.")[2]

"Divination and augury were assiduously practiced and widely trusted" in Rome during John's time. "Astrology . . . magic and sorcery, witchcraft and superstition, charms and incantations, 'portents' and the interpretation of dreams were deeply woven into the tissue of Roman life."[3] John therefore called the evil woman in his vision Mystery Babylon because he saw that she represented all of the evils of false worship not only in Rome but also in all previous and future earthly kingdoms. His conclusion is supported by Isaiah, who saw Satan's evil kingdom in a vision and described it as the "virgin daughter of Babylon" (Isaiah 47:1).

The Mother of Harlots: As noted previously, John's vision describes the evil woman in his vision as the symbolic "Mother of Harlots and Abominations of the Earth." The scriptures often couch the Lord's association with Israel in the guise of a marriage alliance, with the Savior as the husband or bridegroom and his chosen people as the wife or bride—symbolically implying a family relationship.[4] John uses this same type of symbolism to describe the devil's evil kingdom as it imitates the concept of a family relationship when he calls the evil woman "the *mother* of harlots." By this he is saying that the devil's evil kingdom both supports and sustains its adherents as a mother does her family.

The Destruction of the Righteous: John saw the evil woman of his vision "drunken with the blood of the saints" and "of the martyrs of Jesus" (Revelation 17:6). He was witnessing the "destruction" of the righteous by the devil and his advocates. The vision does not specify exactly *how* the righteous are destroyed, but from the descriptions of Satan's kingdom and power, there can be at least three ways:

1.   Physical destruction: destruction of the body through war, persecution, or torture resulting from unrighteous or unholy relationships between men and nations.

2.   Economic destruction: since the devil's kingdom is based on mankind's desire for earthly wealth and power, the righteous in the latter days could be destroyed by their exclusion from the devil's economic organization. Both historically and in modern times, many good people have died from want of the basic necessities when unrighteous regimes have withheld food and money to satisfy their own greed.

3.   Spiritual destruction: this is the devil's major emphasis and ultimate goal. Destruction of spiritual commitment can come in many forms. People can be destroyed spiritually when they substitute the things of the earth for God. A testimony left without nourishment, use of the Lord's name in vain, negligence of the scriptures, disobedience to God's commandments, sins of commission or omission, or trivializing the doctrine of the gospel are all applauded by Lucifer and can all lead to spiritual destruction. Some of the most effective weapons he uses to bring about the spiritual fall of mankind are discouragement, fear of public opinion, laziness, uncontrolled sexual desires, greed, selfishness, dis-

obedience of civil law, feelings of inadequacy, lack of natural af-
fection, self-pity, and unrighteous pride.

John's vision has revealed a series of unbelievably astonishing things to him at this point, and they cause him to sit back and
marvel at the enormous power the devil and his servants possess
and the obvious success they enjoy. The angel directing John's
vision is surprised by John's reaction and asks him, "Wherefore
didst thou marvel?" He then reveals to John the interpretation of
the vision of the evil woman and the "beast that carrieth her"
(Revelation 17:7).

The beast (which John now alludes to as the devil in Revelation 17) came from the "bottomless pit" and would eventually go
to "perdition," along with all those who were not named in the
Lamb's "book of life" (Revelation 17:8). The angel then used an
interesting phrase to describe the existence of the beast. He said
the beast "was, and is not, and yet is" (Revelation 17:8). John has
just been shown the historical development of the devil starting
with his preexistent state, then going through his involvement
with the temporal kingdoms of the earth, and ending with the
prophecies regarding his latter-day kingdom as he struggles to
defeat the Savior. Therefore, the word *was* in Revelation 17:8
would probably refer to Satan's existence in heaven where, as the
intelligent "son of the morning," he had participated in the pre-
earth councils. The phrase "is not" implies the fact that while he
has great powers to tempt men and women during their mortal
probation, his status "is not" as great as it was in heaven during
the premortal period. That he "yet is" appears to signify that he
will yet be as powerful as John's vision portrays.

The angel then explained to John that the seven heads of the
beast were seven mountains where the woman (representing the
devil's kingdom) will sit (Revelation 17:9). Rome has commonly
been assumed to be the locality represented by the seven mountains because it is ringed by seven hills, but that seems to be too
obvious since it does not match the criteria of the other symbolic
representations used in John's vision: i.e., none of them have been
literal. The same misconception has arisen in regards to Isaiah's
statement regarding the Lord's kingdom being established in the
"tops of the mountains" in the latter days (see Isaiah 2:2-3). Isaiah
is not describing a physical place where the Lord's kingdom has

its headquarters. Rather, he is saying that *the Lord's kingdom will be raised up and exalted in the latter days*. In like manner, John's vision is portraying the devil's imitation of such a kingdom. His evil woman is to be elevated on the tops of seven hills, indicating that *Satan's domain will also be raised up and made powerful among all the nations as the Second Coming approaches.*

The angel describes the development of the devil's kingdom through the ages by relating it to seven kings. Five of these kings have existed and fallen at some time in the past, one is in power during John's day (referring to Rome), and "the other is not yet come" (Revelation 17:10). The nations that have "not yet come" are depicted in the interpretation of Nebuchadnezzar's dream as the toes of iron and clay (see Daniel 2:42-43) and the 10 horns of the beast with 7 heads in John's vision. These are the nations which evolve after the breakup of the Holy Roman Empire. According to John's vision, these kingdoms continued for a "short time" until the establishment of Satan's powerful latter-day kingdom. The "short time" is the period of the great Apostasy. It is also the time spent by the righteous woman (the Church) in the wilderness. John symbolically defines this period as "1260 days" (the JST translates this as 1260 "years") (see Revelation 12:6; see also JST, Revelation 12:5).

Finally, the angel defines an eighth kingdom, which is the culmination of all that John has seen. This kingdom represents the Antichrist beast, the false prophet beast, and the woman—the mother of harlots. Next, his vision identifies the source of all their evil and deception—Lucifer—who is identified in this part of the vision as simply "the beast." This eighth kingdom is representative of Lucifer's evil kingdom, which is a derivative of all the kingdoms portrayed in Nebuchadnezzar's vision (Revelation 17:11). From this information we gain the following insight: first, the devil has always been involved in the kingdoms of the earth when those kingdoms based their governance on worldly wealth and power; and second, the ten horns in Revelation 17:12 represent ten kingdoms (depicted by the ten toes of Nebuchadnezzar's vision) which would have "one hour" with the beast: their wicked reigns, though powerful, would be short lived (see also Daniel 7).

What is the intention of the devil's kingdom? To make war against the gospel and the Lamb of God—perhaps not an open

war at first (that will come later), but a war of counterfeit "blessings" based on worldly wealth. Participants in this war will adhere to the belief that if they have sufficient wealth and earthly
possessions, they are blessed, and therefore righteous (even if they
are actually unrighteous). Consequently, they feel that the *source*
of their success (which John clearly defines as being the "beast"
for the wicked) must, by logical deduction, be righteous also. The
Book of Mormon clearly describes cycles wherein people prosper when they are righteous. The devil is obviously able to imi-
tate this process, however, by helping the wicked prosper also
(Chapter 16).

Prior to the Babylonian captivity, the Lord (through the
prophet Jeremiah) condemned the kingdom of Judah for its multitude of sins. The people were committing almost every sin conceivable, but one which the Lord noted with particular anger was
the substitution of things of the world for him. "They are waxen
fat," the Lord declared. "They judge not . . . the cause of the
fatherless, yet they prosper; and the right of the needy do they
not judge" (Jeremiah 5:28). It wasn't just the people who were
guilty of this sin. The Lord further noted through Jeremiah: "The
prophets prophesy falsely, and the priests bear rule by their means;
and my people love to have it so" (Jeremiah 5:31). The wealth of
both the people and their leadership had deadened their sense of
obligation to care for the needs of their fellowman, and it appears
that they even paid their spiritual leaders to tell them that their
actions were justified: "from the least of them even to the greatest
. . . every one [was] given to covetousness; and from the prophet
even unto the priest every one [dealt] falsely" (Jeremiah 6:13).
But the Lord would not allow them to think that their wealth
measured their righteousness. "Shall I not visit for these things?
saith the Lord: and shall not my soul be avenged on such a nation
as this?" (Jeremiah 5:9.) The people's lust for worldly wealth had
overcome their desire to do good, and the Lord pronounced their
judgment in definitive terms: "I will cast you out of my sight, as
I have cast out all your brethren," he said, and then he gave
Jeremiah this unprecedented instruction: "Therefore pray not thou
for this people . . . for I will not hear thee" (Jeremiah 7:15-16).

In the latter days the Lord declared that many are "called,
but few are chosen. And why are they not chosen? Because their

hearts are set so much upon the things of this world " (D&C 121:34-35). From this it is easy to understand what the Lord meant when he warned that even the righteous according to the covenant would hardly escape. Thinking that wealth equates to righteousness is a common deception that is easily believed by the unwary.

In Revelation 17:15, the angel explains to John that the waters whereon the "whore sitteth" represent "peoples, and multitudes, and nations, and tongues." He is describing the tremendous success of the devil's kingdom in the latter days. The effects of the devil's promises on the unwary are succinctly described by Nephi:

> "Eat, drink, and be merry; nevertheless, fear God—he will justify in committing a little sin; yea, lie a little, take the advantage of one because of his words, dig a pit for thy neighbor; there is no harm in this . . . if it so be that we are guilty, God will beat us with a few stripes, and at last we shall be saved in the kingdom of God.
>
> . . . Many . . . shall teach after this manner, false and vain and foolish doctrines . . .
>
> . . . At that day shall he rage in the hearts of the children of men, and stir them up to anger against that which is good.
>
> And others will he pacify, and lull them away into carnal security, that they will say: All is well in Zion; yea, Zion prospereth, all is well—and thus the devil cheateth their souls, and leadeth them away carefully down to hell.
>
> And behold, others he flattereth away, and telleth them there is no hell; and he saith unto them: I am no devil, for there is none—and thus he whispereth in their ears, until he grasps them with his awful chains, from whence there is no deliverance (2 Nephi 28:8, 9, 20–22).

The angel further describes the evil woman in Revelation 17 as "that great city, which reigneth over the kings of the earth" (Revelation 17:18). John was again speaking symbolically. The symbol of a great city reigning over the earth had a least three direct meanings in the vision: (1) It represented the great evil city Babylon as it ruled over its provinces, (2) It represented Rome's rule at John's time, and (3) It represented Rome's future symbolic rule over the nations of the Holy Roman Empire through its consecration and crowning of its kings. In this case, the metaphor also describes an evil entity which rules over, controls, or influences most of the world's economies just prior to the Second Coming. The "great city" is a power (perhaps not an actual city) which describes the center or headquarters of Satan's evil kingdom in the latter days. It is this central entity, under the control of the devil (working through the Antichrist and his prophet), which will enslave all but the Lord's chosen people before the Savior comes again (See Daniel 7).

As great as the devil's kingdom (with its unlimited control over people and nations) will be in the latter days, John begins to see discontentment among its adherents as the Second Coming approaches. The devil's kingdom will become a "city of confusion" (Isaiah 24:10). The angel tells John that the ten horns (which represent nations) begin to "hate the whore." They make her "desolate and naked," they "eat her flesh," and they "burn her with fire" (Revelation 17:16). It is not that the people will ultimately tire of the devil's evil dominion but that they will rebel against the forces that bind and control their economy, their wealth, and their personal freedom.

In the following scriptures, John portrays their greed as they attempt to take control of Satan's organization.

The End of the Devil's Kingdom

Revelation 18

1. And after these things I saw another angel come down from heaven, having great power; and the earth was lightened with his glory.

2. And he cried mightily with a strong voice, saying, Babylon the great is fallen, is fallen, and is become the habitation of devils, and the hold of

every foul spirit, and a cage of every unclean and hateful bird.

3. For all nations have drunk of the wine of the wrath of her fornication, and the kings of the earth have committed fornication with her, and the merchants of the earth are waxed rich through the abundance of her delicacies.

4. And I heard another voice from heaven, saying, Come out of her, my people, that ye be not partakers of her sins, and that ye receive not of her plagues.

5. For her sins have reached unto heaven, and God hath remembered her iniquities.

6. Reward her even as she rewarded you, and double unto her double according to her works: in the cup which she hath filled fill to her double.

7. How much she hath glorified herself, and lived deliciously, so much torment and sorrow give her: for she saith in her heart, I sit a queen, and am no widow, and shall see no sorrow.

8. Therefore shall her plagues come in one day, death, and mourning, and famine; and she shall be utterly burned with fire: for strong is the Lord God who judgeth her.

9. And the kings of the earth, who have committed fornication and lived deliciously with her, shall bewail her, and lament for her, when they shall see the smoke of her burning,

10. Standing afar off for the fear of her torment, saying, Alas, alas, that great city Babylon, that mighty city! for in one hour is thy judgment come.

11. And the merchants of the earth shall weep and mourn over her; for no man buyeth their merchandise any more:

12. The merchandise of gold, and silver, and precious stones, and

of pearls, and fine linen, and purple, and silk, and scarlet, and all thyine wood, and all manner vessels of ivory, and all manner vessels of most precious wood, and of brass, and iron, and marble, and wheat, and beasts, and sheep, and horses, and chariots, and slaves, and souls of men.

14. And the fruits that thy soul lusted after are departed from thee, and all things which were dainty and goodly are departed from thee, and thou shalt find them no more at all.

15. The merchants of these things, which were made rich by her, shall stand afar off for the fear of her torment, weeping and wailing,

16. And saying, Alas, alas, that great city, that was clothed in fine linen, and purple, and scarlet, and decked with gold, and precious stones, and pearls!

17. For in one hour so great riches is come to nought. And every shipmaster, and all the company in ships, and sailors, and as many as trade by sea, stood afar off,

18. And cried when they saw the smoke of her burning, saying, What city is like unto this great city!

19. And they cast dust on their heads, and cried, weeping and wailing, saying, Alas, alas, that great city, wherein were made rich all that had ships in the sea by reason of her costliness! for in one hour is she made desolate.

20. Rejoice over her, thou heaven, and ye holy apostles and prophets; for God hath avenged you on her.

21. And a mighty angel took up a stone like a great millstone, and cast it into the sea, saying, Thus with violence shall that great city Babylon be thrown down, and shall be found no

more at all.

22. And the voice of harpers, and musicians, and of pipers, and trumpeters, shall be heard no more at all in thee; and no craftsman, of whatsoever craft he be, shall be found any more in thee; and the sound of a millstone shall be heard no more at all in thee;

23. And the light of a candle shall shine no more at all in thee; and the voice of the bridegroom and of the bride shall be heard no more at all in thee: for thy merchants were the great men of the earth; for by thy sorceries were all nations deceived.

24. And in her was found the blood of prophets, and of saints, and of all that were slain upon the earth.

God "hath put [it] in [the] hearts [of the wicked] to fulfil his will, and to agree, and give their kingdom unto the beast, until the words of God shall be fulfilled" (Revelation 17:17). This scripture is saying that because of the eternal principle of free agency inherent in the plan of salvation, God allows mankind to choose good or evil. The wicked obviously make the wrong choice, but the Lord promised them agency and he has fulfilled his promise by letting them choose. At the Second Coming the time of their probation will be over, and he will pour out his wrath upon them without measure (see D&C 1:9).[5] There will be no acquittal from their wickedness (see Nahum 1:3); they will be cast out, not redeemed (see Mosiah 16:2); they will receive no mercy (see Mosiah 3:24–27). At that time, the devil's evil deceptions will be revealed (see Isaiah 29:20) and the Lord will conqueror "leviathan . . . that crooked serpent" (Isaiah 27:1), for the Lord will be angry with the wicked (see D&C 63:32)[6] and he will chasten them.

John tells us that the devil's corrupt dominion is responsible for all evil (see Revelation 18:24) and that it will eventually "drink of the wine of the wrath" of its own "fornication" (Revelation 14:8). Its wicked followers will suffer from a plague of "noisome and grievous sore[s]" (Revelation 16:2). They will be gathered as tares to be burned (see D&C 88:94; Matthew 13:38; D&C 101:65–

66) and "cast down by devouring fire" (D&C 29:21).[7] The Antichrist beast, the false prophet beast, and all men and women who bear the beast's "mark" will reap what they have sown (see Revelation 14:9–11), and their final state will be hell (see 1 Nephi 15:32–36), the bottomless pit (see Revelation 20:1–3), where they will become "perdition" (see D&C 76:25–38, 43–49). In spite of its initial and overwhelming success in the latter days, the devil's kingdom will ultimately suffer a violent destruction because, "There is no peace, saith my God, to the wicked" (Isaiah 57:3–13, 20–21).

The scriptures tell us that all nations, kings, and merchants will wax rich with the abundant "delicacies" made available under the devil's reign. He has been and will be (through the influence and power of his economic kingdom) in control, and his evil influence will affect both people and governments as he works to realize his goals. Up until the Second Coming the righteous will be allowed to reside among his denizens, but as the Savior prepares to destroy the devil's kingdom, he will call for the righteous to "come out" from Satan's domain so they will not become "partakers of her sins" and receive of her "plagues" of destruction (see Revelation 18:4).

God knows what Satan's sins are, and he will mete out to him double the punishment for the equivalent reward Satan gives mankind. The Lord will do this because the devil's kingdom "hath glorified herself, and lived deliciously" (Revelation 18:7). She has lusted after all sins and concluded that she could not be stopped. God has judged her, and her death is assured. The "kings of the earth" (representing all nations, entities, and others who pursue the devil's kingdom) will lament her downfall because they love sin more than God (see Revelation 18:9–10). They will see the "smoke of her burning" (Revelation 18:9), which means that they will understand the fullness of her evil and destruction. They will "weep and mourn over her," not because they are repentant, but because "no man buyeth their merchandise any more: gold, and silver, and precious stones . . . pearls, and fine linen . . . purple, and silk . . . scarlet . . . thyine wood . . . ivory . . . brass . . . marble . . . cinnamon . . . odours . . . ointments, and frankincense . . . wine . . . oil . . . fine flour, and wheat . . .beasts, and sheep, and horses and chariots, and slaves," and even the "souls of men" (Revelation 18:11–13). They have allowed the precious things of worldly value to become the "fruits" of their souls. But, the angel declared, all "fruits that thy soul lusted after are departed from thee, and all things which were dainty and goodly are departed from thee, and thou shalt find them no more at all" (Revelation 18:14). Those who succumbed to the devil's kingdom and were made rich by her will cry, "Alas, alas, that great city [Babylon, Satan's kingdom]. . . in one hour is she made desolate" (Revelation 18:16–19). And John sees this final destruction of Babylon in his vision when "another angel" comes to him and cries, "Babylon the great is fallen, is fallen, and is become the habitation of devils, and the hold of every foul spirit" (Revelation 18:2).

In the end, all that are evil shall perish and shall be consumed by the wrath of God (see 1 Nephi 22:15–18).[8] Those who were deceived by Lucifer shall mourn while the heavens rejoice at the destruction of wickedness. Babylon will be "found no more at all" (Revelation 18:20–21). There will no longer be a need for worldly wealth (see Revelation 18:22), and the devil's ability to deceive through mimicry will cease. The righteous will finally overcome the "beast" (see Revelation 15:2) because of their faith according to the covenant, and they will be led by the "Lamb" of God, the "Lord of lords," the "King of kings," as he goes forth into his Millennial reign (see Revelation 17:14).

Part Four

Difficult Times

"And unto you it shall be given to know the signs of the times . . . For verily the voice of the Lord is unto all men, and there is none to escape;

And the rebellious shall be pierced with much sorrow."

Doctrine & Covenants 68:11; 1:2–3

Signs: Both General and Specific

9

> **"And they shall see signs and wonders, for they shall be shown forth in the heavens above, and in the earth beneath."**
>
> **Doctrine & Covenants 45:40**

"The time will come when [mankind] will not endure sound doctrine; but after their own lusts shall they heap to themselves teachers, having itching ears; and they shall turn away their ears from the truth, and [the truth] shall be turned unto fables" (2 Timothy 4:3–4). In this message to Timothy, Paul was speaking not only of the great Apostasy and the many doctrines and teachings that would evolve from it prior to the Second Coming but also of the great flood of false teachings that would occur after the restoration of the gospel in the latter days.

While the Savior was on the earth, he warned his Apostles to "take heed that no man deceive you" (Matthew 24:4). He gave them this warning in answer to their questions concerning his Second Coming and the destruction of Jerusalem, but as was the practice of many of his prophets before him, his comment referenced not only the time of his Apostles but also the time of those who would live after the restoration in the latter days. This latter period was to be a time like no other, a time when the joys of the good life—with its pursuit of worldly wealth—would destroy men's faith on a wholesale basis. Paul warned all mankind of this pitfall when he told Timothy that "the love of money is the root of all evil" (1 Timothy 6:10). He was cautioning us against coveting worldly wealth, lest we "fall into temptation and a snare, and into many foolish and hurtful lusts" which would eventually drown us "in destruction and perdition" (1 Timothy 6:9).

We have already discussed many signs of the Second Coming—signs that have already been fulfilled and some that are yet to be fulfilled. However, there are many more prophesied signs, both *general* and *specific*, that are being and will be fulfilled before the Lord's Advent. Each of these categories presents it own problems of recognition. General signs like wars, rumors of wars, and earthquakes have occurred in many different generations. These general signs occur regularly so that men and women will remain aware of the Lord's prophecies concerning his Second Coming and be encouraged to prepare for it. Furthermore, to compound the difficulty of recognizing general signs, the Lord often made his warnings of them general as well.

Specific signs, on the other hand, let us know with a surety that the Lord's promises will all be fulfilled. Through his Apostles, the Lord has given us the following admonition: "Now learn a parable of the fig tree; when his branch is yet tender, and putteth forth leaves, ye know that summer is nigh: so likewise ye, when ye shall see all these things, [shall] know that [the Second Coming] is near, even at the doors" (Matthew 24:32–33; see also Mark 13:28–29; Luke 21:29–31).

At times, the scriptures seem to explode with signs of the Savior's coming as verse after verse recounts an indiscriminate intermingling of both general and specific signs. For example, the Lord did this in a latter-day revelation wherein he referenced the symbol of the fig tree used in Matthew, and then noted that through its tender leaves and early shoots, mankind would know that his coming was near. He tells us that in that day people will see "signs and wonders" in the heavens and in the "earth beneath" (see D&C 45:40). Then he opens the floodgates and allows the signs to rush out. There will be "blood, and fire, and vapors of smoke . . . before the day of the Lord shall come . . .The sun shall be darkened, and the moon [shall] be turned into blood, and the stars fall from heaven. And the remnant shall be gathered" into one place where they will see the Savior come "in the clouds of heaven, clothed with power and great glory; with all the holy angels; and he that watches not for [him] shall be cut off" (D&C 45:41–44). Further, "the saints that have slept shall come forth to meet" him in a "cloud" (D&C 45:45). "Then shall the arm of the Lord fall upon the nations." He will "set his foot" upon the Mount of Olives, and "it shall cleave in twain, and the earth shall tremble, and reel to and fro, and the heavens also shall shake." In that day "the Lord shall utter his voice, and all the ends of the earth shall hear it; and the nations of the earth shall mourn, and they that have laughed shall see their folly . . . Calamity shall cover the mocker, and the scorner shall be consumed; and they that have watched for iniquity shall be hewn down and cast into the fire." And then the Jews will look at the Savior and say, "What are these wounds in thine hands and in thy feet?" (D&C 45:47–51.) And the Lord will explain to them he received those wounds "in the house of [his] friends." He will then erase all doubt of his Messiahship by declaring, "I am he who was lifted up. I am Jesus that was crucified. I am the Son of God" (D&C 45:52). Finally, in that day "Satan shall be bound," and during the Millennium he "shall have no place in the hearts of the children of men" (D&C 45:55).

With such a litany of signs (and these are but a few), it can easily be concluded that the fig tree has begun to bud. It is now up to each of us to recognize the fulfillment of these specific signs and to accept the ongoing general signs as a reminder that God's hand and the devil's presence are constantly with us. *Spiritual vigilance is the key to preparedness.*

The following are four general signs that we should constantly monitor:

As in the Days of Noah

The Lord tells us in the gospel of Matthew that prior to the Second Coming, men and women will behave as they did in the days of Noah. They will be "eating and drinking, marrying and giving in marriage" (Matthew 24:37-38), and participating in the normal everyday aspects of life. Luke's record supports this, using the people of Sodom and Gomorrah during the days of Lot as his example. Like Sodom and Gomorrah, the people of the latter days will be eating and drinking, buying and selling, and planting and harvesting. Life will go apace. And tragically, most of them will not recognize or heed the warnings and signs given to them so that they can prepare themselves for the Lord's coming (see Luke 17:28–29).

The cities of Sodom and Gomorrah were consumed when fire rained down on them from heaven. Of all their inhabitants, only four souls survived the conflagration and one of those fell because of disobedience. In Noah's time, the flood came and destroyed all but eight of God's children—the rest were too wicked to be saved. "Who then [of mankind] is a faithful and wise servant," the Lord asks, and not like the evil servant who said in his heart, "My lord delayeth his coming" (Matthew 24:45, 48). As a result of the lord's delay in this teaching, the servant began to "smite his fellow servants, and to eat and drink with the drunken," not recognizing that his Lord would come "in a day when he looketh not for him, and in an hour that he [was] not aware of, and [would] cut him asunder." This is exactly what is prophesied to happen at the Second Coming. If men and women ignore the prophesied warnings and signs the Lord has given them, there will be "weeping" and wailing and "gnashing of teeth" when he appears (Matthew 24:49–51).

The fact that the period of time between the restoration and the Second Coming will be as it was "in the days of Noah" is a very general sign of the Lord's Advent, so much so that it is easy to understand why signs of this type are a problem. Life goes on, and we continue to do all of the things that are required for survival, as well as the things that we enjoy. Nonetheless, we can draw one specific thing from this general sign: just as the flood in Noah's time was a worldwide cataclysmic event, so also will the general signs of the Second Coming affect most of mankind, and some will have a devastating effect on the entire earth.

The Good-Times Sin

The days of Noah were times of indescribable evil—so much

so that God was willing to destroy almost all life on the earth and begin again. This period has been used as an example of evil so extreme that it resulted in the Lord pronouncing a catastrophic judgment against the people. (This example is also used as a warning to the people of the latter days regarding their status before God.) The Bible does not describe the sins of Noah's people other than in general terms, but a modern commentary on *The Torah* sheds light on what the people were doing: "The earth [had become] corrupt before God; the earth was filled with lawlessness" (*The Torah*: Genesis 6:11). This lawlessness is interpreted as lawlessness toward God, which "is the manifestation of a social disease" practiced by the antediluvians, and not its cause. "The Midrash speculates that it was *unbounded affluence* that caused men to become depraved, that wealth afforded them the leisure to discover new thrills and to commit sexual aberrations."[1] This, along with the excesses that wealth allowed in all facets of their lives, caused the people to develop an "overbearing attitude toward God."[2] The Lord uses this example in scripture and it completely fits John's prophecies with regards to the devil's use of economics and worldly wealth in the latter days. Thus, the times of Noah, in connection with John's prophecy, illustrate what the good-times sin is: it is a materialistic society eating, drinking, and making merry—to the exclusion of God and spiritual enlightenment (Chapter 8).

Prior to their Babylonian captivity, Israel had this same problem. Isaiah describes the Israelites as a people who overindulged in their pursuits of "joy and gladness." They were "slaying oxen, and killing sheep, eating flesh, and drinking wine," saying "let us eat and drink; for to morrow we shall die" (Isaiah 22:13). As a result of their wicked state of mind, the Lord called for them to weep and mourn, to bald their heads, and to gird themselves with sackcloth as acts of repentance so that he could save their children from future destruction—but Israel would not! (see Isaiah 22:12.) The Lord's reaction to Israel's obduracy was swift: "Surely this iniquity shall not be purged from you till ye die" (Isaiah 22:14).

This pleasure-oriented existence to the exclusion of righteousness was also at the base of Sodom and Gomorrah's destruction, and while "they were accustomed to some form or forms of sexual deviation . . . Jewish tradition stresses social rather than sexual aberrations as the reason for the cities' destruction."[3] In his condemnation of the sins of the kingdom of Judah and the city of Jerusalem (sin was the cause of the Babylonian captivity), Ezekiel compares the people of these cities to those of Sodom and Gomorrah, and he chastens Judah for "pride, fulness of bread, and abundance of idleness . . . [to the extent that she did not] strengthen the hand of the poor and needy" (Ezekiel 16:49). A commentary on *The Torah* expresses the thought that "affluence without social concern is self-destructive; it hardens the conscience against repentance; [and] it engenders cruelty and excess." Sodom and Gomorrah deserved punishment, the Midrash says, "both for their immorality and for their uncharitableness. For whoever grudges assistance to the poor does not deserve to exist in this world, and he also forfeits the life of the world-to-come."[4]

In the New Testament, the Lord depicts perfectly the good-times sin of the people of Noah, Sodom and Gomorrah, and Judah (prior to its Babylonian captivity) through the parable of the foolish rich man:

> And he spake a parable unto them, saying, The ground of a certain rich man brought forth plentifully:
>
> And he thought within himself, saying, What shall I do, because I have no room where to bestow my fruits?
>
> And he said, This will I do: I will pull down my barns, and build greater; and there will I bestow all my fruits and my goods.
>
> And I will say to my soul, Soul, thou hast much goods laid up for many years; take thine ease, eat, drink, and be merry.
>
> But God said unto him, Thou fool, this night thy soul shall be required of thee: then whose shall those things be, which thou hast provided? (Luke 12:16–20.)

This parable points out the relationship between the things of the world and the things of the Spirit. The rich man's ground brought forth an unanticipated abundance of goods, and he wondered what he should do with his newfound wealth. He was not interested in sharing his abundance or even in giving thanks for it; he was only interested in how he could preserve it for himself. He was a selfishly proud, self-indulgent man who placed his personal ease and sensuous enjoyment far above any spiritual values. The Lord purposefully typecast the foolish rich man in this manner so that his audience would recognize the good-times sin that had been inherent in the destruction of Sodom and Gomorrah and the people of Noah, and so that readers of the scriptures in subsequent ages would become aware of the same problems in their time. His parable makes clear the propensities each of us fight against when spiritual values are challenged with temporal desires. The things of the world can make people blind to the things of the Spirit. The foolish rich man only thought to satisfy his physical appetites. He gave no thought to God's commandments and placed worldly desires above the worship of God. By doing so, he broke the first great commandment, and he broke the second great commandment by placing his personal desires above the welfare of his neighbors. He had emphasized all the wrong things in his life: worldly power, riches, self-indulgence; and he had forgotten all the right things: God, his neighbor, the poor. His spiritual impoverishment far outweighed his temporal wealth (see Matthew 6:20–21). As a result, God left him—and us—with this stark warning: "Thou fool, this night thy soul shall be required of thee: then whose shall those things be, which thou hast provided?"[5] (Luke 12:20.) The foolish rich man had made the wrong choice! He had laid up treasure for his earthly pleasure, but he was impoverished toward God and his fellow man. The message is clear: the only things we can take with us when we die are the things of the Spirit—all else is left behind.

The preacher in Ecclesiastes was warning mankind about the good-times sin long before Christ taught the parable of the foolish rich man in Luke. He wrote: "He that loveth silver shall not be satisfied with silver; nor he that loveth abundance with increase: this is also vanity" (Ecclesiastes 5:10). The teachings of the preacher and the parable of the foolish rich man show us how easy it is for the devil to control the hearts and minds of men.

The rich man of the parable thought only of his *fruits*, his *goods*, and his *barn* so that he could "eat, drink and be merry."

In the Book of Mormon, Nephi also described the good-times sin:

> And there shall also be many which shall say: Eat, drink, and be merry; nevertheless, fear God—he will justify in committing a little sin; yea, lie a little, take the advantage of one because of his words, dig a pit for thy neighbor; there is no harm in this; and do all these things, for tomorrow we die; and if it so be that we are guilty, God will beat us with a few stripes, and at last we shall be saved in the kingdom of God (2 Nephi 28:8).

Wrong! Nephi aptly described this rationale as "false and vain and foolish doctrines" (2 Nephi 28:9). Luke warned mankind of the good-times sin by saying,

> And take heed to yourselves, lest at any time your hearts be overcharged with surfeiting, and drunkenness, and cares of this life, and so that day come upon you unawares.

> For as a snare shall it come on all them that dwell on the face of the whole earth.

> Watch ye therefore, and pray always, that ye may be accounted worthy to escape all these things that shall come to pass, and to stand before the Son of man (Luke 21:34–36).

All of this teaches us a great principle: God keeps calling and warning, but our *things* keep getting in the way. He made it clear that we "cannot serve God and mammon" (Matthew 6:24).

Although the good-times sin has occurred throughout the millennia, it is also a general sign of the Lord's Second Coming in the latter days: if we become so involved in the things of the world that we miss the signs of the Lord's prophesied Advent, we will be unprepared for him when he comes. By allowing our hearts to become set on the things of the world, and by justifying the use and aggrandizement of them, the things of God will cease to exist in our hearts. Paul warned the Romans, "Put ye on the Lord Jesus Christ, and make not provision for the flesh, to fulfill the lusts thereof" (Romans 13:14)—a strong warning against the good-times sin. For the Lord declared, "Where your treasure is, there will your heart be also" (Matthew 6:21).

The Effect of Signs on Mankind

Whether we watch for them or not, the signs of the Second Coming will occur! And when they occur, they will confuse and confound mankind by violently disrupting his lifestyle. Their magnitude will be so great that "men's hearts shall fail them" as a result (D&C 45:26). This does not mean that everyone will literally die of a heart attack: the Lord is explaining to us in a graphic manner that the signs announcing his Advent will be so powerful and disruptive that many will be terrified. At that time "all things" will "be in commotion," and "a desolating sickness shall cover the land" (D&C 88:91; 45:31). The Lord has decreed that wars will come "upon the face of the earth, and the wicked shall slay the wicked, and fear shall come upon every man; and the saints also shall hardly escape" (D&C 63:33–34). Luke tells us that the very "powers of heaven shall be shaken" (Luke 21:26). The Doctrine and Covenants is even more graphic: "The sun shall be darkened, and the moon shall be turned into blood, and the stars shall fall from heaven . . . [and] there shall be a great hailstorm sent forth to destroy the crops of the earth" (D&C 29:14, 16). These will not be normal occurrences, and all mankind will be subject to their fury.

With such devastating events occurring, all men and women will fear for their possessions, their loved ones, and their lives. One unfortunate result of these phenomena is that "the love of men shall wax cold" (D&C 45:27). Men and women will become selfish and will withhold assistance from those in need "because their hearts are corrupted." As a result, "the things which they are willing to bring upon others, and love to have others suffer, may come upon themselves to the very uttermost; that they may be disappointed also, and their hopes [of salvation] may be cut off" (D&C 121:13–14). Mankind's fear throughout this period of destruction will cause some to say that God isn't ever going to come (see D&C 45:26), while others may contend that there is no God at all and that the terrors they are experiencing are of their own making. "Iniquity shall abound" during this period, and only those who are not overcome by the world will be saved (see Joseph Smith–Matthew 1:30).

Enoch saw this period of great tribulation and prophesied that mankind would look "forth with fear for the judgments of the Almighty God, which should come upon the wicked" (Moses 7:66). John the Revelator described this fear in vivid terms: "And the kings of the earth, and the great men, and the rich men, and the chief captains, and the mighty men, and every bondman, and every free man [shall hide] themselves in the dens and in the rocks of the mountains; and [they will say] to the mountains and [to the] rocks, Fall on us, and hide us from the face of him that sitteth on the throne, and [hide us] from the wrath of the Lamb" (Revelation 6:15–16). In the Gospel of Mark, the Lord warns us that brother will betray brother, causing his death, and fathers will betray their sons. Even children will "rise up against their parents, and shall cause them to be put to death" (see Mark 13:12).

Zechariah graphically describes those who are found fighting against Jerusalem at the Second Coming: "Their flesh shall consume away while they stand upon their feet, and their eyes shall consume away in their holes, and their tongue shall consume away in their mouth" (Zechariah 14:12). The Lord broadened Zechariah's prophecy to include all the wicked on the earth who would not repent: "Their tongues shall be stayed that they shall not utter against me; and their flesh shall fall from off their bones, and their eyes from their sockets" (D&C 29:19). He stated that he would send flies upon the earth to "take hold of the inhabitants thereof . . . [to] . . . eat their flesh," and he would "cause maggots to come in upon them" (D&C 29:18). He further asserted that these deplorable conditions would cause the "beasts of the forest and the fowls of the air [to come and] devour them up" (D&C 29:20).[6]

Before the Second Coming of the Messiah there will be a great division between the righteous and the unrighteous inhabitants of the earth (see 2 Nephi 30:10–11). The wicked will fear and tremble at this time, but Nephi tells us that the righteous need not fear, for they will not be confounded by anything that occurs during this period (see 1 Nephi 22:22). Jeremiah, the writer of Lamentations, gives us the reason for this: "The Lord is good unto them that wait for him, to the soul that seeketh him. It is good that a man should both hope and quietly wait for the salvation of the Lord" (Lamentations 3:25–26). In other words, the righteous will not necessarily be spared the devastation of the Second Coming, but they will be prepared for it, and their preparation will ensure them a place in the Father's kingdom.

The Lord warns us that by the time of his Advent, the whole of his vineyard will be "corrupted every whit;" there will be "none which doeth good save it be a few; and they [will] err in many instances because of priestcrafts, all having corrupt minds" (D&C 33:4). Nephi tells us that "because of pride, and wickedness, and abominations, and whoredoms . . . [all have] . . . gone astray save it be a few, who are the humble followers of Christ; nevertheless . . . in many instances they do err because they are taught by the precepts of men" (2 Nephi 28:14). The devil frequently disguises his wickedness in the form of pleasurable and even intellectually stimulating things, and it is often difficult for the righteous to recognize his evil enticements.

In the book of Isaiah the Lord declared that he would make "the earth empty, and . . . waste, and turneth it upside down, and scattereth abroad the inhabitants thereof" (Isaiah 24:1). This will involve both the righteous and the wicked, because the Lord "sendeth rain on the just and on the unjust" alike (see Matthew 5:45). Isaiah came to the same conclusion years before: "And it shall be, as with the people, so with the priest; as with the servant, so with his master; as with the maid, so with her mistress; as with the buyer, so with the seller; as with the lender, so with the borrower; as with the taker of usury, so with the giver of usury to him" (Isaiah 24:2). All mankind, both the wicked and the righteous, will be affected by the devastating general signs prior to the Lord's Second Coming.[7] Even the very elect, those elect according to the covenant, need to be cautious.

The Doctrine and Covenants tells us that the prophesied afflictions will devastate mankind in a manner "such as was not from the beginning of the creation," and if the Lord had not told us that he would shorten those days, "no flesh [would] be saved: but for the elect's sake, [those who hear the Savior's voice and 'harden not their hearts' (D&C 29:7)] . . . he hath shortened the days" (Mark 13:19–20). This does not mean that the Second Coming will occur before its decreed time, for that time is mandated in heaven, as was the time of Christ's birth. What it does mean is that the Lord will come before everyone has been destroyed. It is up to each individual to be prepared if he or she wants to be counted among the "elect" who remain. In the parables of the talents and the pounds, the Savior gave a talent or a pound to each of his servants so that he might make preparation for the master's return. But in both of the parables, even though each individual had the opportunity to be an elect of the master, there was one who would not do what was required. Knowing not when the master would return, this individual was unprepared to receive him when he finally did appear.[8] And thus it will be in the last days.

It is also prophesied that false Christs and false prophets will appear before the Lord comes and they will perform "great signs and wonders, insomuch, that, if possible, they shall deceive the very elect, who are the elect according to the covenant" (those who have been endowed with the promised blessings of Abraham) (see Joseph Smith–Matthew 1:22). These signs and wonders will lead some men and women astray, but it is these same signs that will notify them when the Savior "is near, even at the doors," if they are watching for him (Joseph Smith–Matthew 1:39). The devil will continue to practice this art of imitation right to the end. Vigilance is constantly required to maintain righteousness.

The Changing of the Times and Seasons

During the Creation, the Lord set in motion the "lights in the firmament" so that we could determine night from day. He also set them for "signs, and for seasons, and for days, and years" (Genesis 1:14). Their cycles establish our normal times and seasons. The preacher in Ecclesiastes declared: "To every thing there is a season, and a time to every purpose under the heaven: A time to be born, and a time to die; a time to plant, and a time to pluck up that which is planted." He also said there was a time to kill and a time to heal, a time to laugh and mourn and dance, a time to get, a time to lose, a time to keep, and a time to cast away. (See Ecclesiastes 3:1–8.) The preacher obviously recognized the normal sequences of life that God's plan of salvation set in motion. During his ministry, Jesus used these established sequences when he chastised the people for their failure to recognize the signs of the times. He marveled that they had become so acquainted with the normal order of the times and seasons that they could discern the weather: a red sky in the evening meant "fair weather," or a "red and lowring" sky in the morning indicated "foul weather," "but," he continued, "can ye not discern the signs of the times?" (Matthew 16:2–3.) Their reliance on the normal order of the times, seasons, and elements had clouded their ability to recognize the general signs of his first coming; therefore, the Savior declared that they were hypocrites.

The seasonal cycles: summer, winter, spring, fall, rainy, dry etc., have been relied upon throughout the ages and continue to be relied upon today. But God declared that a general sign of the last days would be a change in this normal pattern: "God hath set his hand and seal to change the times and seasons." Why will he do this? "to blind [the minds of the wicked] that they may not understand his marvelous workings; that he may prove them also and take them in their own craftiness" (D&C 121:12). This brings to mind Paul's warning to Timothy wherein Timothy was told to avoid "profane and vain babblings, and oppositions of science falsely so called" (1 Timothy 6:20). Scientists today feel they can predict much of what will occur in nature and tend to explain away all that does occur. In this manner, devastating floods, severe winters, hurricanes, tornadoes, earthquakes and the like become normal or explainable extraordinary events. Therefore, when God changes the times and seasons and makes them unreliable, it becomes a proving to the mind and understanding of man's knowledge. In other words, science may have a logical explanation for the changes that will occur and will not acknowledge them as God's marvelous workings. But eventually they will be proven incorrect, and at that time the scriptures state that great "calamity shall cover the mocker, and the scorner shall be consumed" as God's signs of the times are finally recognized (see D&C 45:50).

It is also possible that the cataclysmic changing of the times and seasons may be the means by which the Lord will bring about the "desolating scourge" which will bring devastation and death to many of the earth's inhabitants just prior to his Second Coming. However, that is yet to be determined. And so we wait, straining to recognize and ever watching "for the signs of the coming of the Son of Man" (D&C 45:39).

Signs: The Earth's Three Phases

> "For the hour is nigh and the day soon at hand when the earth is ripe."
>
> Doctrine & Covenants 29:9
>
> "And the whole earth groans under the weight of its [the inhabitants'] iniquity."
>
> Doctrine & Covenants 123:7

The Earth

"Enoch looked upon the earth; and he heard a voice from [its depths] saying: Wo, wo is me, the mother of men; I am pained, I am weary, because of the wickedness of my children. When shall I rest, and be cleansed from the filthiness which is gone forth out of me? When will my Creator sanctify me, that I may rest?" (Moses 7:48). Whether this scripture is symbolic or literal, it describes the earth as a living entity capable of communicating and feeling both pleasure and pain.

When Adam and Eve were placed on the earth, it was in a state of paradise. But Adam and Eve sinned, and when they fell from the presence of God, the earth also fell. Isaiah described the earth as being "devoured" by this curse and its inhabitants as being desolate, because they were no longer in the presence of God (see Isaiah 24:6). The earth remained defiled because the inhabitants thereof "transgressed the laws, changed the ordinance, [and broke] the everlasting covenant" (Isaiah 24:5). The earth is not capable of sinning, but under the plan of salvation, its condition is affected by its inhabitants; therefore, "the Lord maketh the earth empty, and maketh it waste, and turneth it upside down, and scattereth abroad the inhabitants thereof" (Isaiah 24:1).

There are at least three phases the earth must go through in the latter days before it will be sanctified, made ready to receive its Creator, and have "righteousness for a season [the millennium] abide upon [its] face" (Moses 7:48).

Phase One — Tumults That Will Occur to the Earth

The earth will remain under the curse brought on by the Fall until the Lord comes again. Before that time, however, many signs of his coming will affect it. These general signs, while symbolically bringing great tumults to mind, are described in terms that leave almost everything to the imagination. Isaiah said that the very "foundations of the earth" would shake. The earth would be "utterly broken down . . . dissolved . . . moved," and would "reel to and fro" like a drunken man (Isaiah 24:14–20). A like description given in the latter days adds that the earth will tremble before it reels to and fro as a drunken man (see D&C 45:48; 88:87). Both latter-day revelation and the ancient psalmist declare that the earth will quake or shake at the Lord's Advent (see Psalm 77:18; D&C 29:13; 43:18; 84:118). Joel, an Old Testament prophet, describes these quaking disturbances and declares that they will cause the people to "run to and fro" (Joel 2:9–10). There are many scriptures that predict these shakings and quakings as earthquakes that will occur in diverse places in the latter days (see Mark 13:8; Luke 21:11; D&C 45:33). They are to be a testimony to mankind of the Second Coming, and they will be so severe that men and women will "fall upon the ground" and "not be able to stand" (D&C 88:89). The magnitude of these earthquakes will even cause the "waves of the sea" to heave "themselves beyond their bounds" (D&C 88:90), a description painfully acknowledged by anyone who has ever been near the ocean in an earthquake or who has lived through a tsunami.

Due to the many earthquakes that are predicted, the scriptures indicate that mountains will be made low, valleys will disappear, crooked places will be made straight, and rough places will be made plain, or smooth. (see Isaiah 40:4; D&C 49:23; 133:22.) The scriptures also testify that the mountains will be made to "flow down" at the Lord's presence (see Isaiah 64:1; D&C 109:74),[1] and in another mind-expanding prediction, Isaiah declares that the Lord will shake the heavens and "remove" the earth "out of her place" (Isaiah 13:13). Could this mean that the continents will abruptly change their position or that the earth's orbit will change, or is there some other explanation?

Although the general descriptions of these signs leave the individual to determine when and where they will occur, there is evidence of what will *make* them occur. It is the voice of the Lord! Ezekiel heard the Lord's voice coming from the "east," and it sounded "like a noise of many waters" (Ezekiel 43:2). John the Revelator heard the voice and said it was "as the sound of many waters" (Revelation 1:15; 14:2). Joseph Smith also heard it and described it as "the sound of the rushing of great waters" and "as the voice of a great thunder" (D&C 110:3; 133:22). Are the scriptures saying that the Lord initiates these incidents by the mere *sound* of his voice? Or does he do it by his command? Probably the latter, since the descriptions seem to be symbolic. However, it is the power of his voice that in some way causes the general disasters described (see D&C 133:22), and some of the earth's population will be injured or killed as a result. The primary purpose of these tumultuous general signs, however, is not to kill but to warn the people of the earth that the coming of the Lord is near.

Phase Two—The Physical Cleansing of the Earth

The earth will be cleansed of all wickedness prior to the Second Coming, and while the catastrophes of phase one are designed as a warning and constant reminder of the Lord's pending Advent, the destructions of phase two are specifically intended to destroy the wicked who will not heed the Savior's warnings and repent. The vision of this final cleansing was given to the Apostle John and is recorded in multiple chapters of Revelation.[2]

In Revelation 7:1–3, John introduces us to four destroying angels. These angels are given the power to hurt the earth and the sea. They are ready to begin their cleansing task at once but are restrained by another angel of the Lord. This restraint allows time for the final proselyting of the gospel so that all those who are to be saved prior to the Second Coming will have received the symbolic seal of God in their foreheads. Acceptance or rejection of the gospel will give everyone the opportunity to either be saved from or subject to the wrath of the four angels, and by extension, to either be saved in or cast out of the Father's kingdom (see D&C 77:8). John does not tell us how these four angels will function, and he does not refer to them again until Revelation 9:14.

The balance of the 7th chapter (verses 4–17) deals with those who will receive the seal of God during the proselyting that will occur while the four angels are restrained. These righteous people are symbolically placed into two groups: (1) the 144,000 sealed individuals (12,000 from each of the tribes of Israel) who have received their judgment and had their calling and election made sure (Chapters 12, see also Chapter 2), the multitude of the righteous which John sees as "a great multitude . . . of all nations" who stand before God "clothed with white robes." "These are they," John explains, who "came out of great tribulation, and have washed their robes, and made them white in the blood of the Lamb" (Revelation 7:9, 14). These individuals have also made their calling and election sure and will serve God "day and night in his temple," and will "hunger" and "thirst" no more. The Lord will even "wipe away all tears from their eyes" (Revelation 7:15–17). John's descriptive symbolism indicates that they have been relieved of all their earthly problems: their sins have been forgiven and forgotten, and they will be made joint heirs with Christ in his kingdom.

The Opening of the Seventh Seal

When the seventh seal is opened, the tribulation which will culminate with the Lord's Advent will begin.

Revelation 8

And when he had opened the seventh seal, there was silence in heaven about the space of half an hour. 2. And I saw the seven angels which stood before God; and to them were given seven trumpets.

3. And another angel came and stood at the altar, having a golden censer; and there was given unto him much incense, that he should offer it with the prayers of all saints upon the golden altar which was before the throne.

4. And the smoke of the incense, which came with the prayers of the saints, ascended up before God out of the angel's hand.

5. And the angel took the censer, and filled it with fire of the altar, and cast it into the earth: and there were voices, and thunderings, and lightnings, and an earthquake.

6. And the seven angels which had the seven trumpets prepared themselves to sound.

7. The first angel sounded, and there followed hail and fire mingled with blood, and they were cast upon the earth: and the third part of trees was burnt up, and all green grass was burnt up.

8. And the second angel sounded, and as it were a great mountain burning with fire was cast into the sea: and the third part of the sea became blood;

9. And the third part of the creatures which were in the sea, and had life, died; and the third part of the ships were destroyed.

10. And the third angel sounded, and there fell a great star from heaven, burning as it were a lamp, and it fell upon the third part of the rivers, and upon the fountains of waters;

11. And the name of the star is called Wormwood: and the third part of the waters became wormwood; and many men died of the waters, because they were made bitter.

12. And the fourth

angel sounded, and the third part of the sun was smitten, and the third part of the moon, and the third part of the stars; so as the third part of them was darkened, and the day shone not for a third part of it, and the night likewise.

13. And I beheld, and heard an angel flying through the midst of heaven, saying with a loud voice, Woe, woe, woe, to the inhabiters of the earth by reason of the other voices of the trumpet of the three angels, which are yet to sound!

The opening of the seventh seal is generally thought of as the beginning of the Millennium, but it is evident from John's vision that this is actually the beginning of the final cleansing of the earth *before* the Lord comes. Immediately after the seal is opened, there is a pause before the great calamities begin. The actual time of this pause is short but undefined (described by John as silence in heaven for one-half hour). John now introduces seven new angels, each bearing a trumpet to announce his cleansing efforts. The devastation wrought by these angels will be symbolically initiated when each angel blows his trumpet. They are waiting for the command to "reap down the earth" (D&C 38:12), a harvest that will lead to the lifting of the "curtain of heaven" where the face of the Lord will be revealed (a symbolic description of the Second Coming) (D&C 88:95).

Before explaining the cleansing of the earth by these angels, John interjects "another angel" into his text (see Revelation 8:3–5). This unidentified angel has no part in the cleansing process. His actions are symbolically described in terms of the temple ceremony of John's time. He holds a "golden censer" filled with incense, which he offers (along with the prayers of all the saints) upon a "golden altar" situated before the throne of God. The smoke of the incense represents the prayers or pleas of the Saints who seek redress against the wicked who have destroyed them. When the angel fills the censer with fire from the altar and casts it to the earth, it produces "voices, and thunderings, and lightnings, and an earthquake": the Lord's answer to the prayers of the Saints and a summary description of the destructive events that will follow in Revelation 8:7–13 and Revelation 9 and 10. The imagery in these chapters is vivid and the results are devastating, but John symbolically portrays what will take place rather than describe actual events. Thus begins God's judgment on the wicked and the cleansing of the earth prior to the Second Coming.

The First Angel: The first angel blows his trumpet and something John describes as "hail and fire mingled with blood" falls upon the earth and scorches or destroys a "third part" of the trees and all the "green grass." This symbolism seems to describe an environmental catastrophe of some kind. The earth's ecological cycles are integrally balanced, and if a massive amount of its plant life were suddenly destroyed, it would play havoc with that balance. The animal kingdom would be adversely affected through the loss of a major food supply. There would be a sharp increase in the amount of carbon dioxide in the air, which could affect the earth's ability to sustain animal life as we now know it. Famine, or at least a major impact upon normal agricultural productivity, would also be a predictable result of this type of destruction.

That the "hail and fire" will be "mingled with blood" seems to indicate that many people will be destroyed by this cataclysmic event. It may also indicate that some unusual atmospheric condition could accompany or produce this prophesied *storm* which would cause a third part of all trees and grass to be destroyed. An interesting phenomenon of this type was recorded on September 7, 1841:

> Another shower of flesh and blood is reported in the Boston papers to have fallen in Kensington. 'There had been a drizzling rain during a great part of the day, until about 4 o'clock in the afternoon, when the rain stopped and the dark clouds began gradually to assume a brassy hue, until the whole heavens above seemed a sea of fire. The sky continued to grow more bright until about a quarter past five, when almost instantly it became of burnished red, and in a few moments it rained moderately a thick liquid of the appearance of blood, clothing fields and roads for

two miles in circumference in a blood-stained garment. The bloody rain continued for about ten minutes, when it suddenly cleared away, and the atmosphere became so intensely cold that overcoats were needed.[3]

Whether or not this unusual story is factual, the cleansing by the first angel in the 8th chapter of Revelation will obviously have a devastating effect upon the earth.

The Second Angel: When this angel sounds his trumpet, something like a "great mountain burning with fire" will affect the seas. John states that a "third part" of the living creatures therein and a "third part" of the ships thereon will be destroyed. Whether the "third part" is literal or not, we at least know that a large part of the ocean's life forms will be annihilated and that either a significant number of ships will be destroyed or the use of the oceans for transportation will become significantly impeded.

John's description of a "great mountain burning with fire" could be depicting a gigantic volcanic eruption adjacent to (or in) the ocean. A small prototype of this destruction occurred on August 24, A.D. 79 (John may have known about it). On that day, Vesuvius exploded and "hurled dust and rock high into the air amid clouds of smoke and flashes of flame." Within hours, Pompeii and Herculaneum were buried "to a depth of eight or ten feet" as giant walls of ash and molten rock rolled from the mountain's slopes. Many people were also killed as "tidal waves shut off [the] escape by sea."[4] Volcanic activity of the volume that could fulfil John's vision is readily available in the "Ring of Fire," a geological ring of fault systems and volcanos that surrounds the Pacific Ocean basin.[5] Did John envision this system in a collective explosion? Only time will tell.

John also saw the "sea [become] blood" (Revelation 8:8). This symbolic phrase could refer to either the enormous number of people that will be affected by this cleansing or to the change in the sea water brought about by the "mountain of fire" being cast into it—a change that resembles the plague Moses put on the waters of Egypt when Pharaoh refused to let the children of Israel go free (see Exodus 7:15–21). Such a change would certainly bring death to a high percentage of life forms in the ocean, just as it did to the fish in Egypt's rivers.

The Third Angel: This angel causes "a great star" called "Wormwood" to fall from heaven, "burning as it were a lamp." It will affect an enormous quantity of the earth's fresh water supply, and many men and women will die when it pollutes the waters and makes them "bitter." This is another reference by John to future ecological problems of such magnitude that the earth will have difficulty supporting life as we know it. What is the star John refers to, and why is it named Wormwood? John leaves this to our imagination. It is interesting to note, however, that one of the definitions for *wormwood* in *Webster's New World Dictionary* states that it refers to a "bitter, unpleasant, or mortifying experience"; and *The Torah* describes "wormwood" as "a bitter herb, genus *artemisia* " (see Deuteronomy 29:18).[6]

The Fourth Angel: When the fourth angel sounds his trumpet, something catastrophic will occur to the heavens. John says "the third part" of the sun, the moon, and the stars will be "darkened," and the day will only shine for a "third part of it, and the night likewise." The result of this catastrophe is that day and night will have one-third of their capability or capacity reduced— will they be shortened? While scientifically this is an anomaly, the description makes us aware that not only will the earth be affected by these angelic devastations, the heavens also will not escape.

In the above verses, everything John talks about is either reduced or destroyed by one-third. However, this is undoubtedly a symbolic figure used to represent the vastness of the prophesied destructions, and not a precise one-third measurement of everything. All of these *cleansing* destructions are general signs for the people of the earth. They are given not only to cleanse the earth of all wickedness, but also to warn those who remain of how close the coming of the Lord is. The Lord would like us all to be prepared, yet most of mankind refuses to heed his warnings.

In the last verse of Revelation 8, John sees yet another angel flying through "the midst of heaven" ominously crying, "Woe, woe, woe" to mankind below. He has no trumpet and he causes no destruction—he is symbolic. His purpose is to warn the inhabitants of the earth about the remaining three angels which are "yet to sound" their trumpets and bring more destruction upon the earth. The "woes" begin with the fifth angel in Revelation 9.

The Fifth Angel: When this angel sounds his trumpet, a "star" (the devil) falls from heaven to earth and is given the "key of the bottomless pit." This angel's activities represent the first "woe." (The "woes" of Revelation 9:1–12, along with other specific activities of the devil in the latter days, are discussed in Chapter 7.)

The Sixth Angel:

Revelation 9:13–21

13. And the sixth angel sounded, and I heard a voice from the four horns of the golden altar which is before God,

14. Saying to the sixth angel which had the trumpet, Loose the four angels which are bound in the great river Euphrates.

15. And the four angels were loosed, which were prepared for an hour, and a day, and a month, and a year, for to slay the third part of men.

16. And the number of the army of the horsemen were two hundred thousand thousand: and I heard the number of them.

17. And thus I saw the horses in the vision, and them that sat on them, having breast-plates of fire, and of jacinth, and brimstone: and the heads of the horses were as the heads of lions; and out of their mouths issued fire and smoke and brimstone.

18. By these three was the third part of men killed, by the fire, and by the smoke, and by the brimstone, which issued out of their mouths.

19. For their power is in their mouth, and in their tails: for their tails were like unto serpents, and had heads, and with them they do hurt.

20. And the rest of the men which were not killed by these plagues yet repented not of the works of their hands, that they should not worship devils, and idols of gold, and

silver, and brass, and
stone, and of wood:
which neither can see,
nor hear, nor walk:
21. Neither repented

they of their murders,
nor of their sorceries,
nor of their fornication,
nor of their thefts.

This angel represents the second "woe." When he sounds his trumpet, a voice tells him to release four other angels, who have been prepared for their purposes for a lengthy period that John describes as "an hour, and a day, and a month, and a year." According to Revelation, they have been prepared since the inception of the plan of salvation (see Revelation 4:1). These are the four angels of Revelation 7:1–3 who were previously discussed at the beginning of Phase Two. Their stated purpose is to slay "the third part of men" (again probably meaning a large number and not exactly one-third) (Revelation 9:15). The four angels will accomplish their destruction by means of the great war described in the balance of Revelation 9.

This last great war is portrayed symbolically in John's vision; however, it is not initiated by the four angels. How long it will continue is not revealed, but it will be launched by the devil's evil latter-day kingdom and will culminate against Jerusalem and the kingdom of Judah just before the Second Coming. It is evident from John's description of the carnage it will cause that all peoples of the world will be involved in one way or another. Revelation 16:14 states that the devil's latter-day kingdom will send forth emissaries to the kings of the earth to gather armies for the last great battle against Jerusalem. According to Revelation 17:16, it appears that some resistance to this forced participation will take place, thus causing a worldwide conflict. Nonetheless, the armies that will be arrayed against the Jews will be enormous. They are described by John as numbering 200,000,000 horsemen, and he states that he "heard the number of them"—a comment that fires the imagination.

These horsemen will wear breastplates of fire, jacinth (a dark reddish-purple colored precious stone), and brimstone, and while John states that they will be riding on animals he describes as "horses," the horses' heads will be like the "heads of lions" whose mouths will issue forth "fire and smoke and brimstone," and the

horses' tails will be "like unto serpents" whose heads can "hurt."
The power of these war machines will be in their "mouth" and in
their "tails," and they will be responsible for slaying "the third
part of men."

John is obviously seeing implements of war that he does not
have the vocabulary to describe, so he compares them to the things
he knows. His vivid descriptions leave us with the following
specific information about the war and its evil army:

1.   The army John describes will be extremely large.

2.   The entire destructive force of this army will eventually be
      directed against Jerusalem.

3.   The modern implements of war that John sees will be
      extremely destructive. He could be describing tanks,
      artillery, even atomic weapons, but since this war is yet to
      take place, future weapons may better fit his description than
      existing ones. Regardless, the weapons are not the important
      part of John's vision: it is the destructive force of the war
      and the results of the war that are significant.

4.   The war will kill an enormous number of people. John uses
      the figure of one-third of the earth's population to describe
      the enormity of the destruction that will occur; however, as
      in many other verses in Revelation, this is probably
      representative and not actual. Although this war is
      eventually focused on Jerusalem, John's description indicates
      that all mankind will be involved at one time or another.

5.   The duration of this war (once it converges on Jerusalem)
      will cover the same period of time as that described in
      Revelation 11:1–10 where two special witnesses are called
      to prophesy in Jerusalem; i.e., for three and one-half years
      (Chapter 5).

6.   The information John is giving us is connected with the
      information he received in Revelation 13:1–5 concerning
      Satan's kingdom in the latter-days (Chapter 7).

Amazingly, after all of this colossal devastation, those wicked
men and women yet alive will still not repent! They will continue to worship "the works of their hands," those worldly pos-

sessions symbolically identified as "idols of gold, and silver, and brass, and stone, and of wood" (Revelation 9:20–21). As we saw earlier in Chapter 7 of this text, worldly possessions—things that can neither "see, nor hear, nor walk"—will be the hallmark of the devil's kingdom in the latter days. John sees that through their earthly possessions, people have substituted all types of false gods for the living God. Then, as now, the worship of power and economic wealth will supersede the worship of God. Even after all the destruction that will take place, the people who remain will not repent but will continue to give more credence to temporal power and materialism than they will to the Savior, who can give them a place in his kingdom.

At the height of the devastation caused by the massive conflict, John sees the death of the two special prophets who had been raised up to prophesy to the inhabitants of Jerusalem—and then he sees their miraculous resurrection (see Revelation 11:11–14; and Chapter 5 herein). At this point, he declares that the second woe is past and the third woe will come quickly.

The Seventh Angel:

Revelation 11:15–19

15. And the seventh angel sounded; and there were great voices in heaven, saying, The kingdoms of this world are become the kingdoms of our Lord, and of his Christ; and he shall reign for ever and ever.

16. And the four and twenty elders, which sat before God on their seats, fell upon their faces, and worshipped God,

17. Saying, We give thee thanks, O Lord God Almighty, which art, and wast, and art to come; because thou hast taken to thee thy great power, and hast reigned.

18. And the nations were angry, and thy wrath is come, and the time of the dead, that they should be judged, and that thou shouldest give reward unto thy servants the prophets, and to the saints, and them that fear thy name, small and great; and shouldest destroy

them which destroy the earth.

19. And the temple of God was opened in heaven, and there was seen in his temple the ark of his testament: and there were lightnings, and voices, and thunderings, and an earthquake, and great hail.

The seventh angel brings the third woe, but John now pauses in the vision (as he often does) and inserts information in summary form that he will subsequently detail. As he envisions the closing of the second *woe*, it is obvious that the actual coming of the Lord is near, and he inserts general information about that coming before he proceeds.

He first prophesies that all nations will become subject to the Lord at his Advent and that he will reign over them "for ever and ever" (circumstances that relate specifically to the Second Coming and the beginning of the Millennium, see Revelation 11:15). He next sees the same twenty-four elders that he envisioned at the beginning of his revelation (see Revelation 4:4) speaking with the Lord. They note the anger of the wicked (due to their great tribulation) and the anticipation the righteous have for their resurrection (see Revelation 11:17–18). He then sees God's final judgments upon the wicked, as represented by the trump of the seventh angel with the third *woe*. He does not indicate at this point how the seventh angel will bring his destructions to pass, but he summarily represents them as "lightnings, and voices, and thunderings, and an earthquake, and great hail" that will occur as the "temple of God" is "opened in the heaven" and "the ark of his testament" is exposed to view (Revelation 11:19). The third *woe* will be accomplished by the seventh angel with a trumpet when he releases the seven angels with vials full of the final plagues found in Revelation 16.

John inserts chapters 12, 13, and 14 of Revelation before he returns to the plagues of the seven angels with vials. Chapter 12 is a historical flashback that reveals information about the Great Apostasy, the flight of the gospel into the wilderness (Chapter 2), and the preexistent activities of the devil (Chapter 7). Revelation 13 is John's vision of the devil's great latter-day kingdom (Chapters 7 and 8). Revelation 14 concerns three subjects: the 144,000 righteous individuals who have the "Father's name written in their foreheads" (Chapter 12), the vision of the restoration (Chapter 4), and the final judgment of the devil and those who follow him (Chapter 8). Finally, in Revelation 14:15–20 John returns to the conclusions he recorded at the close of Chapter 11. He sees angels with sickles ready to execute the earth's final cleansing (as presaged in Revelation 11:19): they first declare that "the harvest of the earth is ripe," and then they state that the earth is "reaped." The reaping will be done by the plagues of the seven angels with vials as final preparation is made for the Lord's Advent.[7]

The fifteenth chapter of Revelation is a transition chapter that again introduces us to the seven angels with vials who will control the last seven plagues before the Second Coming.[8] However, before John discusses these angels, he again pauses in his narrative (as if he had begun to write and then suddenly remembered something he had forgotten as he closed chapter 11), and inserts Revelation 15:2–5. These verses record more information about God's heaven and beautifully describe the condition of the righteous who will live there: "And I saw as it were a sea of glass mingled with fire: and them that had gotten the victory over the beast, and over his image, and over his mark, and over the number of his name, stand on the sea of glass, having the harps of God" (Revelation 15:2). The righteous individuals John sees are singing and praising God.

After this insert, John finally returns to the seven angels with vials. He explains that the seven angels received their vials from one of the four beasts that were praising God in Revelation 4:7. Revelation 15 then closes (as if it were a continuation of Revelation 11) by providing us with a witness of God couched in terms reminiscent of his appearances in the Old Testament (see Exodus 40:34–35): his heavenly temple is filled with the smoke of his power as the angels pour out his wrath to completely cleanse the earth of all wickedness, for no one will enter God's kingdom until the seven angels have delivered the seven plagues.

Revelation 16

And I heard a great voice out of the temple	saying to the seven angels, Go your ways,

and pour out the vials of the wrath of God upon the earth.

2. And the first went, and poured out his vial upon the earth; and there fell a noisome and grievous sore upon the men which had the mark of the beast, and upon them which worshipped his image.

3. And the second angel poured out his vial upon the sea; and it became as the blood of a dead man: and every living soul died in the sea.

4. And the third angel poured out his vial upon the rivers and fountains of waters; and they became blood.

5. And I heard the angel of the waters say, Thou art righteous, O Lord, which art, and wast, and shalt be, because thou hast judged thus.

6. For they have shed the blood of saints and prophets, and thou hast given them blood to drink; for they are worthy.

7. And I heard another out of the altar say, Even so, Lord God Almighty, true and righteous are thy judgments.

8. And the fourth angel poured out his vial upon the sun; and power was given unto him to scorch men with fire.

9. And men were scorched with great heat, and blasphemed the name of God, which hath power over these plagues: and they repented not to give him glory.

10. And the fifth angel poured out his vial upon the seat of the beast; and his kingdom was full of darkness; and they gnawed their tongues for pain,

11. And blasphemed the God of heaven because of their pains and their sores, and repented not of their deeds.

12. And the sixth angel poured out his vial upon the great river Euphrates; and the water thereof was

dried up, that the way of the kings of the east might be prepared.

13. And I saw three unclean spirits like frogs come out of the mouth of the dragon, and out of the mouth of the beast, and out of the mouth of the false prophet.

14. For they are the spirits of devils, working miracles, which go forth unto the kings of the earth and of the whole world, to gather them to the battle of that great day of God Almighty.

15. Behold, I come as a thief. Blessed is he that watcheth, and keepeth his garments, lest he walk naked, and they see his shame.

16. And he gathered them together into a place called in the Hebrew tongue Armageddon.

17. And the seventh angel poured out his vial into the air; and there came a great voice out of the temple of heaven, from the throne, saying, It is done.

18. And there were voices, and thunders, and lightnings; and there was a great earthquake, such as was not since men were upon the earth, so mighty an earthquake, and so great.

19. And the great city was divided into three parts, and the cities of the nations fell: and great Babylon came in remembrance before God, to give unto her the cup of the wine of the fierceness of his wrath.

20. And every island fled away, and the mountains were not found.

21. And there fell upon men a great hail out of heaven, every stone about the weight of a talent: and men blasphemed God because of the plague of the hail; for the plague thereof was exceeding great.

In Revelation 16 God commands the seven angels to pour out their "vials of the wrath of God upon the earth." These plagues commence the final destruction of the wicked who cannot abide the Lord's presence at his coming.

First Plague: The *first angel with a vial* will deliver the scourge of a "noisome and grievous sore." Because so much symbolism is used throughout Revelation, we do not know if John is describing an actual "sore," or whether he is just symbolically describing a terrible pestilence of some kind. Three scriptural examples demonstrate God's use of *grievous sores*:

1.   Leprosy is described in the scriptures as a "white reddish sore" (Leviticus 13:42). Under the law of Moses, this disease symbolized exclusion from God. The leper in Israel represented the very epitome of sin and uncleanliness and was used by God as a living example of sin.[9]

2.   Job was afflicted with "sore boils from the sole of his foot unto his crown" (Job 2:7) to test his obedience to God.

3.   In the parable of Lazarus and the rich man, the Lord depicted Lazarus' pitiful condition by describing him as being "full of sores" (Luke 16:20).

This affliction will be widespread and deadly, and it will specifically attack both those who bear the "mark of the beast" and those who worship the beast's image (Chapter 7).

This information gives us insight as to when this plague will occur: each generation looks for the signs of the Lord's coming in the events of its time, thus assigning destructive diseases such as AIDS to the fulfillment of this plague; but the *timing* of the plague preempts any existing or previous "noisome and grievous" sores. This plague will not occur until the devil has established his latter-day kingdom.

Second Plague: The *second angel* will pour out his vial upon the sea. The scriptures state that the sea will become "as the blood of a dead man." It would be difficult to take this prediction literally since that would mean the seas would become coagulated. If taken symbolically, however, this may refer to the verse where John sees a star named Wormwood which destroys a third part of the waters (see Revelation 8:8–11). The Lord told Joseph Smith in latter-day revelation: "Behold, I, the Lord, in the beginning blessed the waters; but in the last days, by the mouth of my servant John, I cursed the waters. Wherefore, the days will come that no flesh shall be safe upon the waters" (D&C 61:14–15). The Lord thereafter forbade general travel upon the waters while the Saints were gathering to Missouri, stating that "the destroyer rideth upon the face thereof" (D&C 61:18–19). The result of this plague on the waters is defined as being so catastrophic that "every living soul" who ventures out upon the sea will die (see Revelation 16:3). The seas will no longer function as they have in the past, which will have a devastating effect upon a vast number of the earth's inhabitants.

Third Plague: The *third angel* will pour his vial into "the rivers and fountains of water" that are found upon the land, and they will also be turned to "blood." In the latter days, the Lord confirms that this plague will occur and gives us the following additional information: "I [will] make the rivers a wilderness; their fish [will] stink, and die for thirst" (D&C 133:68). Neither this latter-day revelation nor John reveals the source of this plague, but their descriptions have some interesting modern-day parallels. Red Tides have caused devastation when their "blooms . . . poisoned the water" and killed fish "by the millions,"[10] and a newly discovered dinoflagellate organism named *Pfiesteria piscicida* (translated as "fish killer") was implicated in the death of more than a billion fish in 1990.[11] Both of these modern-day plagues are attributed to widespread and increased "eutrophication—the abundant accumulation of nutrients—from domestic, agricultural, and industrial effluent . . . " the result, a virtual epidemic of coastal algae blooms.[12]

While these are small examples of John's predicted catastrophic plagues, they readily show how simple it will be for the third angel to "pour out his vial." Something will happen to the earth's fresh water supply—a pollution so severe that the water will no longer be able to sustain life. The angel of the waters in Revelation 16:5 states that the Lord will be justified in destroying the wicked in this manner since "they have shed the blood of saints and prophets." (It is possible that the wicked could literally kill some of the Lord's Saints and his prophets before the Second Coming; however, because of the symbolism found in

Revelation, this is probably a metaphoric representation of the devil's evil kingdom leading people astray—thus "killing" God's influence for good.) If people choose wicked paths, however, they will justify their own eventual destruction.

Fourth Plague: The *fourth angel* will pour out his vial upon the sun, "and power [will be] given unto him to scorch men with fire" and "great heat." John gives no explanation of what this plague is, but in Revelation 8:12 he states that a "third part of the sun [will be] smitten." These two occurrences are related in that they both contribute to an ecological imbalance that could make many areas of the planet uninhabitable. While not stating that it is the potential fulfillment of John's vision and description, there is an interesting natural phenomenon that occurs with the sun every eleven years. Scientists call it the *Solar Maximum* event. During this event the sun emits enormous energy that can affect electronic capabilities on earth—electrical transmission lines, satellites, etc. No one is killed from this solar event, but the environment man has developed (and lives in) and will yet become more dependant upon, may be catastrophically affected by this or a similar event. Perhaps a method God might use to fulfill the prophecy.[13] Mankind's predictable reaction to both of these phenomena is to blaspheme the name of God and repent not. In other words, men and women still will not acknowledge the fact that God is orchestrating the devastation they are experiencing. Interestingly, no deaths are mentioned in this verse. The people seem to survive, indicating that this is not a plague of death but rather of torment. Because the people curse God for the plague and refuse to repent of their wickedness, however, they seal their ultimate fate.

Fifth Plague: The *fifth angel* will pour out his vial upon the "seat of the beast." This plague is unidentified but in some way will fall upon the devil's evil kingdom in the latter days and will cause "darkness," "pain," and "sores" to come upon it (Chapter 7). The darkness is symbolic.

There are several scriptural references to darkness, both actual and spiritual, but there are three specific instances where the Lord uses actual darkness for symbolic purposes: (1) Moses called down three days of darkness upon the Egyptians as one of the plagues (see Exodus 10:22–23); (2) while the Savior hung on the cross, there was darkness "over all the land" from the "sixth hour" until the "ninth hour"(Matthew 27:45); and (3) on the Western Hemisphere, darkness fell upon the land at the Savior's crucifixion (see 3 Nephi 8:19 ff). All of these occurrences are similitudes for the death of the "light of the world," Jesus Christ (see John 8:12)—a death that left the world in spiritual darkness.[14] Therefore, John's envisioned darkness seems to symbolize the spiritual condition of the wicked as compared to those enlightened by the light or knowledge of Christ—much like the condition of the wicked during the Dark Ages (Chapter 3). If spiritual darkness is the interpretation the Lord intended in these verses, this darkness is probably grounded in mankind's desire for earthly power and wealth, certainly not in the wealth of God's kingdom. Perhaps the vial of the fifth angel represents an economic collapse where "no man buyeth [the] merchandise [of the wicked] any more" (Revelation 18:11). Again, John gives no indication what the source is of the pain or sores to be inflicted upon mankind. Perhaps they are also symbolic, representing the trauma suffered by the loss of worldly wealth and power upon which the wicked will come to rely.

Regardless of the interpretation of this plague, it is clear that the discomfort it inflicts will cause the wicked to gnaw "their tongues for pain"—yet again blaspheme God and "[repent] not of their deeds." Even then, they will value their power and possessions more than they will value their God.

Sixth Plague: The *sixth angel* will pour out his vial upon the Euphrates River. The results in the vision are amazing: the river dries up to prepare the way for the "kings of the east"—perhaps symbolically erasing any hindrance in the path of the great evil army that will attack Jerusalem just before the Second Coming. Next, the vision describes three spirits which are like frogs. They will "come out of the mouth of the dragon [the devil], and out of the mouth of the beast [the anti-Christ], and out of the mouth of the false prophet" (see Revelation 13; and Chapter 7). They are the "spirits of devils, working miracles, which go forth unto the kings of the earth and of the whole world, to gather them to the battle of that great day of God almighty" (Revelation 16:14). They appear to be representatives (people or entities) of the devil's kingdom who will go forth to the nations of the earth to gather them for the battle of Armageddon, the last great war against God, Israel, and Jerusalem. The Lord again warns us in Revelation 16 that he comes "as a thief"—emphasizing the fact that the time of his coming is unknown, and mankind must therefore be constantly prepared and vigilant (see also Ezekiel 38:39).

Seventh Plague: Finally, the *seventh angel* will come and pour his vial into the air. A voice will then emanate "out of the temple of heaven, from the throne [of God], saying, It is done" (Revelation 16:17). After the heavenly voice speaks there will be "thunders, and lightnings" and a tremendous earthquake will occur, "such as was not since men were upon the earth." It will be so cataclysmic that John identifies it as a singular event in the earth's history. The earth will be transformed: islands will flee, and mountains will not be found in their place. The entire face of the earth will be changed. In 1831, Joseph Smith received additional information on this transformation:

> And it shall be a voice as the voice of many waters, and as the voice of a great thunder, which shall break down the mountains, and the valleys shall not be found.
>
> He shall command the great deep, and it shall be driven back into the north countries, and the islands shall become one land;
>
> And the land of Jerusalem and the land of Zion shall be turned back into their own place, and the earth shall be like as it was in the days before it was divided (D&C 133:22–24).

The face of the land will change. The physical location of the land masses will be as they were when Adam came out of the Garden of Eden. This massive earthquake will also cause the Mount of Olives to split in two at the conclusion of the great war in Jerusalem, and the Lord will appear in the cleft to the tribe of Judah (Chapter 5). In addition, at or just before the time this massive earthquake takes place, a great hailstorm will occur "out of heaven, every stone about the weight of a talent [a talent equals about 57 pounds, according to the Bible Dictionary]." John does not mention what destruction these massive hailstones will do, nor can we determine if he is again speaking symbolically, but the terrible storm will cause men to blaspheme God "because of the plague of the hail; for the plague thereof [will be] exceedingly great." The people will be so wicked at this point that they will be immune to any influence from the Spirit. Again they will not repent, and they will subsequently be destroyed.

By the end of Revelation 16:21, the seven plagues have been fulfilled—the beleaguered earth will soon rest.

Phase Three—The Earth Returns to Its Paradisiacal Glory

The curse that God placed on the earth because of the Fall of Adam and Eve has continued throughout the millennia because mankind has continued to sin. The great destructions described in phases one and two of this chapter are a consequence of that sin. These destructions will be brought down upon the earth as judgments of God upon the wicked. The destruction of the wicked (especially that destruction related by John in Revelation) is described elsewhere in the scriptures as a *burning* so intense that few men will be left alive after it occurs (see Isaiah 24:6). As a result of these destructions, the present configuration of the earth will come to an end. The earth will literally *pass away*, or die, as it were. This process is described in the scriptures as the earth being "consumed" or "dissolved," melting "with fervent heat" and being "wrapt" or "rolled together as a scroll" (Isaiah 34:4; Revelation 6:14; 3 Nephi 26:3; Mormon 5:23). The Lord declared early in his ministry that the "meek . . . [would] inherit the earth" (Matthew 5:5), and as the Second Coming approaches, it is to this end that these powerful destructive forces will decimate the wicked. Peter said that the day of the Lord would come "as a thief in the night; in the which the heavens shall pass away with a great noise, and the elements shall melt with fervent heat, the earth also and the works that are therein shall be burned up" (2 Peter 3:10). In subsequent verses he again states that the heavens will be "on fire [and will] be dissolved, and the elements [will] melt with fervent heat" (2 Peter 3:12). With these terrifying conflagrations in mind, he asks, "Seeing . . . that all these things shall be dissolved, *what manner of persons ought ye to be?*"[15] (2 Peter 3:11; emphasis added).

The theme of brilliance or fire associated with paradisiacal glory and other of God's works is common in the scriptures. Joseph Smith saw the gate of the celestial kingdom (which itself may have been a metaphor) and described it as the "gate through which the heirs of that kingdom will enter, which [is] like unto circling flames of fire" (D&C 137:2). He also saw and described the "blazing throne of God" (D&C 137:3). In Helaman 5:23–24, the Lord protected Nephi and Lehi from their enemies by encircling them about with a "pillar of fire," and although they stood "in the midst of the fire," they "were not burned." Shadrach, Meshach, and Abednego experienced the same miracle in the "fiery furnace" of Daniel 3:23–25.

The glory of the Lord was first described as a "devouring fire" when the children of Israel gathered at Sinai after their exodus from Egypt (see Exodus 24:17). Isaiah records that the name of the Lord will come "from far, burning with his anger . . . his lips . . . full of indignation, and his tongue as a devouring fire" (Isaiah 30:27). Job used the *fire* and *heat* metaphors quite differently when he said that "leviathan" (a name of the devil or evil) made the "deep to boil like a pot" (Job 41:31). This heat and fire metaphor, as applied by Job, is also used in a latter-day description of the Lord: "for the presence of the Lord shall be as the melting fire that burneth, and as the fire which causeth the waters to boil" (D&C 133:41). All of these descriptions foretell changes that will occur as the curse of Adam is nullified and a renewed earth is transfigured to receive its paradisiacal glory. At that time the earth will become as it was "before [the land] was divided" (D&C 133:24). In the tenth article of faith, Joseph Smith recorded the following: "We believe . . . that the earth will be renewed and receive its paradisiacal glory." The Lord had told Joseph in section 63 of the Doctrine and Covenants that this change to the earth would occur "according to the pattern which was shown unto mine apostles upon the mount [of Transfiguration]; of which account the fulness ye have not yet received" (D&C 63:21).

When the Lord was transfigured on the Mount of Transfiguration, a somnolent Peter, James, and John were suddenly awakened by a great brilliance. It was the Messiah, transfigured and appearing in his glorified state: "His face did shine as the sun, and his raiment was white as the light" (Matthew 17:2).[16] The

Apostles had difficulty describing the Lord in his glory, even when he stood directly before them. In like manner, the prophets down through the ages have had difficulty describing the earth in its paradisiacal glory, let alone the means by which that glory was acquired. They therefore relied upon metaphors to describe the glory of the Lord, his exalted creations, and the paradisiacal earth.

The most detailed description of the earth's paradisiacal transformation at the Lord's Advent was given to Joseph Smith in December 1833. In this revelation, Jesus declared that the day would come when "all flesh" would see him. He then proceeded to give a staccato account of what his Advent would cause:

> Every corruptible thing, both of man, or of the beasts of the field, or of the fowls of the heavens, or of the fish of the sea, that [dwell] upon all the face of the earth, shall be consumed;

> And also that of element shall melt with fervent heat; and all things shall become new, that my knowledge and glory may dwell upon all the earth.

> The enmity of beasts, yea, the enmity of all flesh, shall cease from before my face.

> Whatsoever any man shall ask, it shall be given unto him.

> Satan shall not have power to tempt any man.

> There shall be no sorrow because there [will be] no death [for the righteous]. [Revelation also states that there shall be no pain.]

> An infant shall not die until he is old; and his life shall be as the age of a tree [described by Isaiah as 100 years];

> And when he dies he shall not sleep . . . in the earth, but shall be changed in the twinkling of an eye, and shall be caught up, and his rest shall be glorious.

> Yea, verily I say unto you, in that day when the
> Lord shall come, he shall reveal all things—
>
> Things which have passed, and hidden things
> which no man knew, things of the earth, by which
> it was made, and the purpose and the end
> thereof—
>
> Things most precious, things that are above, and
> things that are beneath, things that are in the earth,
> and upon the earth, and in heaven (see D&C 101:
> 24–34; see also Isaiah 65:17–25; Revelation 21:4).

These verses truly reveal a promised paradise for mankind, but what will the physical earth be like after all these changes? The scriptures again give us detailed information. They reveal that the mountains will "flow down" at the Savior's presence (see D&C 133:40, 44), or, according to Isaiah, they will "depart" (see Isaiah 54:10). Every valley will be "exalted," every "mountain and hill" will be made "low," the "crooked" will be made "straight," and the "rough places" will be made smooth (Isaiah 40:4). Whether this scripture is describing a flat earth or a reconfigured earth, only time will tell. As for the waters, the great seas will return to the "north countries, and the islands [will] become one land" (D&C 133:23). John confirms this reunification of the land masses by stating that there will be "no more sea" (Revelation 21:1). He further states that the islands will be gone (see Revelation 16:20), "moved out of their places" (Revelation 6:14), which latter day revelation defines as becoming "one land" (D&C 133:23). At the time of the Garden of Eden the land was apparently all in one place, and it remained that way until "the earth was divided" in the days of Peleg (Genesis 10:25; 1 Chronicles 1:19). At or just before the Savior's coming, the land will return to its former place and "be like it was in the days before it was divided" (D&C 133:24). How will this change take place? Some of it will undoubtedly be caused by the great earthquake John describes (see Revelation 16:18), but the balance of the changes will be caused by the transfiguration of the earth at the Lord's coming.

The transfiguration descriptions, if taken literally when they speak of "fervent heat," might lead to the conclusion that a great fire will rain down from heaven such as fell upon Sodom and Gomorrah (see Genesis 19:24), or that a cataclysmic man-caused infernal heat—perhaps of a nuclear type[17]—might occur. But more likely these descriptions are symbolic because the prophets who saw the glory of the Lord and his cleansing works did not have the vocabulary to describe them; therefore, they had to compare them to the things they knew. It is obvious that if these descriptions of destruction were literal, no man, plant, animal, or element would survive without the direct intervention of the Lord.

The description of the earth's destruction is a recurring theme, both in regards to the cleansing of the earth by the destruction of the wicked, and in regards to the changes the earth will experience in preparation for the Lord's coming.[18] We know with certainty that the coming of the Lord will physically change the earth and restore it to the way it was in the days of Eden—with a twist, for it will also possess the glory of the Messiah. Who will inherit this new earth? The righteous! (See D&C 59:2.) It will be given to those who have been faithful to God's covenants and who have not been deceived by the devil, as represented by the faithful virgins of the parable[19] (see D&C 45:56–57; 63:20). These will have the Lord in their midst, and their children will be blessed to grow thereafter in righteousness from generation to generation (see D&C 45:57–59; 56:20).

Signs: Increased   11
Devastations

"For behold, and lo, vengeance cometh
speedily upon the ungodly as the whirlwind;
and who shall escape it?"

Doctrine & Covenants 97:22

The Desolating Scourge

One of the most interesting general signs of the Second Coming is described in scripture as a "desolating scourge" that will
go forth upon mankind. The scourge is not portrayed as a singular event, nor is it considered a unique event in any given period
of time. Indeed, it is just the opposite. It can and does take many
forms. The Lord states that it will "go forth among the inhabitants of the earth, and shall continue to be poured out [upon them]
from time to time, if they repent not, until the earth is empty" (D&C
5:19; emphasis added).

In one section of the Doctrine and Covenants, the "desolating scourge" is defined as a "desolating sickness" which will
"cover the land" (D&C 45:31), and while this may incline us to
look for a specific illness to fit this description, this scripture may
in fact refer to many different disorders—anything from the "black
death" of the 14th century to the influenza, AIDS, or ebola epi-

demics of the 20th century. Perhaps it refers to some future scourge—or it could refer to them all! That is what makes this sign so difficult to identify.

In the 29th section of the Doctrine and Covenants, the mysterious "desolating scourge" adversely affects the heavens. Because of it "the sun shall be darkened, and the moon shall be turned into blood, and the stars shall fall from heaven, and there shall be greater signs in heaven above and in the earth beneath." It causes a great hailstorm that will be "sent forth to destroy the crops of the earth," and it causes flies to come "upon the face of the earth," flies "which shall take hold of the inhabitants thereof, and shall eat their flesh, and shall cause maggots to come in upon them . . . [until] their flesh shall fall from off their bones, and their eyes from their sockets." As a result, "the beasts of the forest and the fowls of the air shall devour them up" (see D&C 29:14–21).

More devastating scourges are found in Revelation 16 wherein the great plagues of the seven angels are described (Chapter 8). These scourges include wars, pestilence, and earthquakes, and their specific purpose is to cleanse the earth for the last time in preparation for the Lord's coming (see Joseph Smith–Matthew 1:39). Another scourge in Revelation is described as a "noisome and grievous" sore which will be inflicted upon those in the latter days who bear the mark of the beast (see Revelation 16:2). Other nonspecific scourges recorded in the scriptures are blood and fire, smoke,[1] vapors of smoke, thunder and lightning,[2] and famine (see D&C 29:16; Joseph Smith–History 1:45). The "desolating scourge" of famine will be the fulfillment of John's vision of a black horseman who holds a "pair of balances in his hand:" balances which signify a famine so devastating that the value of food will be far greater than the value of money (see Revelation 6:5–6). This condition is described by Joseph Smith as having also occurred during the third thousand years of the earth's existence—prior to Christ's birth (see D&C 77:7).

One problem mankind has with these scourges (besides having to live through them) is recognition, since the devil uses them to deceive mankind just as the Lord uses them to remind mankind of his coming. The righteous men and women of the latter days will have to rely upon spiritual insight to recognize the difference between the normal occurrences of nature and God's hand moving upon the wicked. Science (or the natural man) is always ready with a plausible explanation for unusual natural occurrences—such as shifts in El Nino's current, unusual sun spots, erosion of the ozone layer, or a new virus—and science may be right. However, scientists may fail to recognize that God also has the power to cause scourges—through natural means or otherwise.

Isaiah perceived the problem of the Lord using scourges as warnings while the devil uses them to deceive (he cannot create or cause them) as a "covenant" with death and hell. While addressing the Jewish leadership the Lord said through Isaiah, "Ye have said, We have made a covenant with death, and with hell are we at agreement; when the overflowing scourge shall pass through, it shall not come unto us: for we have made lies our refuge, and under falsehood have we hid ourselves" (Isaiah 28:15). What he is explaining is that the devil can use our own intelligence and sophistication to deceive us. Many of the "scourges" that befall mankind are just normal life's circumstances and can be explained as such; however, because of their supposed intelligence or sophistication, mankind may also attempt to explain away those scourges that come from God, and that is the key to Isaiah's comment. We can easily be deceived into believing that any or all of the scourges that befall mankind have a natural explanation and have nothing to do with God's condemnation of the wicked. Conversely, we may attribute God's vengeance to a given scourge when in reality, it is only one of life's circumstances. This problem can subject us to one of two consequences: *first,* we may rely upon our own knowledge and scientific sophistication to explain away God's signs as natural phenomena, thereby rejecting the possibility of God's involvement and possibly withdrawing ourselves from his kingdom; or *second,* we may justify our own righteousness by citing the destruction of others as a scourge from God upon the wicked, when in fact they may have only fallen subject to a normal occurrence.

An interesting example of not recognizing God's influence in our lives is found in the New Testament. Herod Agrippa had been promoted by Rome for his allegiance to the empire. He was allowed to take the title of king, and following the death of Philip was given Philip's territory as part of his kingdom. Soon thereafter he dressed himself in formal royal attire, sat upon his throne, and delivered an oration to the people. Apparently the Spirit influenced his talk and the people listening recognized it, for his audience declared that the speech had come from God. But Herod did not recognize Deity's hand and failed to give God the glory for the speech. As a result, "the angel of the Lord [immediately] smote him, because he gave not God the glory: and he was eaten of worms, and gave up the ghost" (Acts 12:21–24).

During the latter days, God will send devastating scourges through what may appear to be normal and natural processes as he changes the times and seasons and puts the general signs of the Second Coming into place. But through the self-serving, obdurate, and dishonest characteristics of humankind (the covenant with death and hell), they will reject the signs of the times and the admonitions of the prophets. Isaiah warned mankind that "your covenant with death shall be disannulled, and your agreement with hell shall not stand; when the overflowing scourge shall pass through, then ye shall be trodden down by it" (Isaiah 28:18). The scourges which will assail men and women prior to the Second Coming may have the power to destroy them physically, but their disbelief in God will have the power to destroy them spiritually.

Wars and Rumors of War

Wars and rumors of war have always been a part of earth's history. In a double-reference prophecy found in Matthew, the Lord warned his Apostles about the impending destruction of Jerusalem and the great calamities of war in the last days: "And ye shall hear of wars and rumors of wars: see that ye be not troubled . . . For nation shall rise against nation, and kingdom against kingdom . . . [and] . . . all these are [but] the beginning of sorrows" (Matthew 24:6–8, see also D&C 45:26).

The last days began with the restoration of the gospel, and it is from that time forward that the double-reference portion of the prophecy applies. On Christmas day in 1832, Joseph Smith, the prophet of the restoration, received the following prophecy concerning war in the latter days:

Verily, thus saith the Lord concerning the wars
that will shortly come to pass, beginning at the
rebellion of South Carolina, which will eventually
terminate in the death and misery of many souls;

And the time will come that war will be poured
out upon all nations, beginning at this place.

For behold, the Southern States shall be divided
against the Northern States, and the Southern
States will call on other nations, even the nation
of Great Britain, as it is called, and they shall also
call upon other nations, in order to defend
themselves against other nations; and then war
shall be poured out upon all nations.

And it shall come to pass, after many days, slaves
shall rise up against their masters, who shall be
marshaled and disciplined for war (D&C 87:1–4).

The Civil War marked the beginning of "wars and rumors of
wars" in the latter days (see D&C 45:63). It was the fulfillment of
John the Revelator's vision of the red horseman, to whom was
given the power to "take peace from the earth" so that mankind
would "kill one another" (Revelation 6:4). (Again, this is a condition that Joseph Smith described in Doctrine and Covenants 77:7
as having also occurred in the second thousand years of the earth's
existence. A pattern of repetition that appears throughout history.) John's vision of warning was confirmed in 1831 when the
Lord stated that his Advent was "nigh at hand," that peace would
be "taken from the earth, and [that] the devil [would soon] have
power over his own dominion" (D&C 1:35).

In 1839, seven years after he received the revelation on the
Civil War, the prophet Joseph Smith declared: "The Saints and
the world will have little peace from henceforth . . . [for] . . . wars
are at hand."[3] Again referring to the Civil War he said:

I saw men hunting the lives of their own sons,
and brother murdering brother, women killing
their own daughters, and daughters seeking the
lives of their mothers. I saw armies arrayed

against armies. I saw blood, desolation, fires. The Son of Man has said that the mother shall be against the daughter, and the daughter against the mother. These things are at the doors. They will follow the Saints of God from city to city. Satan will rage, and the spirit of the devil is now enraged. I know not how soon these things will take place; but with a view of them, shall I cry peace? No! I will lift up my voice and testify of them.[4]

From the time of the Civil War forward, the Saints were repeatedly warned of wars in other nations and in their own land, and the scriptures tell us that these wars will continue until the whole earth is in commotion (see D&C 38:29; 45:26, 63).

On April 2, 1843, Joseph Smith gave the following prophecy to the Saints:

I prophesy, in the name of the Lord God, that the commencement of the difficulties which will cause much bloodshed previous to the coming of the Son of Man will be in South Carolina.

It may probably arise through the slave question. This a voice declared to me, while I was praying earnestly on the subject, December 25th, 1832 (D&C 130:12–13).

Doctrine and Covenants 87:1–4 and 130:12–13 are reminiscent of Samuel the Lamanite's prophecy to the Nephites concerning the Savior's coming birth and death (see Helaman 13–15). Both prophecies identify very specific information. Why was the Lord so definite about the Civil War being a sign? Because wars and rumors of wars have been so common throughout the ages that believers and nonbelievers alike may not recognize them in the latter days as a sign of the Second Coming. However, the specific prophecy of the Civil War initiated the fulfillment of this sign in the latter days, and the sign will not be fulfilled until war is poured out upon *all* nations (see Joel 3:9–14). Nonetheless, in the Gospel of Luke the Lord comforts us by telling us to "be not terrified: for these things must first come to pass; but the end is not by and by" (Luke 21:9).

Although the *general* prophecies concerning wars will be fulfilled, there will still be *one last specific war* before the Savior's coming. It will center around Jerusalem (Chapter 5), for the Lord has declared that Jerusalem will become "a burdensome stone for all people" in the last days (Zechariah 12:3). Through this war (and all other wars and rumors of wars) "the inhabitants of the earth [will] be made to feel the wrath, and indignation, and chastening hand of an Almighty God, until the consumption decreed hath made a full end of all nations" (D&C 87:6).

The Hailstorm

In Revelation 11:19, John said there would be "lightnings, and voices, and thunderings, and an earthquake, and great hail" just prior to the Second Coming. In Revelation 16:18–21, he refers to this great hailstorm and states that it will occur in association with a massive earthquake—an earthquake that will change the face of the land.

There are several references to the Lord's use of hailstorms throughout the scriptures. They were used symbolically when the false prophets in Ezekiel's time prescribed a belief in a counterfeit peace (a situation Ezekiel described as a wall created with "untempered mortar"). Ezekiel prophesied that the Lord would send "an overflowing shower in [his] anger, and great hailstones in [his] fury to consume" the symbolic wall and destroy the prophesied peace (Ezekiel 13:13).

Ezekiel again spoke of a great hailstorm when he had a vision of the same storm John had seen. While prophesying of the terrible latter day invasion of Israel and Jerusalem by an army he called "Gog," he cited the same great earthquake John had seen and stated that God would send "great hailstones" (among other natural calamities) to afflict the wicked (Ezekiel 38:19–22).

When Mosiah recorded God's judgments against the wicked people of King Noah's time, he stated that the Lord would send "hail among them" to "smite them" (Mosiah 12:6). In the dedicatory prayer of the Kirkland Temple, Joseph Smith asked the Lord to send hail as a judgment upon those who were slandering the

Saints of his time (see D&C 109:30). In his battle with the five kings at Gibeon, Joshua records that the Lord discomforted the enemies of Israel by casting down "great stones from heaven " upon them. In this storm, there were more soldiers "which died with hailstones than they whom the children of Israel slew with the sword" (Joshua 10:11).

However, the hailstorm seen in vision by John and Ezekiel will make all former hailstorms pale in comparison. The severity of this storm will cause men to suffer greatly and to blaspheme God "because of the plague of the hail" (Revelation 16:21). This is not an unwarranted assumption since John describes the weight of the hailstones as that of a "talent," and while the weight of a talent has differed historically depending upon how it was used, its minimum weight was approximately 57 pounds.[5]

Whether the weight of these hailstones is symbolic or literal, it is unquestionable that they will be extremely large and destructive. Their purpose will be twofold: to destroy the crops of the earth (see D&C 29:16) and to plague the army (Gog) which will assail Judah just prior to the Second Coming (see Ezekiel 38:19).

The Nations

There are many scriptures that describe the suffering that the nations of the earth will experience prior to the Second Coming. Luke predicts that nation will "rise against nation and kingdom against kingdom, and there shall be signs in the sun, and in the moon, and in the stars; and upon the earth distress of nations" (Luke 21:10, 25). The word *distress* is used metaphorically to describe all judgments that will come upon the nations because of their wickedness. In another scripture, the Lord said all nations would "tremble" at his coming (see D&C 34:8) and that after the establishment of Zion, they would "tremble because of her [Zion]" and would "fear because of her terrible ones" (D&C 64:43). Independence, Missouri—the City of Zion—is where people will flee for protection from the great conflicts that will occur between the nations, because they will be "the only people that shall not be at war one with another" (D&C 45:68–69) at a time when there will be "wars and rumors of war among all the nations" (1 Nephi 14:15).

Isaiah saw the great destruction that will occur among the nations in the latter days and described it in *historical double-reference prophecy* (prophecy written as if it has already occurred, yet which actually applies to two or more time periods in the future). His vision of the tribulations that will come upon nations is written in Isaiah 13–23. The fulfillment of these prophecies started shortly after Isaiah's prediction, and they will continue to be fulfilled with the distress which the Lord will bring upon all nations prior to his Second Coming (see Zechariah 9:1–8).

Through double-reference prophecy, Isaiah described both the destruction which God would bring upon the nations surrounding Israel during Isaiah's time, and the destruction that will occur to those nations and all other nations in the latter days. In his writings, the nation of Israel (meaning the covenant people consisting of the twelve tribes) represents the kingdom of God (see Exodus 19:5–6; Ephesians 2:12; 1 Peter 2:9). The double-reference prophecy in his visions (which he calls "burdens") describes the afflictions which the Lord will place upon *all* nations of the earth that fight against the kingdom of God (see Isaiah 13–23). John, in Revelation, sees the latter day distress of the nations in terms of the devil's latter day kingdom as it opposes the kingdom of God.

When discussing the distress of nations in Isaiah and Revelation, it should be remembered that Israel and the kingdom of God are synonymous and include not only the state of Israel and the tribe of Judah but also the other eleven tribes of Israel (as well as any entity, including the Church, which represents the gospel or the covenant people in the last days).

Chapters 13 through 23 of Isaiah testify of the following salient points concerning the distress of nations:

1. The Lord sometimes uses outside nations or entities to *punish* the tribes of Israel. A latter day example of this involves the establishment and abandonment of Zion in Missouri by the early Church. The Lord gave instructions for the establishment of Zion and specified its location (see D&C 57:2–3), and while the Saints gathered there, they soon found persecution heaped upon them to such a degree that they were forced to abandon the promised city. Why? Because of the transgression of the Saints (see D&C 101:2; 103:4; 105:9). And what was the nature of their offense? "They sinned against the Lord, . . . they sinned against

each other . . . they failed to live in accordance with the high moral and spiritual law of the Gospel; they failed to meet the conditions on which God was pledged to their maintenance upon the land of Zion, and hence were left in the hands of their enemies."[6] And what did the Lord use to evict the Saints from Zion? The state of Missouri and its people, "including the Governor and Lieutenant Governor, and finally . . . the state legislature."[7]

2. The Lord sometimes uses the nations of the earth to *punish* each other. The Missouri expulsion of the Saints also provides us with an example of this Isaiah principle. While it is true that the Lord used both the state of Missouri and its inhabitants to expel the Mormons and to punish them for their iniquity and disobedience, he also punished Missouri—both the state and the people—for the sins they committed against the Saints. During the Civil War "all the hardships the Missourians had inflicted upon the Saints were now visited upon their heads, only more abundantly."[8] And by whom? The United States of America!

3. While the Lord used the nations surrounding Israel to punish her, he did not accept any of them as her replacement. He rejected them because of their wickedness and idolatry.

4. Double-reference prophecy involves the following aspects of the Lord's relationship to the nations of the earth:

    a.   They will again be punished for their wickedness prior to the Second Coming.

    b.   They will reject the Lord, even though he has prophesied to them of his coming.

    c.   Their Savior is Christ, just as he is the Savior of the covenant people.

    d.   As Israel's God, the Messiah is superior to the gods of other nations.

5. The most important aspects of Isaiah's double-reference prophecies are the references to the judgments that will come upon all nations of the earth prior to the Second Coming.

6. The judgments of the Lord upon the nations of the latter days will occur for the same reasons that they did historically: the nations of the earth will (a) reject God, (b) afflict Israel, (c) worship false gods, and (d) revere material things over spiritual truths.

7. All material power, political power, false gods of whatever nature, and all nations will fall before the wrath of God; only the blessings of the Lord's covenant people will remain.

Zechariah confirms Isaiah's prophecies regarding the fate of nations although he couches his prophecies in terms of all those nations that had "vexed" Israel (see Zechariah 9:1–8).

Although Isaiah's prophecies involve all nations, it is interesting to note the Lord's particular interest in Egypt. In his visions, Isaiah views Egypt's past, present, and future (see Isaiah 19). He foresaw Israel's reliance upon treaties with Egypt for protection and warned them against such alliances: those that would imminently occur (see Isaiah 30:2–7), those that would occur during the Babylonian captivity (see Isaiah 30:7; Jeremiah 37:5, 7), and those that would yet occur during the latter days (see Isaiah 19:23–24). Isaiah warned Israel against alliances with Egypt—or any worldly nation—as opposed to her alliance with God, and he reiterated the Lord's promise to Israel that he would protect her if she would but rely upon him (see Isaiah 31:1–5). Only God can protect the chosen people—worldly alliances will prove false (see Isaiah 31). Isaiah further notes that in spite of the judgments that will come upon Egypt, the Lord loves the Egyptian people and will yet send the Savior to them after their repentance and punishment (see Isaiah 19:20).

The judgment of the nations is, in most instances, another general sign of the Second Coming. However, it is not easy to determine whether a nation's particular distress is the result of the Lord's judgment or whether it is based upon natural causes. Only through the Spirit can we make this determination.

Six Signs: Beginning with the Church

"Therefore, thou son of man, say unto the
children of thy people, The righteousness of
the righteous shall not deliver him in the day
of his transgression."

Ezekiel 33:12

Beginning with the Church

In the early years of the restoration of the gospel, the Lord
gave a warning to two eager members of the Church: "Wherefore, be faithful," he said, "praying always, having your lamps
trimmed and burning, and oil with you, that you may be ready at
the coming of the Bridegroom" (D&C 33:17). The Lord is referring to the parable of the ten virgins in this admonition (see Matthew 25:1–13), and since the bridegroom represents the Savior
and the ten virgins represent his followers, this parable applies
directly to the status of the members of The Church of Jesus Christ
of Latter-day Saints at the time of the Second Coming (see D&C
45:56–59).

Initially, all of the virgins in the parable are prepared to join
the wedding feast, as was the custom in Christ's time. But when
the bridegroom tarried (the time of the Savior's coming is unknown), their oil (the spiritual preparation required to be mem-

bers of Christ's Church under the covenant) diminishes. The parable tells us that five of the virgins were adequately prepared to wait for the bridegroom—no matter how long it took. They had "received the truth, and [had] taken the Holy Spirit for their guide, and [had] not been deceived" (D&C 45:57)—this was their extra oil. And while the other five virgins had participated in all that was required of them to get them to the point where they were *entitled to wait* for the bridegroom, they were not prepared for the duration of the wait—they could not *endure to the end*. Consequently, they would not be able to enter in with the bridegroom (join the Lord in his kingdom) when he came.

To be spiritually prepared means that an individual has a personal testimony of Jesus Christ and a thorough knowledge of the gospel and will constantly and consistently subject his or her own will to God's will. These individuals are "agents unto themselves" with the power to do "much righteousness," and they must not wait to be commanded to do good lest they find themselves damned—shut out from the presence of the Lord at his coming (see D&C 58:26–29). Five virgins had the depth of spiritual preparedness necessary to gain the kingdom and five did not. Whether or not the split between those prepared and those not prepared is literally fifty-fifty, this figure at least indicates that a substantial number of Church members will not be ready to greet the Savior. They will be destroyed in the cleansing of the earth and will not be allowed to enter his kingdom.[1]

The Lord declared early in the restoration of the gospel that the great calamities which will come upon the earth to judge the inhabitants and destroy those who cannot abide the Second Coming will begin with the Church. "Upon my house shall it begin, and from my house shall it go forth, saith the Lord" (D&C 112:25). This warning applies directly to the members of the Church identified in the parable as the five foolish virgins who "professed to know [his] name," but still "blasphemed against [him]" (D&C 112:26). How do members of the Church blaspheme against Christ today? By accepting the covenant of Abraham via baptism (Chapter 3) and then failing to live according to God's commandments. They are like the scribes and Pharisees of Christ's day who were "like unto whited sepulchres, which indeed appear beautiful outward, but are within full of dead men's bones, and of all uncleanness." They are men and women who "outwardly appear righteous unto men, but within . . . are full of hypocrisy and iniquity" (Matthew 23:27–28). These scribes and Pharisees were also like the five foolish virgins. They accepted the covenant and outwardly lived the law to perfection, but their personal reasons for living the law were unacceptable to the Lord. They used their outward perfection to justify their failure in complying with the weightier matters of the law, and the parable of the virgins makes it clear that in like manner, many Latter-day Saints will be judged and found wanting by the Lord in the last days.

The judgment of unfaithful members at the Second Coming will resemble the Lord's judgment of his covenant people at the time of Micah. Through Micah, he declared that he had "a controversy with his people" (Micah 6:2), because he had required them "to do justly, and to love mercy, and to walk humbly with [their] God" (Micah 6:8), but they had not kept his commandments. Members of the Church today, as well as all mankind, will not be judged by outward appearances. God sees the heart, and he will judge by the spirit of the law and our reasons for living it. At his coming, he will "recompense unto every man according to his work [how well men and women live the first great commandment], and measure to every man according to the measure which he has measured to his fellow man [how well they live the second great commandment]" (D&C 1:10).

While warning the Church in general (meaning all members) of the need for righteousness if they were to survive the destructive judgment in preparation of the Second Coming, the Lord also narrowed the warning specifically to Priesthood holders. This warning has been couched in identified terms of priest, prophet, rights, men and watchmen, and described specifically, metaphorically, and symbolically.

Isaiah contended that some of the priesthood of his day had "erred, . . . the priest and the prophet have erred . . . they err in vision, they stumble in judgment," (Isaiah 28:7). He uses the metaphor of strong drink to represent errors of judgment and the unrighteous use of power, stating that "through strong drink, they are swallowed up of wine, they are out of the way through strong drink . . . For all [their] tables are full of vomit and filthiness, so that there is no place clean" (Isaiah 28:7–8). These statements are graphically symbolic. The Lord clarified some of Isaiah's symbolic prophecy in terms of the rights of priesthood in the latter days as follows:

> The rights of the priesthood are inseparably connected with the powers of heaven, and . . . the powers of heaven cannot be controlled nor handled only upon the principles of righteousness.
>
> That they may be conferred upon us, it is true; but when we undertake to cover our sins, or to gratify our pride, our vain ambition, or to exercise control or dominion or compulsion upon the souls of the children of men, in any degree of unrighteousness, behold, the heavens withdraw themselves; the Spirit of the Lord is grieved; and when it is withdrawn, Amen to the priesthood or the authority of that man.
>
> Behold, ere he is aware, he is left unto himself, to kick against the pricks, to persecute the saints, and to fight against God.
>
> We have learned by sad experience that it is the nature and disposition of almost all men, as soon as they get a little authority, as they suppose, [that] they will immediately begin to exercise unrighteous dominion (D&C 121:36–39).

The unrighteous dominion of priesthood holders is the unrighteous use of power, position, and authority—from the least to the greatest in the priesthood. Isaiah again warns priesthood holders (whom he refers to as watchmen):

> His watchmen are blind: they are all ignorant, they are all dumb dogs, they cannot bark; sleeping, lying down, loving to slumber.
>
> Yea, they are greedy dogs which can never have enough, and they are shepherds that cannot understand: they all look to their own way, every

one for his gain, from his quarter (Isaiah 56:10–
11).

Priesthood holders have a special calling in the plan of salvation for the human family and must not only *teach* righteousness,
they must also *be* righteous as they explicate the requirements of
the kingdom. The Lord expressed this thought and teaching when
he instructed his Apostles (and by application all of his priesthood holders) that they were the "salt of the earth: but if the salt
have lost his savour, wherewith shall it be salted? It is henceforth
good for nothing, but to be cast out . . ." (Matthew 5:13). Salt was
the great preservative of his day. To the Jews salt specifically
symbolized fidelity and hospitality—it was an evidence of their
covenant with the Lord, and it was used in every meat offering
under the Law. (See Leviticus 2:13; Numbers 18:19; 2 Chronicles
13:5) The salt (all priesthood holders and by application all members) had to be pure, any object which adulterated it caused it to
lose its savor. Therefore the disciples would lose their savor if
they became fainthearted or slothful or if they broke the commandments. By so doing they would lose their worth to the kingdom of God and thereafter be cast out. In the restored application of this warning the Lord put it this way in the Doctrine and
Covenants:

> No power or influence can or ought to be
> maintained by virtue of the priesthood, only by
> persuasion, by long-suffering, by gentleness and
> meekness, and by love unfeigned;
>
> By kindness, and pure knowledge, which shall
> greatly enlarge the soul without hypocrisy, and
> without guile—
>
> Reproving betimes with sharpness, when moved
> upon by the Holy Ghost; and then showing forth
> afterwards an increase of love toward him whom
> thou hast reproved, lest he esteem thee to be his
> enemy;
>
> That he may know that thy faithfulness is stronger
> than the cords of death.

> Let thy bowels also be full of charity towards all
> men, and to the household of faith, and let virtue
> garnish thy thoughts unceasingly; then shall thy
> confidence wax strong in the presence of God; and
> the doctrine of the priesthood shall distil upon
> thy soul as the dews from heaven (D&C 121:41–
> 45).

All men and women are subject to God's judgments, from the newest convert to the highest authority. The scriptures teach us that being a member of the Church does not mean that all we do is automatically correct or justified. Isaiah put it simply: "And it shall be, as with the people, so with the priest; as with the servant, so with his master" (Isaiah 24:2)—all are equally responsible to God under the covenant—but "of him unto whom much is given much is required; and he who sins against the greater light shall receive the greater condemnation" (D&C 82:3).

As members of the Church, we have all been invited to the wedding supper which the Lord of the vineyard has scheduled. Let us look to our preparation that we may be ready to enter in with the Lord at his coming—appropriately dressed[2] and secure in the knowledge that our lamps are sufficiently full of oil.

The 144,000

Revelation 7:4 records that there are 144,000 children of Israel (12,000 from each tribe) who have received the seal of God in their foreheads. This seal of God is mentioned again by John in Revelation 9:4, where it is symbolic of those who have made their calling and election sure and will return to the Father's presence at the final judgment.

When John listed the twelve tribes of Israel (each of which will supply 12,000 men), he listed Manasseh and Joseph as separate tribes and excluded the tribe of Dan. There has been discussion about why he listed the tribes in this manner, but it would appear to have been for one of two simple reasons: (1) he may have made an error as he recorded his revelation, or (2) scribes over the centuries may have made an error while transcribing his text. One of these two reasons seems likely since John notes that the 144,000 are to come from *all* of the tribes of Israel. Therefore, it is probable that the listing of the names is nothing more than an inconsequential error. This theory seems to be born out by the revelation Joseph Smith received, as recorded in the 77th Section of the Doctrine and Covenants: "What are we to understand by sealing the one hundred and forty-four thousand, out of *all* the tribes of Israel—twelve thousand out of *every* tribe?" (D&C 77:11; italics added.) The Lord did not correct the error in John's list nor enumerate the tribes in his answer. But he did direct that the selection would be from *all* of the original twelve tribes, just as John's use of the word *all* indicates.

The answer Joseph records to this question sheds more light on the 144,000:

> We are to understand that those who are sealed are high priests, ordained unto the holy order of God, to administer the everlasting gospel; for they are they who are ordained out of every nation, kindred, tongue, and people, by the angels to whom is given power over the nations of the earth, to bring as many as will come to the church of the Firstborn (D&C 77:11).

In a revelation given in November 1831, the Lord revealed that the 144,000 would be with him upon Mount Zion (see D&C 133:18)—in other words, they will be with Christ at his coming. Although Joseph did not discuss John's revelation often, in February 1844 at a prayer meeting he "made some remarks respecting the one hundred and forty-four thousand mentioned by John the Revelator, showing that the selection of the persons to form that number had already commenced."[3]   No other details are given.

From this limited information concerning the 144,000, we learn the following:

1.   They are high priests.

2.   There are 12,000 from each of the twelve tribes of Israel.

3.   They are "sealed," or have the name of God in their foreheads, meaning that their calling and election is sure.

4.   They are not "defiled with women; for they are virgins"
       (see Revelation 14:4) (which may mean that they are
       pure and holy rather than unmarried).

5.   They are as Nathaniel, without guile, or perfect (see
       Revelation 14:5).

6.   They are to "administer the everlasting gospel."

7.   They are ordained by angels.

8.   Their work is to bring as many into the "church of the
       Firstborn" as will come.

9.   They will be with Christ at his coming.

Any other information would be conjecture.

The Last Laborers

The Lord has given his Church of the latter days the same
charge that he gave his Apostles before he ascended into heaven:
"Go ye therefore, and teach all nations . . . and, lo, I am with you
alway[s], even unto the end of the world" (Matthew 28:19–20).
Before the Millennium is ushered in, the Lord has said that the
Church must declare "the voice of warning . . . unto all people by
the mouths of [his] disciples whom [he has] chosen in [the] last
days "(D&C 1:4). They are to go forth to the inhabitants of the
earth so that "all that will hear may hear" (D&C 1:11), for "it is
the eleventh hour, and the last time" that the Lord will "call laborers into [his] vineyard" (D&C 33:3). This last great call will
prune the vineyard and gather all the righteous out of the wickedness of the world prior to the great judgment that God will
pour out upon the wicked before the Second Coming. This gathering of the righteous need not be to a central, geographical location. They will be gathered to the covenant of Abraham, or the
Church.

The Lord has always called his children to repentance before
cataclysmic judgments came upon them: Noah was sent to warn
the people before the Flood (see Moses 8:17–30); Lot was sent to
his unrepentant sons-in-law to warn them of the destruction of
Sodom and Gomorrah (see Genesis 19:12–15); Isaiah and Micah
were sent to warn the Israelites before the Northern Kingdom of

Israel was destroyed; Jeremiah, Lehi, and "many prophets" were sent to call Judah to repentance and to warn her of Jerusalem's destruction before she was destroyed and carried off into Babylon (see the book of Jeremiah; 1 Nephi 1:4); and in the latter days, the final pruning and nourishing of the vineyard before the ultimate destruction of the wicked is recounted in Jacob's great vineyard allegory found in the Book of Mormon (see Jacob 5:71–75).

Exactly who are those who are called to labor for the last time? All those who desire to serve! (See D&C 4:3.) Perhaps the 144,000 spoken of by John will be established to assist in this work (see D&C 133:18), or perhaps their number simply represents a righteous multitude of missionaries that will be called to serve in this final gathering. The Lord confirms by revelation that he has "committed the keys of [his] kingdom, and a dispensation of the gospel for the last times" (D&C 27:13). Therefore, the Lord leaves us with this command: "Labor ye in my vineyard for the last time— for the last time call upon the inhabitants of the earth . . . For . . . I come upon the earth in judgment, and my people shall be redeemed . . . For the great Millennium . . . shall come" (D&C 43:28–30).

The Heavens

While many signs of the Second Coming will occur upon the earth, even greater signs will occur in the heavens. These signs will cause "weeping and wailing among the hosts of men" (D&C 29:15). Many references describe these heavenly occurrences as signs and wonders (see Joel 2:30; Acts 2:19; D&C 45:40) or declare that while the earth will "shake," "the starry heavens shall tremble" (D&C 84:118: Joel 2:10). Occasionally the scriptures reverse the descriptive words or combine them (see D&C 43:18; Joel 3:16), leaving the exactness of the sign undefined.

Isaiah declares that "all the host of heaven shall be dissolved, and the heavens shall be rolled together as a scroll: and all their host shall fall down, as the leaf falleth off from the vine, and as a falling fig from the fig tree" (Isaiah 34:4). He further states that the Lord will "rend the heavens" at his coming (Isaiah 64:1), and latter-day revelation says that "the curtain of heaven [will be] unfolded, as a scroll is unfolded after it is rolled up" (D&C 88:95, see also Revelation 6:14). The Lord states that all of these events will occur as the "heavens" pass away (3 Nephi 26:3) to the accompaniment of great "lightnings, and voices, and thunderings, and an earthquake, and great hail" (Revelation 11:19; 16:18; D&C 88:90). No wonder men will become fearful (see Luke 21:11) and have their hearts "fail them;" the "powers of Heaven" will be shaken (Luke 21:26). These descriptions are very general, however, and just *how* these events will be fulfilled is left up to the imagination. Only one thing is attested to by the prophets over and over again: something devastating is going to happen to the heavenly orbs, and the prophets describe the cataclysmic results of these events with great clarity.

> The *sun* will be "darkened," "hide its face and . . . refuse to give light."[4] It will hide its face in "shame"[5] and it will be gone,[6] because the Lord will become our "everlasting light . . . [when] . . . the days of [our] mourning shall be ended" (Isaiah 60:20).

> The *moon* will "turn into blood"[7] or be "bathed in blood"[8] and become "dark."[9] It will withhold its light[10] and be "confounded."[11] "Neither for brightness shall the moon give light unto thee: but the Lord shall be unto thee an everlasting light" (Isaiah 60:19).

> Finally, the *stars* will "fall"[12] and be "darkened" so that they "withdraw their shining."[13] They will become "angry" and "cast themselves down,"[14] they will "not give their light" (Isaiah 13:10), and they will be "hurled from their places" (D&C 133:49).

These signs of heavenly destruction defy description, and perhaps that is why the prophets have given us such generalized reports of their occurrence. All that can be factually determined is that these signs will occur *after* the cleansing of the earth and *before* the Savior's specific sign of the Second Coming (Joseph Smith–Matthew 1:36; Mark 13:24–26).

The Rainbow

After the great flood wherein all men and women were destroyed because of their wickedness (save eight righteous souls), the Lord spoke with Noah and reestablished his covenant with him. He declared at that time that "neither shall all flesh be cut off any more by the waters of a flood; neither shall there any more be a flood to destroy the earth" (Genesis 9:11). The token God gave to Noah of this promise was the rainbow. "This is the token of the covenant . . . I do set my bow in the cloud . . . [as an] . . . everlasting covenant between God and every living creature of all flesh that is upon the earth" (Genesis 9:12–16). Joseph Smith declared that when the rainbow no longer appears in the heavens, the Second Coming will be imminent. He states:

> I have asked of the Lord concerning His coming; and while asking the Lord, He gave a sign and said, 'In the days of Noah I set a bow in the heavens as a sign and token that in any year that the bow should be seen the Lord would not come; but there should be seed time and harvest during that year: but whenever you see the bow withdrawn, it shall be a token that there shall be famine, pestilence, and great distress among the nations, and that the coming of the Messiah is not far distant.[15]

Joseph asked the Lord about his coming because a Father Miller had prophesied that the Savior would come in 1844. After he received the above statement, he further stated: "But I will take the responsibility upon myself to prophesy in the name of the Lord, that Christ will not come this year, as Father Miller has prophesied, for we have seen the bow."[16]

The only knowledge we are left with is that the disappearance of the rainbow for one year is a sign of the Savior's coming. No information is given as to whether this disappearance will be local or worldwide, only that it will cause "famine" (since rainbows are created by rain in the atmosphere), "pestilence, and great distress among nations." We can draw the logical conclusion that as long as the rainbow is with us, the Second Coming will be at some future time.

Adam-ondi-Ahman

On May 19, 1838, the Lord designated "Spring Hill, Daviess County, Missouri" as the location of Adam-ondi-Ahman (see D&C 116). Joseph received this revelation while in the process of "selecting and laying claim to a city plat" at that location.[17] This is the place where Adam "called together his children and blessed them with a patriarchal blessing" prior to his death.[18] All the righteous of Adam's posterity were gathered there. The Lord Jesus Christ (whose name is also declared to be Son Ahman [see D&C 95:17]) appeared to them and blessed Adam, and declared him to be Michael—the prince and archangel. The Lord comforted Adam and set him forever at the head of the human family (see D&C 107:53–57).

The Old Testament prophet Daniel declared that there would be another great council at Adam-ondi-Ahman prior to the Second Coming. He saw it in a vision wherein he described Adam as the "Ancient of days." He saw Adam dressed in a garment as "white as snow." "The hair of his head [was] like the pure wool: [and] his throne was like the fiery flame." Adam was at this council to set in order the books of life for the final judgment (see Daniel 7:9–14). Of this great council Joseph Smith declared:

> Daniel in his seventh chapter speaks of the Ancient of Days; he means the oldest man, our Father Adam, Michael, he will call his children together and hold a council with them to prepare them for the coming of the Son of Man. He (Adam) is the father of the human family, and presides over the spirits of all men, and all that have had the keys must stand before him in this grand council . . . The Son of Man stands before him, and there is given him glory and dominion. Adam delivers up his stewardship to Christ, that which was delivered to him as holding keys of the universe, but retains his standing as head of the human family.[19]

Who will attend this great council? According to the statements of Daniel and Joseph, a great multitude! It will include all those who have ever held the "keys of the priesthood" plus all of the righteous (presumably all the righteous who have ever lived upon the earth). Daniel describes their number as "a thousand thousands . . . and ten thousand times ten thousand" (Daniel 7:10). When will this council meeting take place? After the destruction of the devil's earthly kingdom and the cleansing of the earth in the latter days (see Daniel 7:22), but before the coming of the Lord.

Part Five

The End Draweth Nigh

"Wherefore gird up the loins of your mind, be sober, and hope to the end for the grace that is to be brought unto you at the revelation of Jesus Christ."

1 Peter 1:13

The Three Cities   13

"Blessed are they that do his commandments,
that they may have right to the tree of life, and
may enter in through the gates into the city."

Revelation 22:14

Three holy cities will play an integral part in the Lord's Second Coming: the translated City of Enoch, the City of Zion on the Western Hemisphere, and Jerusalem on the Eastern Hemisphere. At one time or another, all three of these cities have been referred to by the name *Zion* (see Moses 7:19; D&C 57:2; 2 Samuel 5:7). In fact, as the following chart shows, at least seventeen different doctrines or entities are referred to as *Zion* in the scriptures.

Zion used to represent:	Specific doctrine or entity being described:	Scriptural reference:
A mountain	Mt. Zion (Sion)	Deuteronomy 4:48
A city	The City of David	2 Samuel 5:7
A city	City of Enoch	Moses 7:19
A struggle	Birth of a nation	Isaiah 66:8

Zion used to represent:	Specific doctrine or entity being described:	Scriptural Reference:
A system	Gospel of Salvation	1 Nephi 13:36–37
A sense of security	All's well doctrine	2 Nephi 28:21
Future city of Zion	The New Jerusalem	D&C 84:2
A city	The City of God	D&C 97:19
A people	The pure in heart	D&C 97:21
As a kingdom	The Kingdom of God	D&C 105:32
A religious tenet	The Gospel	D&C 133:9
The Lord's people	A united people	Moses 7:18
An Article of Faith	Zion/New Jerusalem	A of F 1:10
A geographical description	Land	D&C 64:30
A synonym	"She" or a person/ place/city	D&C 97:25–26
An entire country	America	HC 6:318–319

From the examples listed above, it is obvious that care must be taken to determine what is being referred to when the scriptures reference the name *Zion*. The same care must be exercised with the name *New Jerusalem*. While it can be seen in the table that the term *Zion* is sometimes interchanged with the term *New Jerusalem* when referencing both the City of Zion on the Western Hemisphere and the City of Enoch, there are other scriptural references where the determination of what is being referred to is left up to the reader. (An example of this is found in Ether 13:3, 10.) For the purposes of discussion in this chapter, the three cities will be identified as follows:

The City of Enoch was established by Enoch during his ministry and was later translated into heaven in anticipation of the great Flood at the time of Noah. This city is prophesied to return at the Second Coming of the Savior, and while its return is probably symbolic in regards to its buildings, streets, and so forth, it is literal in regards to the righteous people who were translated, both at the time of Enoch and thereafter until the time of the Flood.

The City of Zion is the city that will be built on the Western Hemisphere in Jackson County, Missouri. It will be one of the two cities from which the Lord will govern during the Millennium. Zion is the eventual focal point for the gathering of all the tribes of Israel except Judah, and the future center place of the promised land of the restoration.

The City of Jerusalem is the ancient holy city that is located in Israel (the promised land of the Children of Israel in antiquity). It is the other city from which the Lord will govern during the Millennium and is the focal point for the gathering of the tribe of Judah in the last days.

The City of Enoch

Enoch was an ancient prophet, the "seventh from Adam." His father's name was Jared, and his only known son was named Mathusala (Methuselah) (see Luke 3:37). The biblical record concerning Enoch is scanty. In addition to his lineage, however, we know that he was a righteous man since he "walked with God" (Genesis 5:18–24) and was *taken* by God (Genesis 5:24), which could give rise to much speculation save for Paul's text to the Hebrews wherein he stated: "By faith Enoch was translated that he should not see death; and was not found, because God had translated him" (Hebrews 11:5). The only other mention of Enoch in the Bible is by Jude, who uses Enoch's teachings as an example of God's future judgments upon the ungodly (see Jude 1:14–15).

The book of Moses in the Pearl of Great Price and other latter-day revelation gives us more in-depth information about Enoch. They state that he was taught the ways of God by his father, Jared (see Moses 6:21), that he was twenty-five years old when he was ordained by Adam and that he was sixty-five when Adam blessed him (see D&C 107:48). His son Methuselah was born when Enoch was sixty-five years old; it was at this time that "the Spirit of God descended out of heaven, and abode upon him," thus calling him to be a prophet. Enoch's response to his prophetic call is interesting: "Why is it that I have found favor in thy sight, and am but a lad [he was sixty-five years old], and all the people hate me; for I am slow of speech; wherefore am I thy servant?" But the Lord comforted Enoch with this response: "Go forth and do as I have commanded thee, and no man shall pierce thee. Open thy mouth, and it shall be filled, and I will give thee utterance, for all flesh is in my hands, and I will do as seemeth me good" (Moses 6:25–26, 31, 32).

Enoch went on to become a powerful prophet. He was given the power to move mountains, to turn rivers from their course, and to cause the "roar of the lions [to be] heard [in] the wilderness" (Moses 7:13). He received tremendous visions wherein he "beheld the spirits that God had created . . . for the space of many generations" (Moses 7:4). He saw Noah and the great Flood and heard the earth lament, "Wo, wo is me, the mother of men;" because of the wickedness of mankind (Moses 7:48). In anguish of soul he wept for the earth's sorrows and asked the Lord to never again bring such terrible devastation upon mankind.

Enoch also saw "the Lord . . . before [his] face" and spoke with him "as a man talketh one with another" (Moses 7:4). He saw the Savior crucified on the cross, and he observed the ensuing Dark Ages give way to the light of the Restoration. He beheld the great tribulations that would precede the Second Coming, and he saw the Millennial reign of Christ. He was privileged to see "all things, even unto the end of the world" (Moses 7:67).

In obedience to God's command, Enoch successfully called his people to repentance and with his righteous followers, he founded a city that was called the "City of Holiness, even Zion" (Moses 7:19). The Lord blessed Enoch's city—but he cursed the rest of the people. When enemies came against Enoch and his people, he merely spoke "the word of the Lord" and the earth "trembled, and the mountains fled" (Moses 7:13). "So powerful was the word of Enoch" that he caused land to come up out of the "depth of the sea" (Moses 7:14). The wicked were astonished and feared him, and "all men were offended because of him" (Moses 6:37). They declared that a "seer" was among them as a "strange thing in the land," and accused him of being a "wild man" (Moses 6:38).

The righteous who gathered to Enoch's city were in the "process of time . . . taken up into heaven" (Moses 7:21). Thereafter, angels continued to bear testimony "of the Father and Son," and "the Holy Ghost fell on many." These souls were also translated, "caught up by the powers of heaven into Zion" (Moses 7:27) in anticipation of the Flood that would cleanse the earth of the wicked. The Lord revealed to Joseph Smith that Enoch's city had been translated, thus confirming the fact that he was "the same [God] which [had] taken the Zion of Enoch into [his] own bosom" (D&C 38:4).

The scriptures tell us that the City of Enoch will eventually return to the earth when "a day of righteousness [the Second Coming] shall come" (D&C 45:12). Ether prophesied that at his Advent, the Lord would come to Zion on the Western Hemisphere and the City of Enoch would also "come down out of heaven" to Zion on this, the American continent (see Ether 13:3–4).

John the Revelator was carried away by God to a "great and high mountain" where he saw Enoch's city descend from heaven (Revelation 21:10). It came "down from God out of heaven, prepared as a bride adorned for her husband" (Revelation 21:2), a *metaphoric* description of its great beauty and the happiness of its inhabitants. The city was encompassed with the glory of God, and its light was like a most precious stone, "a jasper stone [diamond], clear as crystal" (Revelation 21:11). Its wall was high, symbolic of the security its people enjoyed. There were twelve gates in the wall representing the twelve tribes of Israel, and "the wall of the city had twelve foundations, and in them the names of the twelve apostles of the Lamb" (Revelation 21:14). This symbolic description reveals the purity of the city's inhabitants and the fact that they are the covenant people of the Lord (as represented by twelve gates, one for each tribe of Israel). They had fulfilled all of the requirements of the gospel as it was taught by the twelve Apostles after Jesus' death.

John also observed that the city gates were never closed, that "glory and honor" from the nations of the earth were brought to it, and that nothing could defile it. He further records, "For there shall be no night there." The inhabitants will have no need for a "candle, neither light of the sun . . . neither of the moon, to shine in it: for the glory of God [will] lighten it, and the Lamb [will be] the light thereof" (see Revelation 21:10–14, 23, 25–27; 22:5).

The City of Zion

"We believe in the literal gathering of Israel and in the restoration of the Ten Tribes; *that Zion (the New Jerusalem) will be built upon the American continent;* that Christ will reign personally upon the earth; and, that the earth will be renewed and receive its paradisiacal glory" (Articles of Faith 1:10; emphasis added).[1] Joseph Smith's astonishing declaration pertaining to the location of the City of Zion represented a radical departure from the apostate belief concerning Zion, for at that time Zion was—and continues to be—interpreted as a synonym for old Jerusalem and its environs. This is one of the major reasons for the misinterpretation of the scriptures surrounding the latter days involving Zion and Jerusalem.

For the gospel to be true (and not just another reformation of an apostate Christianity), its restoration had to include a promised land—not the *old* promised land, which was reserved for the gathering and restoring of Judah, but a *new* promised land for the establishment of the restored covenant of Abraham and a gathering place for all of the tribes of Israel *except* Judah. Ether saw this land in vision hundreds of years before the time of Christ. He called it a "New Jerusalem" and stated that it would be established "upon this land," meaning the Western Hemisphere (Ether 13:4–6).

The location of the New Jerusalem (or the City of Zion—also called Zion) has been specifically defined (see D&C 45:66–67). But the Lord led his early latter-day followers slowly through the following step-by-step process, building their anticipation before he revealed the city's location to them:

1.   He first declared its existence in September 1830 when he said, "No man knoweth where the city Zion shall be built, but it shall be given hereafter. Behold, I say unto you that it shall be on the borders by the Lamanites" (D&C 28:9).

2.   In February 1831, the Lord commanded the elders of the Church to move westward from Kirtland, Ohio, building "up [his] church in every region" until the time that Zion would be prepared for the gathering, "that ye may be my people and I will be your God" (D&C 42:8–9). The land for the city was to be purchased (see D&C 42:35) so that the people could be gathered and

the Lord could come to his temple (see D&C 42:36). But the Savior still did not tell the Saints where the city would be located, only that its exact location would be revealed "in [his] own due time" (D&C 42:62).

While the Lord designates the city as *Zion* (see D&C 45:67), he also calls it the *New Jerusalem*. It will be "a land of peace," and it will be "a city of refuge, [and] a place of safety for the saints" (D&C 45:66). Both the glory and the terror of the Lord will be there, and the wicked will not "come unto it" (D&C 45:67). Those numbered in it will be from every nation of the earth, and it will be the only city where the people will "not be at war one with another" (D&C 45:69). The righteous who gather to the city will sing "songs of everlasting joy" under the Lord's protection, and the wicked will refuse to go up against it, contending that "the inhabitants of Zion are terrible" (D&C 45:70–71).

3. In Doctrine and Covenants 48, the Lord was still not ready to reveal Zion's location, but he promised to do so after some of the brethren returned to Kirtland, Ohio, from the east. At that time, "certain men" would be "appointed" to know the place (D&C 48:5), and the Lord would "hasten the city in its time" since its location was currently in the land of their "enemies" (D&C 52:42–43).

4. Finally, on July 20, 1831, the Lord revealed to Joseph Smith the exact location of Zion. Pursuant to the Lord's command, the prophet and others had traveled to Missouri in June 1831 to join another company of Saints (see D&C 52:1–3). Upon their arrival, Joseph pondered the great differences between what he called the "highly cultivated state of society in the east" and the "degradation, leanness of intellect, ferocity, and jealousy of the people that were nearly a century behind the times" in Missouri. While under the influence of these opinions, he cried to the Lord saying, "When will Zion be built up in her glory?"[2] In response, the Lord declared:

> Hearken, O ye elders of my church . . . who have assembled yourselves together, according to my commandments, in this land, which is the land of Missouri, which is the land which I have

appointed and consecrated for the gathering of the saints.

Wherefore, this is the land of promise, and the place for the city of Zion.

And thus saith the Lord your God, if you will receive wisdom here is wisdom. Behold, the place which is now called Independence is the center place; and a spot for the temple is lying westward, upon a lot which is not far from the courthouse (D&C 57:1–3).

Thereupon, Sidney Rigdon was appointed to "consecrate and dedicate" the land for the establishment of Zion (D&C 58:57), which he did on August 2, 1831.[3] On August 3, 1831, Joseph Smith dedicated a spot for the temple;[4] however, according to his plat, the completed city would eventually have a total of twenty-four temples within its boundaries to ensure that the Lord's work would go forth.[5] The building up of the city was to begin from the original "temple lot" which, while not being in mountainous country, was designated by the Lord as Mount Zion (see D&C 84:2–4)—a term symbolically referring to the exaltation or lifting up of Christ's gospel upon the earth.

After the dedication of the land, the Saints proceeded to move into Missouri, acquiring territory for the establishment of Zion as they arrived. But Zion was not to be redeemed in their time. Severe persecutions befell them and this oppression culminated when Lilburn W. Boggs, then governor of Missouri, conspired with mobbers and other persecutors of the Church to issue his infamous *Extermination Order*. This order expelled the Saints from the State of Missouri.[6] Still, the Lord recognized the diligence and hard work of those early Saints. He acknowledged the obstacles their enemies had placed in their way when he relieved them of the duty to build Zion at that time, and he severely cursed those who had hindered his work:

Verily, verily, I say unto you, that when I give a commandment to any of the sons of men to do a work unto my name, and those sons of men go with all their might and with all they have to perform that work, and cease not their diligence, and their enemies come upon them and hinder them from performing that work, behold, it behooveth me to require that work no more at the hands of those sons of men, but to accept of their offerings.

And the iniquity and transgression of my holy laws and commandments I will visit upon the heads of those who hindered my work, unto the third and fourth generation, so long as they repent not, and hate me, saith the Lord God.

Therefore, for this cause have I accepted the offerings of those whom I commanded to build up a city and a house unto my name, in Jackson county, Missouri, and were hindered by their enemies, saith the Lord your God.

And I will answer judgment, wrath, and indignation, wailing, and anguish, and gnashing of teeth upon their heads, unto the third and fourth generation, so long as they repent not, and hate me, saith the Lord your God (D&C 124:49–52).

God's judgment and wrath befell the people of Missouri because they hindered the establishment of this holy city in the early days of the Restoration so severely that "all the hardships the Missourians had inflected upon the Saints were now visited upon their heads, only more abundantly."[7] While discussing his arrest and pending trial during his incarceration in Liberty Jail, Joseph Smith prophesied to A. W. Doniphan (his attorney) that "God's wrath hangs over Jackson County . . . The Lord of Hosts will sweep it with the besom of destruction. The fields and farms and houses will be destroyed, and only the chimneys will be left to mark the desolation."[8] This remarkable prophecy was fulfilled with the destruction that came upon Missouri and its people prior to and during the Civil War. Governor Robert W. Stewart reported that several of Missouri's western counties were made desolate "and almost depopulated, from fear of a bandit horde" which had been and were committing "depredations—arson, theft, and foul murder."[9] General Sterling Price, who had custody of and mistreated Joseph Smith and many other members of the Church,[10] "destroyed upwards of 'ten million dollars worth of property,' a fair share of which belonged to his friends," during his Civil War skirmishes in Missouri.[11] And under Military Order No. 11 issued from Kansas City by General Thomas Ewing, the very people who had expelled the Saints from Missouri by driving them from their homes and confiscating their personal property were themselves driven and expelled from their homes. "Their dwellings [were] burned, their farms laid waste, and the great bulk of their movable property handed over, without let or hindrance, to the Kansas 'jayhawkers.'"[12] During the first nineteen months of the war, between April 20, 1861, and November 20, 1862, "over three hundred battles and skirmishes were fought within the limits of the State . . . [and probably] half as many more" during the last two years[13]—the result of which was to depopulate "a large part of the western border."[14]

Did God smite Missouri because it hindered his work? He most certainly did! The ancient prophet Mormon warned those who would attempt to prevent the progress of God's work: "He that shall breathe out wrath and strifes against the work of the Lord, and against the covenant people of the Lord who are the house of Israel . . . the same is in danger to be hewn down and cast into the fire" (Mormon 8:21). Missouri itself, from the governor down to the common citizen, had been "made to feel the wrath, and indignation, and chastening hand of an Almighty God" (D&C 87:6).

While visiting the Western Hemisphere after his resurrection, the Lord prophesied of Zion's future existence. He declared that it would be established "in this land," meaning America (see 3 Nephi 20:22), and that both the "remnant of Jacob" and the Gentiles would assist in its construction (see 3 Nephi 21:22–23). Enoch viewed its establishment after his translation into heaven (see Moses 7:62). But it was the Lord's ancient prophets who foresaw and described its glory. Isaiah and Micah saw it as one of the two world capitals from which the Lord would govern during the millennium: "for out of Zion shall go forth the law," they declared, and as Joel metaphorically described it, "the Lord also shall roar out of Zion" (Isaiah 2:3; Micah 4:2; Joel 3:16).

Although the City of Zion is yet to be established, when the time comes it will be located exactly where the Lord said it would be: Independence, Missouri! It will be ready for him when he comes in his glory. It will be ready when "the graves of the saints shall be opened; and they shall come forth and stand on the right hand of the Lamb, when he shall stand upon Mount Zion, and upon the holy city, the New Jerusalem" (D&C 133:56). The righteousness of the Saints will prevail over the wicked and the Lord will cleanse "the daughters of Zion" in preparation for his coming (see Isaiah 4:1–4). The City of Zion and ancient Jerusalem will become a haven for the righteous (see Isaiah 33:20–24) as these two cities regain the paradisiacal glory that was once enjoyed by Adam and Eve and return to the geographical locales they occupied before the earth was divided (see D&C 133:24; Articles of Faith 1:10). The Lord will come and "stand in [their] midst," and the lost tribes of Israel will return "unto the children of Ephraim" where they will be "crowned with glory, even in Zion" (D&C 133:25–32), and shall receive (along with "as many of the Gentiles as shall comply") all the blessings of the new and everlasting covenant of Abraham.[15]

The Temple in Zion: When the Lord revealed the location for the City of Zion, he also revealed that there would be a temple there. The temple would be "lying westward, upon a lot which is not far from the court-house" (D&C 57:3). On August 3, 1831, shortly after this revelation, Joseph Smith dedicated the "spot for the Temple."[16] In June 1833, Joseph described the plat of the City of Zion which contained not only the temple referenced above, but twenty-three other temples as well. Joseph also *named* these temples and described their construction and use.[17] In August 1835, it was declared that the "Elders [had] failed in the outset to fill their great and important mission" pertaining to the construction of the temple. It was then declared that "Zion could not be redeemed" until the temple was built and endowments were taking place.[18]

While it is evident that the Lord desires both the City of Zion and its temple to be "redeemed," it will not be done until the Lord commands it. Then, and only then, will the way be opened to acquire the latter-day *promised land* of Zion.

The City of Jerusalem

Ancient Jerusalem "has known the hosts of thirty-six wars. She has been reduced to ashes seventeen times. She has risen eighteen."[19] Her beauty has always been renowned. "It is said the world has ten measures of beauty and nine of these belong to Jerusalem."[20] She is loved deeply by three religious cultures— Christian, Jew, and Muslim—but the "Jews have always loved her the most." This love has remained deeply ingrained throughout the centuries, ever since David first made Jerusalem his capital. "It is the longest, deepest love affair in all of history."[21]

We know little about the City of Enoch and the City of Zion (the New Jerusalem), but much is known about ancient Jerusalem. To detail its history would take volumes, but a brief chronology showing its development is interesting.

B.C.

3000	Earliest discovered remains of habitation at Jerusalem [discovered] on the hill of Ophel
1850	Jerusalem referred to in Egyptian Execration Texts
1280	Exodus from Egypt
1250	Conquest of Canaan under Joshua
1013–973	King David makes Jerusalem the capital of the united kingdom of Israel
973–933	King Solomon builds the First Temple
928	United kingdom splits into Judah and Israel
715–687	King Hezekiah of Judah builds tunnel from Gihon Spring to Pool of Siloam and strengthens the city walls
587	Nebuchadnezzar, King of Babylon, conquers Jerusalem, destroys the Temple and exiles Jews to Babylonia
538	Cyrus, King of Persia, conquers Babylon and allows Jews to return to Jerusalem
537–332	THE PERSIAN PERIOD

515	Completion of the Second Temple
445	Nehemiah, Governor of Judea, rebuilds the walls of Jerusalem
332–167	THE HELLENISTIC PERIOD
331	Alexander the Great passes through Palestine and perhaps visits Jerusalem
198–128	RULE OF THE SELEUCIDS OF SYRIA
172	Jerusalem becomes a Hellenistic polis named Antiochia
169	Antiochus IV Epiphanes, Seleucid king, plunders the Temple. Practice of Judaism forbidden
167–63	THE HASMONEANS (MACCABEES)
167–141	Maccabean war of liberation
139	Roman Senate recognizes independence of Judea
131	Siege of Jerusalem by Antiochus VII
63 B.C.– A.D. 324	THE ROMAN PERIOD
63	The Roman General Pompey conquers Jerusalem and destroys the Temple
40–37	Romans ousted briefly by Zealots
37–4	Reign of Herod the Great, who rebuilds the Temple
A.D.	(CHRISTIAN ERA)
26–36	Pontius Pilate procurator
30	Crucifixion of Jesus
41–44	Agrippa I, King of Judea, builds new city wall know as the "third wall"
66–70	First great Jewish revolt against the Romans
67	Vespasian arrives; the Zealots take over in Jerusalem
70	Destruction of the Second Temple by Titus and fall ofJerusalem

132–135	Bar Kochba's war of freedom; Jerusalem again Jewish capital; second revolt of the Jews
135	Emperor Hadrian's total destruction of Jerusalem. Building of new city called Aelia Capitolina. Jews banned from the city
324–638	THE BYZANTINE PERIOD
326	Emperor Constantine declares Christianity the state religion. His mother, Queen Helena, visits Jerusalem and names Christian sites. Building of the Church of the Holy Sepulchre begins
614	Persian conquest of Jerusalem
638–1099	THE MOSLEM PERIOD
638	Caliph Omar enters Jerusalem; city falls to Arabs
691	Dome of the Rock completed
996–1020	Church of the Holy Sepulchre destroyed
1037	Church of the Holy Sepulchre rebuilt
1099–1187	THE CRUSADER KINGDOM
1099	Crusaders capture Jerusalem; Jews and Moslems banned
1099–1187	Jerusalem capital of the Latin Kingdom
1187	Saladin captures Jerusalem from the Crusaders
1250	The Mamelukes, slave kings of Egypt, seize the city
1516	Ottoman conquest of Jerusalem
1838	First consulate (British) opened in Jerusalem
[1841	October 4, Orson Hyde's dedicatory prayer on the *Mount of Olives*]
1861	First Jewish settlement outside the city walls
1898	Visit by Dr. Theodor Herzel, founder of World Zionist Organization

1917	November 2, Balfour Declaration; December 11: British conquest; General Allenby enters Jerusalem
1923	British Mandate confirmed by League of Nations
1947	United Nations resolution recommending the partition of Palestine into Arab and Jewish states
1948	British Mandate ends and State of Israel proclaimed
1948–1949	Israel's War of Independence (May 1948–January 1949), the first Arab-Israeli War, ending with a divided city. New City of Jerusalem remains intact but Jewish Quarter in Old City falls (May 28, 1948). Signing of Israel-Transjordan armistice agreement in which Jerusalem is divided between the two countries (April 1949). West Jerusalem declared the capital of Israel
1967	Six-Day War in which Israeli troops capture the Old City from the Jordanians. Jerusalem liberated and reunited.[22]

This outline of the history of the Lord's holy city was summarized (with some additional items not significant to this topic excluded) by Leon Uris in his book, *Jerusalem Song of Songs*; and while totally unintentional (after inserting Orson Hyde's dedicatory prayer date), the outline confirms the following prophetic utterances:

1. Christ's prophecy of the destruction of Jerusalem (see Matthew 24:1–3).

2. Paul's prophecy of the apostasy from the truth of the gospel (see 2 Thessalonians 2:1–3).

3. Daniel's prophecy of the end of sacrifice (see Daniel 11:31).

4. The prophecies of many prophets regarding the scattering of both Israel and Judah (Chapter 2).

The above historical outline clearly shows the establishment of Jerusalem, its adoption by David as the holy city, its place in Israel until the end of sacrifice, the destruction of the temple by

the Romans, the end of the kingdom of Judah through the scatterings, the false prophets predicted by Jesus and his Apostles
(the most conspicuous being Bar Kochba),[23] and the Jews being
prohibited from returning to their holy city until after the dedicatory prayer of Orson Hyde.

Except for brief periods of peace, Jerusalem, since it came into
existence, has been a city under siege for thousands of years. The
prophecies of the Lord and his prophets have thus far been fulfilled (and will continue to be fulfilled) with the result that Jerusalem will continue to be embroiled in conflict and war until the
Second Coming.

Isaiah and Micah declared that Jerusalem will be one of the
two cities from which the Lord will govern during the millennium: "The word of the Lord [will go forth] from Jerusalem"
(Isaiah 2:3; Micah 4:2). The many signs of the Second Coming
that are yet to be fulfilled concerning Jerusalem were discussed
in chapter 5 of this text. It is the glory of what the city and its
inhabitants will become, however, that now interests us.

Isaiah describes Jerusalem in his historical prophecy of the
last days *as if its exaltation had already occurred.* In the 62nd chapter of his text he begins by identifying both Zion and Jerusalem,
but in the third verse he shifts to a singular noun and thereafter
speaks only of Jerusalem. He describes the scattered and forsaken Jews as becoming "Hephzibah," or *delightful,* and they are
"Beulah," or *married*—united to the land. He again uses the anal-
ogy of a marriage covenant, with Jesus as the husband and Israel
(the Jews in this instance) as the bride, for the Lord will "set watchmen upon [the] walls . . . till he make[s] Jerusalem a praise in the
earth" (Isaiah 62:1–7). The people shall then be called "the holy
people," and Jerusalem will be "sought out, A city not forsaken"
(Isaiah 62:12). Isaiah made this declaration toward the end of his
book, but he began his book with a double-reference prophecy
that Jerusalem and Zion would be restored "as at the first." In
other words, Isaiah's beloved Jerusalem will again be favored of
the Lord (see Isaiah 1:26–27; 33:20).

The remnant of the Jews that survive the last great battles
around Jerusalem just prior to the Second Coming will be delivered from annihilation by the Lord himself (see Joel 2:32). Judah
will again be cleansed by her Master (see Joel 3:20–21) and be

able to produce "excellent and comely" fruit (see Isaiah 4:1–4). Jerusalem will finally be restored as a great "city of truth" and peace. Her inhabitants will be the Lord's people, and he "will be their God, in truth and in righteousness" (Zechariah 8:1–8). The land Jerusalem occupies will also return to its "own place, and the earth shall be like as it was in the days before it was divided" (D&C 133:24). Isaiah writes an eloquent description of this millennial Jerusalem:

> Violence shall no more be heard in thy land, wasting nor destruction within thy borders; but thou shall call thy walls Salvation, and thy gates Praise.
>
> The sun shall be no more thy light by day; neither for brightness shall the moon give light unto thee: but the Lord shall be unto thee an everlasting light, and thy God thy glory.
>
> Thy sun shall no more go down; neither shall thy moon withdraw itself: for the Lord shall be thine everlasting light, and the days of thy mourning shall be ended.
>
> Thy people also shall be all righteous: they shall inherit the land for ever (Isaiah 60:18–21).

Zechariah describes this desirable time in personal terms: "There shall yet old men and old women dwell in the streets of Jerusalem, and every man with his staff in his hand for *a multitude of days*. And the streets of the city shall be full of boys and girls playing in the streets thereof" (Zechariah 8:4–5; italics indicates alternative language used). These are visions of pure joy.

Then, as Ether declares, there will be a "new heaven and a new earth" (Ether 13:9) and the three glorious cities shall be as one. Zion in America will be joined by the City of Enoch from its heavenly abode, "and then also cometh the Jerusalem of old; and the inhabitants thereof, blessed are they, for they have been washed in the blood of the Lamb; and they are they who were scattered and gathered in from the four quarters of the earth, and from the north countries, and are partakers of the fulfilling of the covenant which God made with their father, Abraham" (Ether 13:11).

And then shall the Lord reign forever and ever.

The Coming of   *14*
 the Lord

> "Blow ye the trumpet in Zion, and sound an alarm in my holy mountain: let all the inhabitants of the land tremble: for the day of the Lord cometh, for it is nigh at hand;
>
> ". . . for the day of the Lord is great and very terrible; and who can abide it?"

Joel 2:1, 11

The Great and Terrible Day of the Lord

The *great* and *terrible* day of the Lord—seemingly an oxymoron—is a perfect description of the Lord's Advent. For the righteous it will be a *great* day, a day long awaited and eagerly anticipated; for the wicked, however, it will be a *terrible* day of fear and trembling for the cold fact is, *the Atonement will not apply to the unrepentant sinner.*

The catastrophic devastations preceding the Lord's Second Coming will undoubtedly cause some of the righteous pain and even death, but the wicked will be completely annihilated—none will escape—for no unclean thing can enter into the Lord's presence.

Through the prophet Zephaniah, the Lord speaks of his coming as "a day of wrath." A day of "trouble . . . distress . . . wasteness . . . desolation . . . gloominess . . . and thick darkness." He describes the wicked as those who "walk like blind men" and whose "blood shall be poured out as dust." He states that their flesh will be "as the dung," and that "neither their silver nor their gold shall be able to deliver them in the day of the Lord's wrath," for instead of being clothed in garments of righteousness, they will be "clothed with strange apparel" (See Zephaniah 1:2–18).

In the parable of the marriage of the king's son, the Lord confirmed the warning of Zephaniah when he invited all mankind to come into his kingdom (represented in the parable as the marriage feast). Those initially invited to attend the feast refused and responded with pathetic excuses for their absence, and they both abused and killed the Lord's servants who had been sent with the invitation. They were unwilling to comply with the requirements of righteousness needed to gain admission to the feast, so the Lord invited others to the celebration. As the new guests came, they were given an appropriate "wedding garment;" which indicated that they had clothed themselves in righteousness in compliance with the Savior's commandments. When the guests were seated, however, one of them was found to be clothed in "strange apparel" (Zephaniah 2:8). This guest had attempted to enter the feast without complying with the entrance requirements, even though they had been readily available to him. When questioned he was speechless: he had no defense. The Lord's kingdom can only be enjoyed by those who comply with its prerequisites. *There are no valid excuses for unrighteous choices!* Therefore, the king bound his errant guest and cast him out of his presence (see Matthew 22:1–14).[1] (See also Matthew 24:16–23.)

When Moroni came to Joseph Smith in 1823 to declare the glorious news of the coming forth of the Book of Mormon, he reemphasized the need for spiritual preparation and reinstated the warning of Malachi to the world:

For behold, the day cometh that shall burn as an oven, and all the proud, yea, and all that do wickedly shall burn as stubble; for they that come shall burn them, saith the Lord of Hosts, that it shall leave them neither root nor branch (Joseph Smith–History 1:37; see also D&C 29:9).

The allegory of the wicked being burned is used over and over again in the scriptures.[2] Some have speculated that the *burning* could be literal—the possible result of a nuclear holocaust.[3]

But the Lord is probably speaking symbolically. He states in another revelation: "For after today [the latter days] cometh the burning—this is speaking *after the manner of the Lord*" (D&C 64:24; emphasis added). He also uses the symbolism of burning to describe the state of the wicked after the final judgment[4] and the ultimate fate of the earth itself, descriptions that lend credence to the position that the burning is not literal (see D&C 101:23–25). However, one of the most interesting and descriptive of these symbolic scriptures is found in Zephaniah. "Wait ye upon me," the Lord declares as he describes through Zephaniah what he will do to the evil kingdom prior to his coming, "until the day that I rise up to the prey: for my determination is to gather the nations, that I may assemble the kingdoms, to pour upon them mine indignation, even all my fierce anger." He concludes with a warning; *"all the earth shall be devoured with the fire of my jealousy"* (Zephaniah 3:8; emphasis added—this verse also gives us a glimpse into the Lord's personality). (See also Isaiah 13:6-9, 11–12.)

The Savior's Second Coming is almost always couched in terms of fear and devastation in an attempt to warn the wicked (see D&C 133:63–74) because the righteous will *"not* be hewn down and cast into the fire"—they "shall abide the day" of the Savior's Coming, whether in life or in death (D&C 45:57; emphasis added). In regards to the wicked, however, the scriptures provide the following conclusions:

(a)   The Lord does not like disobedience.

(b)   He will "punish the world for evil, and the wicked for their iniquity, . . . arrogancy . . . [and] haughtiness" (2 Nephi 23:11)—and for other like reasons as detailed in scripture[5]—and he will do it "speedily . . . as the whirlwind" (D&C 97:22), trampling the wicked in his "fury" and "anger" (D&C 133:51).[6]

The Lord has described the great anger he feels for disobedience in language mankind can easily comprehend. He has expressed this anger in both general and symbolic terms as he warns the wicked that they will be afflicted "with famine, and plague, and earthquake," all of which will issue forth from the "chastening hand of an Almighty God, until the consumption decreed hath made a full end" and men have seen the "salvation of their God"

(D&C 87:6; 133:3). The great consolation for the righteous is that even if they are destroyed physically in these devastations, they will die unto the Lord and their reward will be great.

The Lord Delayeth His Coming

"Fear ye not, stand still, and see the salvation of the Lord, which he will show to you to day" (Exodus 14:13). Moses delivered this admonition to the children of Israel as they fearfully stood on the shores of the Red Sea and watched the armies of Pharaoh descend upon them. After 430 years of captivity, Pharaoh had finally been persuaded by the Lord's plagues[7] to let the Israelites leave Egypt; but they had barely departed the city gates before Pharaoh asked himself, "Why have we done this, that we have let Israel go from serving us?" (Exodus 14:5.) So he pursued them to the shores of the Red Sea. The children of Israel "were sore afraid: and . . . cried out unto the Lord. And they said unto Moses, Because there were no graves in Egypt, hast thou taken us away to die in the wilderness? . . . Is not this the word that we did tell thee in Egypt, saying, Let us alone, that we may serve the Egyptians? For it had been better for us to serve the Egyptians, than that we should die in the wilderness" (Exodus 14:10–12). Thus the faithless Israelites complained against Moses and against the Lord, in spite of the miracles they had witnessed as the Lord delivered them.

There is an interesting parallel in the Book of Mormon to this example of faithlessness. Samuel the Lamanite was sent to call the wicked Nephites to repentance. They initially cast him out, but he ultimately delivered his message by ascending the walls of the city and preaching from their heights. He prophesied to the Nephites that the Savior's birth would take place in exactly five years, and he told them that this miraculous event would be accompanied by a sign: "one day and a night and a day, as if it were one day and there were no night . . . for ye shall know of the rising of the sun and also of its setting . . . nevertheless the night shall not be darkened" (Helaman 14:4). He then predicted the Savior's death and its accompanying sign: the "sun shall be darkened and refuse to give his light unto you; and also the moon and the stars; and there shall be no light upon the face of this land . . . for the space of three days" (Helaman 14:20).

As the time for the first sign approached, many disbelievers claimed that "the time [appointed for the Savior's birth] was [already] past," and they began to "rejoice over their brethren saying: Behold the time is past, and the words of Samuel are not fulfilled" (3 Nephi 1:5–6). They decreed a certain date wherein those who believed in Christ's birth would be "put to death except the sign should come to pass" (3 Nephi 1:9).

Of course, the sign occurred and the righteous were spared, but shortly thereafter "the people began to forget those signs and wonders which they had heard, and began to be less and less astonished at a sign" (3 Nephi 2:1). As the time for the sign of the Savior's death approached, there again "began to be great doubtings and disputations among the people, notwithstanding [that] so many signs had been given [to them]" (3 Nephi 8:4). But again the sign was given as prophesied, and with devastating results! (See 3 Nephi 8–10.)

Why use these two stories in a book about the Second Coming? Because they exemplify what the mind-set of civilization will be like in the days prior to the Lord's final Advent. Like the Israelites and Nephites of old, people will again be faithless and disbelieving. They will be like the people in the days of Noah "before the flood . . . eating and drinking, marrying and giving in marriage," and paying no attention to Noah until he entered the ark and the flood came and destroyed them. "So shall also the coming of the Son of man be" (Matthew 24:38–39).

Belief and faith have always been complicated, and they will continue to be complicated in the latter days. We anticipate the Second Coming, but we don't know when that day will be. The signs we are given are predominately nonspecific, and many of them involve disturbances that have been occurring since the dawn of time. Prophets foresaw this difficulty and prophesied what people's reaction to it would be. Peter declared: "There shall come in the last days scoffers, walking after their own lusts, And saying, Where is the promise of his coming? for since the fathers fell asleep, all things continue as they were from the beginning of the creation" (2 Peter 3:3–4).

Peter then recites the evidences of the Lord's presence from the creation of the earth to the final judgment, and he warns us that "the Lord is not slack concerning his promise, as some men count slackness; but is longsuffering to us-ward, not willing that any should perish, but that all should come to repentance. But the day of the Lord will come as a thief in the night" (2 Peter 3:9–10).

Even after the tribulation when "the whole earth shall be in commotion, and men's hearts shall fail them," there will be disbelievers who will claim that "Christ delayeth his coming" (D&C 45:26; Matthew 24:48). There is no question that recognizing the signs as they occur may be a problem, and there may even be confusion as to which signs have already occurred, *but the real problem mankind will face is a lack of faith that the Savior will come at all!*

Just as the signs of the Messiah's First Coming were fulfilled, so will the signs of his Second Coming be fulfilled. And in spite of all the devastation that will occur, his coming will be as simple as his ascension: "This same Jesus, which is taken up from you into heaven, shall so come in like manner as ye have seen him go into heaven" (Acts 1:9–11).

When Will the Lord Come?

When will the Lord come? What is the exact date? Almost every biblical prophet since Enoch has pondered these questions. Enoch saw a vision of the Lord's coming in Moses 7:65 and John the Revelator closed his book with it in Revelation 19–22, but the Old Testament prophet Daniel appears to have been the first to record the question, "When?"

Daniel was given a great vision showing the destruction of the temple in Jerusalem (which ended daily sacrifice) and the destruction of Jerusalem itself (See Daniel 11:1–34). He described this destruction as the *abomination of desolation* because:

1. It destroyed the Jewish kingdom (which to Daniel represented Israel).

2. It desecrated the holy temple, thereby defiling the God of Israel.

3. It laid waste the holy city (see Daniel 11:35–45).

His vision continued to the "time of the end" (Daniel 12:4, 9), where he saw Michael lead the great battles against evil that resulted in terrible consequences for the wicked. Finally, he saw the resurrection of both the just and the unjust (see Daniel 12:1–3). As these great visions closed, he was commanded to "seal the book even to the time of the end" (Daniel 12:4). But in spite of the power of these visions, Daniel was left without definition as to when they would take place, so he asked the angel, "How long shall it be to the end of these wonders?" (Daniel 12:6.) The angel responded, "It shall be for a time, times, and an half; and when he shall have accomplished to scatter the power of the holy people, all these things shall be finished" (Daniel 12:7).

A bewildered Daniel stated, "I heard, but I understood not." He again asked, "O my Lord, what shall be the end of these things"? (Daniel 12:8.)

But the vision was over. The angel said, "Go thy way, Daniel: for the words are closed up and sealed till the time of the end. Many shall be purified, and made white, and tried; but the wicked shall do wickedly: and none of the wicked shall understand; *but the wise shall understand*" (Daniel 12:9–10; emphasis added).

Then the angel again expressed the time of the end in terms of the vision: "And from the time that the daily sacrifice shall be taken away, and the abomination that maketh desolate set up, there shall be a thousand two hundred and ninety days" (Daniel 12:11; in the JST, Joseph changed "days" to "years").

Although the Savior fulfilled the law of Moses in his final sacrifice upon the cross, the Jews as a whole continued to function under the law's requirements (through the Roman conquest in A.D. 70, and on up to the present time), even though they have not been able to perform the ritual of sacrifice since the Romans destroyed the temple. According to Daniel's prophecy, it is the destruction of the temple, of Jerusalem, and of the kingdom of Judah (the "abomination that maketh desolate"), together with the cessation of daily sacrifice, that provides the *key* to the "time of the end." (This prophecy is reinforced by the Savior as he speaks to his Apostles in the 24th chapter of Matthew.)

The angel in Daniel 12 then added another specific time period to his prophecy: that it would be 1,290 days from the destruction of Jerusalem until the "time of the end." He continued, "Blessed is he that waiteth, and cometh to the *thousand three hun-*

dred and five and thirty days" (Daniel 12:12; emphasis added)—a *different* period of time. Daniel was left with two conflicting time periods which were scheduled to begin after the destruction of Jerusalem (obviously clues to the time of the Second Coming), but the angel gave no further explanation.

Daniel was dismissed from the vision with the promise that he would "rest, and stand in [his] lot at the end of the days" (Daniel 12:13). He was not given the "time of the end," but he was told that he would be present when it occurred and that he would be counted among the righteous at that time.

The same curiosity which prompted Daniel to ask "when" was also aroused in the Lord's Apostles shortly after the Savior's scathing comments to the Jewish leadership during his last public discourse (see Matthew 23). After his discourse, the Lord and his Apostles left Jerusalem, crossed through the valley of Kidron, and climbed the Mount of Olives. The Savior's ministry was coming to a close and as he stood upon the mount, he gazed back at the beauty of Jerusalem and its magnificent temple and prophesied of their future destruction. The Apostles asked the Lord, "When shall these things be? and what shall be the sign of thy coming, and of the end of the world?" (Matthew 24:3.) This same question had also been asked by the Lord's enemies, the Pharisees, earlier in his ministry (see Luke 17:20). He would not give them a direct answer because they did not believe in him; however, even though his Apostles did believe in him, he did not give them a direct answer either. Instead, he gave them the great double-reference sermon recorded in Matthew 24 which describes both the destruction of the Jewish kingdom as seen by Daniel and the cleansing of the earth prior to the Second Coming.[8]

After the Savior's resurrection, the Saints at Thessalonica became concerned about the immediacy of the Second Coming. In response to their concern, Paul wrote the following:

> For the Lord himself shall descend from heaven with a shout, with the voice of the archangel, and with the trump of God: and the dead in Christ shall rise first:
>
> Then *we which are alive and remain* shall be caught up together with them in the clouds, to meet the

> Lord in the air: and so shall we ever be with the
> Lord.
>
> Wherefore comfort one another with these words.
>
> But of the times and the seasons, brethren, ye have
> no need that I write unto you.
>
> For yourselves know perfectly that the day of the
> Lord so cometh as a thief in the night (1
> Thessalonians 4:16–18; 5:1–2; emphasis added).

Paul wrote as if this occurrence would take place immediately, which caused the Saints in Thessalonica to misunderstand him. They literally anticipated that they would be "caught up together . . . in the clouds, to meet the Lord in the air" during their lifetime. Some of the Saints may have even quit their occupations and sold their possessions in anticipation of this glorious event. They became "busy-bodies" (2 Thessalonians 3:11) in the Church in the sense that they spent much of their time talking about and planning for the Second Coming.[9] As a result of this incorrect belief, Paul again dealt with the subject in a second letter:

> Now we beseech you, brethren, by the coming of
> our Lord Jesus Christ, and by our gathering
> together unto him,
>
> That ye be not soon shaken in mind, or be
> troubled, neither by spirit, nor by word, nor by
> letter as from us, as that the day of Christ is at
> hand.
>
> Let no man deceive you by any means: for that
> day shall not come, except there come a falling
> away first, and that man of sin be revealed, the
> son of perdition (2 Thessalonians 2:1–3).

Thus, Paul made it clear that the day of Christ's coming would not be an immediate event but would occur sometime far in the future.

Curiosity concerning the time of the Second Coming has not been limited to the members and prophets of Christ's ancient

Church. Joseph Smith had a similar interest and asked the same question as that posed by Daniel and the early Apostles:

I was once praying very earnestly to know the time of the coming of the Son of Man, when I heard a voice repeat the following:

> Joseph, my son, if thou livest until thou art eighty-five years old, thou shalt see the face of the Son of Man; therefore let this suffice, and trouble me no more on this matter.
>
> I was left thus, without being able to decide whether this coming referred to the beginning of the millennium or to some previous appearing, or whether I should die and thus see his face.
>
> I believe the coming of the Son of Man will not be any sooner than that time (D&C 130:14–17).

The Lord has made it clear that the time of his coming is known only to the Father, but it still excites such curiosity among individuals both in and out of the Church that many have ventured to speculate on it.

In the early history of the restored Church, a man named William Miller founded a Christian belief known as *Millerism*. It was based on his calculations for the date of the Second Coming, which he derived from the books of Daniel and Revelation. His first proposed date was general—between March 21, 1843, and March 21, 1844,[10]—but he later identified April 3, 1843, as an exact date. However, the day came and went without event, as Joseph Smith noted with some sarcasm.[11] Father Miller, as he was known, then reworked his calculations and derived a new date for the Lord's Advent: October 22, 1844. Anticipation again surged among his followers, only to end in disappointment when the prophecy failed a second time.[12]

In 1949 a small group called the Children of Light left Canada in search of immortality. After sixteen years of wandering from area to area, their preacher declared that Jesus had visited her and that she had seen the name "Agua Caliente" spelled out in the clouds. She proclaimed that this was the place where her followers should settle to await the Apocalypse. So in 1967 the group moved to Agua Caliente, Arizona. At the date of this writing, the apocalypse has not yet arrived, and only seven of the original group remain alive. They are all in their 70s or 80s.[13]

The detail found in the book of Daniel and the book of Revelation, along with the many numerical anomalies of the scriptures (such as the use of the numbers 7 and 12; the cycle of 40 days; the cycles of 40, 70, 430, 490, and 2,520 years; and the fact that many of the major events in Israel occurred on these cycles and correlate with many of their major anniversaries: i.e., the Passover, the Day of Atonement, and the Feast of Tabernacles) has led many to speculate on the date of the Lord's coming. They use these cyclical biblical numbers in an attempt to mathematically calculate and manipulate the Jewish, Roman, and Christian calendars in order to predict the date of Christ's Advent. Most, if not all of the current prognosticators, settled on the fall of the year 2000.[14] Again, nothing happened.

Not all modern predictions of the Lord's Advent come from apostate Christianity. Even the Prophet Joseph Smith could not resist. In February 1835 he declared that it was time for the last pruning of the vineyard, and that the "coming of the Lord . . . was . . . nigh." He stated that "fifty-six years should wind up the scene."[15] On another occasion he said: "There are those of the rising generation who shall not taste death till Christ comes," and "the Son of Man will not come in the clouds of heaven till I am eighty-five years old." Joseph then read Revelation 14:6–7 and the sixth chapter of Hosea and stated that 2,520 years would "bring it to [the year] 1890."[16] The method of his calculation and the means by which he determined his beginning date are left unexplained, but his revelation from the Lord intimated that if Joseph lived until he was eighty-five years of age, he would see the Lord's face (see D&C 130:15). This seems to have had an influence upon his calculations.

Many of the early Brethren believed that the Second Coming would be in the lifetime of those present in their audiences—especially the children. Wilford Woodruff stated this over the pulpit four times between 1871 and 1898,[17] and Lorenzo Snow said it in 1901.[18] In 1873, Charles C. Rich stated:

> I did not expect forty-seven years to pass away before the prophecies would be fulfilled concerning the second coming of the Savior, and the end of the world. I expected the Savior would come . . . before this time . . . We are not accustomed to hear the Lord speak, and when he spoke of a short time, we understood it according to our use of the language.
>
> It takes a long time according to our reckoning to do the work the Lord has decreed concerning the children of men in this last dispensation.[19]

With all of the calculations that have been made and the many speculations that have failed in their accuracy, the question still remains: *when* will the Lord come? The answer remains the same: "But of that day and hour knoweth no man, no, not the angels of heaven, but my Father only" (Matthew 24:36; see also Mark 13:32; D&C 133:10–11). This utterance was made at the close of the Lord's ministry almost 2,000 years ago. Without question the time is nearer now than when the statement was made, but the exact date remains unknown.

On November 4, 1830, the Lord revealed to Joseph Smith that "the time is soon at hand that I shall come in a cloud with power and great glory" (D&C 34:7). In February 1831 he continued: "For in mine own due time will I come upon the earth in judgment, and my people shall be redeemed and shall reign with me on earth" (D&C 43:29). But lest anyone anticipates his coming as the Thessalonians did, the Lord gave the following caution in the forty-ninth section of the Doctrine and Covenants: "The hour and the day no man knoweth, neither the angels in heaven, *nor shall they know until he comes*" (D&C 49:7; emphasis added).

Obviously, the time of his coming will remain a mystery—and there is a purpose for this. The anticipation of Christ's appearance motivates devout men and women to constantly strive for righteousness in thought and action so that they might be found worthy of his presence when the time comes. The Lord explained it this way:

> Watch therefore: for ye know not what hour your Lord doth come.

> But know this, that if the goodman of the house had known in what watch the thief would come, he would have watched, and would not have suffered his house to be broken up.

> Therefore be ye also ready: for in such an hour as ye think not the Son of man cometh (Matthew 24:42–44).

The righteous will be rewarded at the Lord's coming, but the wicked, thinking that the "Lord delayeth his coming" will procrastinate their repentance and be "cut . . . asunder." Their portion will be with the "hypocrites . . . [where] there shall be weeping and gnashing of teeth" (Matthew 24:48–51).

Blessed is the man or woman who will be caught up to meet the Savior at his Advent, but as the Lord cautioned, our meeting with him might occur sooner than that since we can die at any time. Therefore, "pray always that you enter not into temptation, that you may abide the day of his coming, *whether in life or in death*. Even so. Amen" (D&C 61:39; emphasis added). We would be well advised to heed the advice of Paul to the Thessalonians and let the Lord direct our hearts "into the love of God, and into the patient waiting for Christ" (2 Thessalonians 3:5).

The Bridegroom Cometh

All of the signs and prophecies of the Second Coming have been given so that man can anticipate and prepare himself for entrance into God's kingdom. The parable of the ten virgins gives us insight into that preparation,[20] and the Lord announced in March 1831 that the parable would be fulfilled when he came in his glory (see D&C 45:56).

As we have previously discussed, the ten virgins (representing the Church) await the bridegroom (who is the Lord). Half of the virgins are wise and have properly prepared themselves to receive the bridegroom, no matter how long it takes. They have "received the truth, and have taken the Holy Spirit for their guide, and have not been deceived" (D&C 45:57). The other virgins are foolish and unprepared and will remain so right up to the hour of his coming when there will be a "separation of the righteous and the wicked" (D&C 63:54). Recognizing that the Lord is talking directly to the members of the Church today, it becomes especially important that we listen to his counsel: "Wherefore, be faithful, praying always, having your lamps trimmed and burning, and oil with you, that you may be ready at the coming of the Bridegroom" (D&C 33:17).

In December 1832, in a revelation known as the "olive leaf," he reemphasized this admonition: "Prepare ye, prepare ye, O inhabitants of the earth; for the judgment of our God is come. Behold, and lo, the Bridegroom cometh; go ye out to meet him" (D&C 88:92). Nearly 200 years have passed since the Lord gave this warning. Many have already passed on to meet him, but among those who remain alive, the wise are prepared.

The Sign of the Son of Man

The Lord will come after all the great signs of his Advent have been completed and the wicked have been destroyed (see D&C 49:23)—after the sun is darkened and the moon stops giving her light and the stars have fallen from heaven. He will come at a time when all the "powers of the heavens shall be shaken" (Matthew 24:29). Only then will the angel of God sound his trump to prepare the earth for his arrival (see D&C 88:92). And that is when the "sign of the Son of man" will appear in heaven (Matthew 24:30)—"a great sign" that "all people shall see . . . together" (D&C 88:93).

Just as John the Baptist recognized the Savior by the sign of the dove, so shall we recognize the Savior by the "sign of the Son of man."[21] All mankind will recognize it as the veil is lifted from our minds, for it is a sign we all learned in the preexistence. The Savior shall appear and his glory "shall be revealed, and all flesh shall see it together" (Isaiah 40:5). He will come in the clouds of heaven, clothed "with power and great glory" (D&C 34:7) with "all the holy angels" (D&C 45:44), and "every eye shall see him" (Revelation 1:7). The tribes of the earth will mourn as they see him appear (see Matthew 24:30), for "the nations are as a drop of a bucket, and are counted as the small dust of the balance . . . All nations before him are as nothing; and they are counted to him less than nothing, and vanity" (Isaiah 40:15–17).

His glory will be like "a pillar of fire" (D&C 29:12), and he warns us not to be deceived (see Matthew 24:4; D&C 49:23) since he will not come "in the form of a woman, neither of a man traveling on the earth" (D&C 49:22). He will not come in secret; rather, his appearance will be dramatic: "For as the light of the morning cometh out of the east, and shineth even unto the west, and covereth the whole earth, so shall also the coming of the Son of Man be" (JST, Matthew 1:26; see also Matthew 24:27).

Dressed in Red

John the Revelator described the Savior's miraculous Advent symbolically in the 19th chapter of Revelation:

> And I saw heaven opened, and behold a white horse; and he that sat upon him was called Faithful and True, and in righteousness he doth judge and make war.
>
> His eyes were as a flame of fire, and on his head were many crowns; and he had a name written, that no man knew, but he himself.
>
> And he was clothed with a vesture dipped in blood: and his name is called The Word of God.
>
> And the armies which were in heaven followed him upon white horses, clothed in fine linen, white and clean.
>
> And out of his mouth goeth a sharp sword, that with it he should smite the nations: and he shall rule them with a rod of iron: and he treadeth the winepress of the fierceness and wrath of Almighty God.
>
> And he hath on his vesture and on his thigh a name written, KING OF KINGS, AND LORD OF LORDS (Revelation 19:11–16).

Isaiah also saw the Lord dressed in red apparel at his coming:

> Who is this that cometh from Edom, with dyed garments from Bozrah? this that is glorious in his apparel, travelling in the greatness of his strength? I that speak in righteousness, mighty to save.
>
> Wherefore art thou red in thine apparel, and thy garments like him that treadeth in the winefat?
>
> I have trodden the winepress alone; and of the people there was none with me: for I will tread them in mine anger, and trample them in my fury; and their blood shall be sprinkled upon my garments, and I will stain all my raiment (Isaiah 63:1–3).

The Lord himself confirmed his vesture in November 1831:

> And it shall be said: Who is this that cometh down from God in heaven with dyed garments; yea, from the regions which are not known, clothed in his glorious apparel, traveling in the greatness of his strength?
>
> And he shall say: I am he who spake in righteousness, mighty to save.
>
> And the Lord shall be red in his apparel, and his garments like him that treadeth in the wine-vat.
>
> And so great shall be the glory of his presence that the sun shall hide his face in shame, and the moon shall withhold its light, and the stars shall be hurled from their places.
>
> And his voice shall be heard: I have trodden the wine-press alone, and have brought judgment upon all people; and none were with me;
>
> And I have trampled them in my fury, and I did tread upon them in mine anger, and their blood have I sprinkled upon my garments, and stained

all my raiment; for this was the day of vengeance
which was in my heart (D&C 133:46–51).

The Lord's robes will be red at the Second Coming representing the fact that he has suffered the sins of the world, bled the
blood of the Atonement, and with vengeance destroyed the unrepentant sinner. The blood of his (and their) suffering has symbolically stained his garments red.

The Messiah will "reign over all flesh" (D&C 133:25). He will
be in the midst of the righteous (see D&C 29:13). "His glory shall
be upon them, and he will be their king and their lawgiver" (D&C
45:59). He will strengthen the weak and those that are infirm. He
will comfort the fearful, heal the blind, and unstop the ears of the
deaf. The lame shall walk and the "tongue of the dumb [shall]
sing." Waters shall break forth in the wilderness and streams
appear in the desert (see Isaiah 35:3–7), and the Dead Sea will be
healed (see Zechariah 14:8).[22] In that day the Lord "shall be king
over all the earth" (Zechariah 14:9).

He will appear in the exalted form of a man, with flesh and
bones as tangible as a man's (see D&C 130:1, 22); and the righteous who are with him, and all who know him, shall sing the
song of his coming:

> The Lord hath brought again Zion;
> The Lord hath redeemed his people, Israel,
> According to the election of grace,
> Which was brought to pass by the faith
> And covenant of their fathers.
> The Lord hath redeemed his people;
> And Satan is bound and time is no longer.
> The Lord hath gathered all things in one.
> The Lord hath brought down Zion from above.
> The Lord hath brought up Zion from beneath.
> The earth hath travailed and brought forth her strength;
> And truth is established in her bowels;
> And the heavens have smiled upon her;
> And she is clothed with the glory of her God;

For he stands in the midst of his people.
Glory, and honor, and power, and might,
Be ascribed to our God; for he is full of mercy,
Justice, grace and truth, and peace,
Forever and ever, Amen (D&C 84:99–102).

Judgment

"For the Father judgeth no man, but hath committed all judgment unto the Son."

John 5:22

When God the Father presented the plan of salvation to his spirit children at the great premortal council, he laid out its purpose and the standard by which all mankind would be judged: "And we will prove them herewith," he declared, "to see if they will do all things whatsoever the Lord their God shall command them" (Abraham 3:25). This standard of judgment is relatively simple: we must do only what our Father tells us to do!

Judgment in the Preexistence

Our judgment began early. After being educated by our Father in the preexistence, and after having Lucifer's dissent from the Father's plan, we arrived at a point in our progression where we were required to choose whom we would follow: God or Satan. The plan required us to follow God, but we were free to make our own decision. However, once we exercised that choice, a judgment came into play: those who chose to follow God would continue on to a temporal existence under the plan of salvation; those who chose to follow Satan would not because a final judgment was pronounced upon them that prohibited them from coming to the earth to receive a physical body. They were doomed to eventually reside in outer darkness, a kingdom devoid of the Father's glory, and because of that, wherein there is "everlasting . . . endless . . . eternal punishment," a place where the "worm dieth not, and the fire is not quenched, . . . [and] the end, the width, the height, the depth, and the misery thereof" cannot be understood by any except those who find themselves under this "condemnation" (D&C 76:43–49; see also D&C 76:25–39; Abraham 3:22–28).

A degree of judgment also appears to have been exercised upon some of those who accepted God's plan while they were yet in their preexistent state, as evidenced by the following experiences of Abraham and Jeremiah. After Abraham came to earth, he received a personal revelation from God wherein he spoke with God "face to face" (Abraham 3:11). It was during this revelation that God made a great covenant with him—the Abrahamic covenant. During this vision, God showed Abraham many preexistent spirits and told him that some of those spirits had been chosen to be leaders on the earth because they had been "noble and great" in their premortal existence. God informed Abraham that he was one of these noble and great spirits and that he had been chosen before he was born (see Abraham 3:22–23).

Jeremiah was also told about his preexistent state. The scriptures indicate that the Lord "knew" him before he was born and had "sanctified" and "ordained" him to be a prophet to the nations (see Jeremiah 1:5). It would be reasonable to assume that all of the great ancient prophets were so distinguished. In addition, Joseph Smith declared that all who were called to minister to the people of the world were designated to receive such a call *before the world was*.[1]

This evidence leads us to the conclusion that some type of judgment in the preexistence could have affected our earthly circumstances. However, it should be remembered that we left the extent of this judgment or knowledge behind the veil at our birth. In most instances, we can only speculate as to whether there is a relationship between our mortal circumstances and what we did in the preexistence.

Judgment on Earth

We all make judgments. This is one way we comprehend our relationship with God and our fellowman. Our parents and other adults exercised judgment over us as children regarding our food, our clothing, our friends, our recreation, and our religion. "Train up a child in the way he should go:" the scripture says, "and when he is old, he will not depart from it" (Proverbs 22:6). As we became adults, we began making our own judgments. However, our judgments are not always sound, and the wisdom so simply expressed in Proverbs is often lost in the results of our actions. God will ultimately judge our choices in this life by the same standard that he judged our premortal choices. Whenever he commands, we are expected to obey.

We are all familiar with the *sin-disease-punishment* and *obey-success-blessing* relationships recorded in the scriptures. Mormon records what seems to be a direct relationship between sin-poverty and righteousness-riches as he records the history of the Book of Mormon cultures,[2] yet the very wealth they considered a blessing of righteousness became a curse to them when they sinned as a result of it.[3]

The Jews at the time of Jesus were trained to regard different types of suffering as necessary or consequential to a corresponding sin.[4] They had even determined that many situations of suffering or apostasy were consequential to undisclosed or known sins. For example, "up to thirteen years of age a child was considered, as it were, part of his father, and as suffering for his guilt. More than that, the thoughts of a mother might affect the moral state of her unborn offspring, and the terrible apostasy of one of the greatest Rabbis, had, in popular belief, been caused by the sinful delight his mother had taken when passing through an idol-grove. Lastly, certain special sins in the parents would result in specific diseases in their offspring, and one is mentioned as causing blindness in the children."[5]

With regard to the relationship between worldly riches and righteousness, the Jews taught the following: "The good man, if prosperous, was so as the son of a righteous man; while the unfortunate good man suffered as the son of a sinful parent. So, also, the wicked man might be prosperous, if the son of a goodly parent; but if unfortunate, it showed that his parents had been sinners."[6] The Savior disavowed this cause and effect theory when he healed a man who had been born blind (see John 9). On this occasion the Apostles asked, "who did sin, this man, or his parents, that he was born blind?" Jesus answered that in this case, *neither* had sinned. The man had been born blind to manifest the works of God (see John 9:1–3).[7]

On another occasion, some people told the Savior about some "Galilaeans" whose blood had been mingled with Pilate's sacrifices. "Jesus answering said unto them, Suppose ye that these Galilaeans were sinners above all the Galilaeans, because they suffered such things? I tell you, Nay." He also made it clear that the eighteen men who were killed when a tower in Siloam fell on them had not died because of sin. They had simply been in the wrong place at the wrong time (See Luke 13:1–5). While we should give thanks to God for all of our blessings, material or otherwise, we do not necessarily receive worldly wealth and health because of our righteousness—nor are we necessarily poor, unhealthy, or accident prone because of our unrighteousness. Man developed the *sin-disease-punishment, obey-success-blessing* formulas—not God!

The statement "Go thy way and sin no more," occasionally uttered or inferred by a forgiving Lord to those caught in transgression, makes it clear that he *does* judge us in this life.[8] But these passing judgments are predicated on the repentant state of the individual. The Lord recognizes that even after he has extended forgiveness to those who sin, they can still fall from grace if they make the wrong choices.

There are two judgments potentially given during the earth life of the recipient that *do* have eternal consequences: they involve the *state of our individual righteousness or wickedness* and whether our *calling and election is made sure* for either exaltation or condemnation. Either judgment can take place while we are yet in the flesh. To achieve the blessing of having one's calling and election made sure for exaltation, an individual must become so righteous that the Lord will *advance* his or her day of judgment and "reward" the individual not with earthly wealth, but with the riches of eternal life. According to Peter, this blessing will be received by the "more sure word of prophecy" (2 Peter 1:19)—in other words, testimony extended and sealed by the Holy Ghost that this judgment has been given. Joseph Smith explained that this is "knowing that [an individual] is sealed up unto eternal life, by revelation and the spirit of prophecy, through the power of the Holy Priesthood" (D&C 131:5). Peter advised each Saint to "give diligence to make your calling and election sure: for if ye do these things, ye shall never fall" (2 Peter 1:10).

When Joseph Smith was teaching from the text in 2 Peter, he noted that once an individual's calling and election has been made sure, "they [are] sealed in the heavens and [have] the promise of eternal life in the kingdom of God."[9] He explained that *knowledge* is the key to the acquisition of this blessing, for "it is impossible for a man to be saved in ignorance" (D&C 131:6). "Knowledge through our Lord and Savior Jesus Christ" and "knowledge of the priesthood," Joseph declared, are the keys that will unlock the "glories and mysteries of the kingdom of heaven." It is clear from the comments of both Peter and Joseph that *knowledge* and *obedience* are the keys to accomplishing this advanced judgment. This is not an ordinance or blessing given by a priesthood holder, but the fact that it is through the priesthood that the ordinances and knowledge of the plan of salvation are upon the earth. *We make our calling and election sure by perfecting our obedience to God in the gospel and relying upon his grace,* and Joseph exhorted the Saints to "continue to call upon God" until they all made their calling and election sure.[10] On May 12, 1844, he again advised "all [members of the Church] to go on to perfection, and [to] search deeper and deeper into the mysteries of Godliness. A man can do nothing for himself," he maintained, "unless God direct[s] him in the right way; and the priesthood is for that purpose."[11]

On the other hand, John teaches us in Revelation that individuals can become so wicked that they can *advance* the day of their judgment (a negative calling and election making their condemnation "sure"), thereby sealing themselves to the devil and his kingdom in outer darkness—a condemnation from which they cannot escape! (Chapter 8; see also Revelation 13:16–18.) In each of these two instances, God makes the determination to advance judgment; however, individual men and women are responsible for bringing that judgment upon themselves.

The problem we all face in this life is knowing when we have received a judgment from God. In all probability, we would not misidentify a witness from the Spirit regarding our "calling and election," yet even here we may be deceived (see Joseph Smith–Matthew 1:22). When speaking of the relationship between reward and punishment as pertaining to righteousness and wickedness, it is difficult to determine if God is giving us a blessing or a punishment, or whether we just made a wise or an unwise decision. After all, it was the widow in her poverty who gave two mites and was judged by the Lord to be righteous, not the wealthy who only gave of their abundance (see Mark 12:42–44). Isaiah gives us a superb description of our personal relationship with sin: "For the bed [representing sin] is shorter than that a man can stretch himself on it: and the covering narrower than that he can wrap himself in it" (Isaiah 28:20). We are not always qualified to determine our own righteousness, let alone the blessings we feel we deserve, or have, or have not received. We are especially unqualified to determine the state of righteousness of others or to ascertain what blessings they should receive. It is sufficient to know that this life is a determining factor in our final judgment and that the judgment we receive will be based on our individual wickedness or righteousness. God, through his Son, will be our ultimate judge.

John the Revelator saw the "small and great" standing before God at the final judgment. He records that the "books were opened," even "the book of life," and that it was from these books that all mankind would be judged (Revelation 20:12). He informs us that God knows what our thoughts and actions are and why we think and act as we do. Malachi used this same image when he said that "a book of remembrance was written before [the Lord]" from which those "that feared the Lord, and that thought upon his name" were remembered (Malachi 3:16). The book motif was carried forward from Adam (see Moses 6:5–8) to the latter days when the Lord declared, "All they who are not found written in the book of remembrance shall find none inheritance in" the day of judgment (D&C 85:9).

The scriptures tell us that as a person "thinketh in his heart, so is he" (Proverbs 23:7). God knows what is in our hearts and understands the reasons for our actions; therefore, it behooves us to ask by what standard he will judge us. We are aware of his commandments and we know that those commandments must be obeyed. When we have faith in God, we want to obey him. However, obedience requires action, and action implies work. James confirms that "faith without works is dead" (James 2:26). Why? Because it is by our works that our faith is demonstrated. But *works* alone will not get us to heaven.

Faith is the term used throughout the scriptures to characterize the degree of our commitment and obedience to God. Our *faith* is the *standard* by which the Lord will judge us. However, the evidence of our faith and our obedience is our *works*, works that are performed for the right reasons. Thus, our faith gives rise to action, but we must act for the right reasons if we are to be judged righteous in the Lord's sight.

Early in the restoration of the gospel, the Lord testified that at the day of judgment he would "come to recompense unto every man according to his work, and measure to every man according to the measure which he has measured to his fellow man" (D&C 1:10). *Recompense* is an interesting word in this scripture. It means "to give compensation for" or "to repay or reward."[12] Therefore, we are going to receive compensation in kind for our works as a result of two things:

One our work for God. This work is objective. We know exactly what we have to do to fulfill the commandments. This work measures our absolute obedience to the first great commandment since nothing comes before God and our obedience to his commandments.

Two how we "measure" or "treat" our fellow man. This work is subjective, undefined, and without limits. This work demonstrates how well we keep the second great commandment. After reciting the parable of the ten virgins[13] and the parable of the talents[14] to his Apostles, the Lord gave this warning and explanation of his future judgment:

Then shall the King say unto them on his right hand, Come, ye blessed of my Father, inherit the kingdom prepared for you from the foundation of the world:

For I was an hungred, and ye gave me meat: I was thirsty, and ye gave me drink: I was a stranger, and ye took me in:

Naked, and ye clothed me: I was sick, and ye visited me: I was in prison, and ye came unto me.

Then shall the righteous answer him, saying, Lord, when saw we thee an hungred, and fed thee? or thirsty, and gave thee drink?

When saw we thee a stranger, and took thee in? or naked, and clothed thee?

Or when saw we thee sick, or in prison, and came unto thee?

And the King shall answer and say unto them, Verily I say unto you, Inasmuch as ye have done it unto one of the least of these my brethren, ye have done it unto me.

Then shall he say also unto them on the left hand, Depart from me, ye cursed, into everlasting fire, prepared for the devil and his angels:

For I was an hungred, and ye gave me no meat: I was thirsty, and ye gave me no drink:

I was a stranger, and ye took me not in: naked, and ye clothed me not: sick, and in prison, and ye visited me not.

Then shall they also answer him, saying, Lord, when saw we thee an hungred, or athirst, or a stranger, or naked, or sick, or in prison, and did not minister unto thee?

Then shall he answer them, saying, Verily I say
unto you, Inasmuch as ye did it not to one of the
least of these, ye did it not to me.

And these shall go away into everlasting
punishment: but the righteous into life eternal
(Matthew 25:34–46).[15]

We are all responsible for our actions: we will reap as we have
sown (see D&C 6:33), we will be repaid according to our deeds
(see Isaiah 59:18), and we will reap a reward from our works. "If
they have been righteous" works, we will reap exaltation; but "if
they have been evil" works, we will reap "the damnation of [our]
souls" (Alma 9:28). We will have restored to us exactly what we
have done to God and to our fellow man (see Alma 41:2–5).

Judgment is simple!

Judgment at Death

When we die, our spirits move on to either the paradise of
God or to a spirit prison. The judgment as to where we will reside in this phase of our existence will be determined by our
earthly righteousness and knowledge.

A notable example of judgment at death is found in the stories of Enoch and Noah. The world was judged by God prior to
the Flood and found sorely wanting. As a result, the righteous
were taken and translated with Enoch and his city into heaven
until only eight righteous people were left on the earth—Noah
and his family. Noah had warned the people of God's impending judgment. He had told them about the Flood that would
come upon them if they did not repent. But they would not listen. Consequently, Noah built the Ark, the flood came, and only
"eight souls were saved" alive (1 Peter 3:20). The balance—all of
the people of the earth—died in the flood.

During the centuries between the time the City of Enoch was
taken into heaven and the time Noah built his ark, many righteous people made their calling and election sure and were translated into Enoch's city to await the resurrection. The wicked who
lived during the same period, however, including those who died
in the floodand thereafter, went to the spirit prison to await the
mercies of God (Isaiah 24:21–22). Missionary work to these im-

prisoned souls was initiated by the Lord during his stay in the spirit world following his crucifixion.[16] Peter describes this event, indicating that the Savior arranged for the gospel to be preached to those spirits "which sometime were disobedient, when once the long suffering of God waited in the days of Noah." The Doctrine and Covenants gives us further insight into how this missionary work is being carried out and expands this work to include *all* disobedient spirits who reside or will reside in the spirit prison (see 1 Peter 3:18–20; D&C 138).

Judgment at the Second Coming

The wicked of Noah's time were drowned in a universal flood. The wicked on the Western Hemisphere died in the massive destruction that occurred when the Savior of the world was crucified. And prophecy tells us that *all* the wicked of the earth (those unable to abide the Lord's presence) will again be destroyed in the devastation that will occur prior to the Lord's Second Coming.

The Savior will come "with ten thousands of his saints, to execute judgment upon all . . . that are ungodly" (Jude 1:14–15). He will purge the earth to gather the righteous and destroy the wicked (D&C 133:56–74), as described in the parable of the wheat and tares (see Matthew 13:24–30).[17] John's vision of the Second Coming indicates that "one . . . like unto the son of man" will receive this instruction: "Thrust in thy sickle, and reap: for the time is come for thee to reap; for the harvest of the earth is ripe." And the vision says he "thrust in his sickle on the earth; and the earth was reaped" (Revelation 14:13–16).

Judgment at the Second Coming will complete the two great harvests of the righteous. The first harvest occurred at Jesus' resurrection when all the righteous who had previously died were themselves resurrected. This resurrection is *part* of the first resurrection and is the first resurrection Alma looked forward to (see Alma 40:16). All who die after this resurrection (except those few men who had work to do in the Restoration) will sleep until the general resurrection at the Lord's Second Coming. This is the resurrection we commonly refer to as the first resurrection. These two resurrections reflect major judgments that have taken place to separate the righteous from the wicked—the wicked being destroyed temporally to await a later resurrection, and the righteous being resurrected when the Lord comes.

In addition to those who are resurrected at his coming, the righteous living upon the earth at his Advent will be caught up to meet him. But these individuals will not be resurrected at this time, for if they were, there would be no righteous men or women left upon the earth to carry on his work during the Millennium. These righteous disciples, and other worthy people living during the Millennium, will automatically be resurrected when they reach "the age of a tree." They will then be "caught up" to the Lord's kingdom, and their "rest shall be glorious" (D&C 101:30–31).

At this time, the Lord will "bring to light the hidden things of darkness, and will make manifest the counsels of the hearts" (1 Corinthians 4:5). Isaiah describes this condition:

> The vile person shall be no more called liberal, nor the churl said to be bountiful.
>
> For the vile person will speak villany, and his heart will work iniquity, to practise hypocrisy, and to utter error against the Lord, to make empty the soul of the hungry, and he will cause the drink of the thirsty to fail (Isaiah 32:5–6).

This means that there will be no deception possible at this time. People will actually be what they appear to be.

Delegated Judgment

The Lord is our supreme judge. However, he has delegated some preliminary judgment to others. There are several specific references where he delegates the responsibility of judgment to certain people or groups:

The Original Twelve Apostles: The Lord delegated judgment of the entire twelve tribes of Israel to his original Twelve Apostles:

And again, verily, verily, I say unto you, and it hath gone forth in a firm decree, by the will of the Father, that mine apostles, the Twelve which were with me in my ministry at Jerusalem, shall stand at my right hand at the day of my coming in a pillar of fire, being clothed with robes of righteousness, with crowns upon their heads, in glory even as I am, to judge the whole house of Israel, even as many as have loved me and kept my commandments, and none else (D&C 29:12).

From this scripture it would appear that Judas Iscariot is included in this edict; however, because he fell from his position and became a "son of perdition" (John 17:12), he will not serve as a judge over Israel. After Christ's ascension, the Twelve met in council to choose a new member. They selected "of these men which have companied with us all the time that the Lord Jesus went in and out among us" (Acts 1:21). Two candidates were considered, and their names were presented to the quorum for final selection. They were "Joseph called Barsabas, who was surnamed Justus, and Matthias" (Acts 1:23). Both men were disciples who had traveled with Jesus and the Apostles throughout the Lord's ministry; because of this, the man selected would be considered as one of the Twelve who were with Jesus "in [his] ministry at Jerusalem" (D&C 29:12). Matthias was the disciple subsequently selected to replace Judas Iscariot as one of the Lord's Apostles.

The Nephite Disciples: The Lord chose these twelve men to minister to the Nephite people after his visit to the Western Hemisphere. They were to administer the gospel to their people in a manner similar to that of the Apostles on the Eastern Hemisphere. Nephi saw these men in vision during his early ministry:

> And I also saw and bear record that the Holy Ghost fell upon twelve others; and they were ordained of God, and chosen.
>
> And the angel spake unto me, saying: Behold the twelve disciples of the Lamb, who are chosen to minister unto thy seed.
>
> And he said unto me: Thou rememberest the twelve apostles of the Lamb? Behold they are they who shall judge the twelve tribes of Israel; wherefore, the twelve ministers of thy seed shall be judged of them; for ye are of the house of Israel.
>
> And these twelve ministers whom thou beholdest shall judge thy seed. And, behold, they are righteous forever; for because of their faith in the

> Lamb of God their garments are made white in
> his blood (1 Nephi 12:7–10).

The relationship between these twelve disciples and the Twelve Apostles on the Eastern Hemisphere seems clear from this scripture, but to ensure clarity, Mormon added the following: "And I write also unto the remnant of this people, who shall also be judged by the twelve whom Jesus chose in this land; and they shall be judged by the other twelve whom Jesus chose in the land of Jerusalem" (Mormon 3:19). Thus, the twelve disciples and their people will also be judged by the Lord's Apostles on the Eastern Hemisphere, who will judge all Israel as well (see Matthew 19:28; Luke 22:30).

The Bishop: During the restoration of the gospel in the latter days, the Lord established the priesthood office of bishop. The individual holding this office is to "be a judge in Israel, like as it was in ancient days." Initially, bishops were instructed to oversee the division of lands under the United Order so that these divisions would be equitable and to ensure that each individual who received land would be accountable for it. He was also authorized to "judge his people by the testimony of the just, and by the assistance of his counselors, according to the laws of the kingdom which are given by the prophets of God" (D&C 58:16–18).[18] These scriptures indicate that a bishop is authorized to judge the temporal affairs of Church members and to help maintain the integrity of the Church. The bishop, therefore, can judge whether each member of his congregation is worthy to participate in the blessings the Church has to offer: the priesthood, temple attendance, membership, callings, and similar opportunities. But it is the Lord who judges the intent and honesty of each individual as he deals with the bishop.

The Elders: There is an interesting scripture concerning missionaries pronouncing judgment upon people:

> And in whatsoever house ye enter, and they
> receive you, leave your blessing upon that house.
>
> And in whatsoever house ye enter, and they
> receive you not, ye shall depart speedily from that

house, and shake off the dust of your feet as a testimony against them.

And you shall be filled with joy and gladness; and know this, that in the day of judgment you shall be judges of that house, and condemn them;

And it shall be more tolerable for the heathen in the day of judgment, than for that house; therefore, gird up your loins and be faithful, and ye shall overcome all things, and be lifted up at the last day. Even so. Amen (D&C 75:19–22).

This scripture declares that missionaries can potentially judge the people they proselyte. This judgment is limited, however, by the type of contact the missionaries make at the time of their visit. The following circumstances have to be taken into consideration: (1) Were the missionaries in the proper spirit and did they take ample time to indicate who and what they were representing (as well as bear their testimonies to the truthfulness of their representations)? (2) What was the condition of the contact (represented in the scriptures as the "house") at the time the visit was made? (3) Did the Holy Ghost bear witness to the contact, and did he or she knowingly rejected it? (4) Did the contact continue to reject the gospel, or did he or she later repent and embrace it? It seems obvious that any judgment which affects the eternity of the soul should be used judiciously and should require a confirmation from the Lord. Only God knows the intentions of the heart.

Judgment is always difficult when it concerns the eternal disposition of the soul, but we come from a loving Father who is always willing to forgive those who repent. Through the Atonement of Christ and by his grace all mankind can be saved (see Articles of Faith 1:3; 2 Nephi 25:23). We all have a tendency to be hard on ourselves when we evaluate our lives, but "if our heart condemn us," know that "God is greater than our heart, and knoweth all things" (1 John 3:20). We can place our confidence and trust in the Lord, for all his judgments will be correct and just.

Millennial Peace, War, and Resurrection

"There shall be time no longer, . . .
. . . and they shall not any more see death."

Doctrine & Covenants 88:110, 116

Millennial Judgment

Judgment will continue during the Millennium as the human life cycle continues. Men and women will be born and will live to the "age of a tree" (or as Isaiah notes, "100 years"); then they will die and be caught up and changed in the "twinkling of an eye." The righteous will enjoy instant resurrection and their "rest shall be glorious," but those who are unworthy to be in God's kingdom will be "accursed." They will die and go into the spirit world to await their resurrection at a later time (see Isaiah 65:20; D&C 63:49–51; 101:31).

Great changes will occur to the earth as the Millennium is ushered in. The world as we know it will no longer exist. The earth will return to its paradisiacal glory and will become a new earth (Articles of Faith 1:10). "Old things shall pass away, and all things [will] become new" (D&C 63:49). "In that day the enmity of man, and the enmity of beasts, yea the enmity of all flesh, shall cease from before [God's] face" (D&C 101:26). "The wolf . . . shall dwell with the lamb, and the leopard shall lie down with the kid; and the calf and the young lion and the fatling [shall live] together; and a little child shall lead them." Wild and domestic animals will be able to live together in peace, and children will be able to play by the "hole of the asp" and the "cockatrice' den" without being harmed (Isaiah 11:6–9). Man and beast will be in harmony.

There will be an explosion of knowledge during the Millennium. When the Lord comes "he shall reveal all things—things which have passed, and hidden things which no man knew, things of the earth, by which it was made, and the purpose and the end thereof—things most precious, things that are above, and things that are beneath, things that are in the earth, and upon the earth, and in heaven" (D&C 101:32–34). The gospel will continue to be preached until all men "either come into the Church, or kingdom of God, or the wicked die and pass away."[1] Temples will also continue to be built as the ordinances of salvation continue.

During the Millennium Satan will not have the power to tempt mankind; furthermore, there will be no sorrow because for the righteous there will be no death (see D&C 101:26–30). God will remove all curses from the earth: the curse of weeds and thistles instituted after the Fall (see Genesis 3:18), the curse on Cain and his seed (see Genesis 4:11–15), and the curse on the waters (see Revelation 16:3–5; D&C 61:14)—all curses shall become null and void (see Revelation 22:3; 2 Nephi 30:17).

Zephaniah tells us that the Lord will return a "pure language" to the people living during the Millennium so that they can all call upon him "to serve him with one consent" (Zephaniah 3:9); Ezekiel tells us that the Dead Sea will be "healed" and full of many kinds of edible fish (see Ezekiel 47:1–12); Isaiah states that the deserts will blossom as a rose (see Isaiah 35:1–2, 7); the Doctrine and Covenants describes "pools of living water" that will appear in "barren deserts" (D&C 133:29); Christ will rule the earth in his glory and all people will both see him and hear his voice (see D&C 29:7; 133:21); all that the Lord has said and promised will be accomplished, for his words will not pass away unfulfilled (see Matthew 24:35); and there will be no king but God (see D&C 38:21), who will resolve all sorrows (see Revelation 21:4).

John informs us that everyone who is judged worthy to inherit the celestial kingdom will be given a "white stone" bearing the inscription of a new name. He writes, "To him that overcometh will I give to eat of the hidden manna, and will give him a white stone, and in the stone a new name written, which no man knoweth saving he that receiveth it" (Revelation 2:17). Joseph Smith gives the following commentary on this subject:

> Then the white stone mentioned in Revelation 2:17, will become a Urim and Thummim to each individual who receives one, whereby things pertaining to a higher order of kingdoms will be made known;
>
> And a white stone is given to each of those who come into the celestial kingdom, whereon is a new name written, which no man knoweth save he that receiveth it. The new name is the key word (D&C 130:10–11).

Two world capitals will be in existence during the Millennium: Zion and Jerusalem (see Isaiah 2:3). Those inhabiting these cities, as well as all others who inhabit the earth during the Millennium, will enjoy a wonderful quality of life. Anger and pain will be swept away. There will be no more weeping (see Isaiah 65:19). People will see "eye to eye" (D&C 84:98). They will understand each other, and deception will not be possible. Everyone will be exactly as they *appear* to be (see Isaiah 32:5–6). People will build and inhabit their houses and plant, harvest, and eat their food in peace, and no one will be able to take these things away from them (see Isaiah 65:21–22). Men and women will be able to perpetrate sin and evil through their agency, but Satan will be bound (see Revelation 20:2–3). He will not have the power to "tempt any man," and only peace will prevail (see D&C 101:28). There will be no more war during the Millennium, and swords will be turned into plowshares (see Isaiah 2:4; Joel 3:10; Micah 4:3–5). The great prophet-poet Isaiah puts all of this in his own words:

> For, behold, I create new heavens and a new earth:
> and the former shall not be remembered, nor come
> into mind.

But be ye glad and rejoice for ever in that which I create: for, behold, I create Jerusalem a rejoicing, and her people a joy.

And I will rejoice in Jerusalem, and joy in my people: and the voice of weeping shall be no more heard in her, nor the voice of crying.

There shall be no more thence an infant of days, nor an old man that hath not filled his days: for the child shall die an hundred years old; but the sinner being an hundred years old shall be accursed.

And they shall build houses, and inhabit them; and they shall plant vineyards, and eat the fruit of them.

They shall not build, and another inhabit; they shall not plant, and another eat: for as the days of a tree are the days of my people, and mine elect shall long enjoy the work of their hands.

They shall not labour in vain, nor bring forth for trouble; for they are the seed of the blessed of the Lord, and their offspring with them.

And it shall come to pass, that before they call, I will answer; and while they are yet speaking, I will hear.

The wolf and the lamb shall feed together, and the lion shall eat straw like the bullock: and dust shall be the serpent's meat. They shall not hurt nor destroy in all my holy mountain, saith the Lord (Isaiah 65:17–25).

The prophet Nephi saw this same vision and described it in similar terms:

And then shall the wolf dwell with the lamb; and the leopard shall lie down with the kid, and the calf, and the young lion, and the fatling, together; and a little child shall lead them.

And the cow and the bear shall feed; their young ones shall lie down together; and the lion shall eat straw like the ox.

And the sucking child shall play on the hole of the asp, and the weaned child shall put his hand on the cockatrice's den.

They shall not hurt nor destroy in all my holy mountain; for the earth shall be full of the knowledge of the Lord as the waters cover the sea.

Wherefore, the things of all nations shall be made known; yea, all things shall be made known unto the children of men.

There is nothing which is secret save it shall be revealed; there is no work of darkness save it shall be made manifest in the light; and there is nothing which is sealed upon the earth save it shall be loosed.

Wherefore, all things which have been revealed unto the children of men shall at that day be revealed; and Satan shall have power over the hearts of the children of men no more, for a long time (2 Nephi 30:12–18).

Men will act for themselves during the Millennium, without excuse, and will receive in kind according to their actions.

The Little Season of Judgment and War

After the Millennium is over, there will follow what has been described as a "little season." Some have inferred that it will also last for a thousand years,[2] but the scriptures do not specifically define its length. During this time the righteous and the wicked will become strongly divided, but toward the end of the "season" they will gather to fight the last great battle of Gog and Magog (see Revelation 20:7–10; D&C 88:111–16).

The Battles of Gog and Magog: There are two great battles that will occur known as the battles of Gog and Magog. The terms

Gog and *Magog* are used symbolically in the scriptures to represent the armies and countries that will oppose the forces of good at two climatic points in history.[3] One battle will take place before the Second Coming and will lead to the battle at Armageddon. This will be an actual war conducted between armies and nations. The second battle will take place after the Millennium and at the end of the "little season." It will not involve actual warfare, but is merely a symbolic representation of the final conflict between the devil and his followers, and Michael (the archangel of God) and the righteous—a final conflict between good and evil.

In Ezekiel's description of the first battle of Gog and Magog, Gog appears to be the prince of a country identified as Magog. Gog and the armies from Magog come from the north (see Ezekiel 38:2), a land located adjacent to that of Togarmah (known as Armenia today; Ezekiel 38:6) and only a short distance from "the isles" (perhaps the maritime regions of Europe; Ezekiel 39:6). A large battle takes place between these armies and the people of Israel—armies that are armed with bows and arrows (see Ezekiel 39:3) and that have cavalry (see Ezekiel 38:15). While Ezekiel may initially be speaking of a battle that took place in his own time involving the Scythians,[4] he is also speaking in double-reference prophecy since he declares that this war will take place "in the latter days" (Ezekiel 38:16).

This latter-day war of Gog and Magog will occur just prior to the Second Coming (this war is also referred to by other Old Testament prophets besides Ezekiel).[5] It will lead to the Second Coming battle at Armageddon, where great earthquakes will ravage the land as the Lord destroys the armies of Gog and Magog in his fight for Israel. The battle will climax when the Mount of Olives splits in two and the Lord physically appears to save his people (Chapter 5). It is at the conclusion of this devastating battle that the Millennium will be ushered in.

When the Millennium ends, the devil will again be free upon the earth for a "little season." His main objective will be to "gather together his armies" one last time (D&C 88:110). John the Revelator saw this time and gave a brief description of it:

> And when the thousand years are expired, Satan shall be loosed out of his prison,
>
> And shall go out to deceive the nations which are in the four quarters of the earth, Gog and Magog, to gather them together to battle: the number of whom is as the sand of the sea.
>
> And they went up on the breadth of the earth, and compassed the camp of the saints about, and the beloved city: and fire came down from God out of heaven, and devoured them.
>
> And the devil that deceived them was cast into the lake of fire and brimstone, where the beast and the false prophet are, and shall be tormented day and night for ever and ever (Revelation 20:7–10).

From John's description of the second battle of Gog and Magog, it is evident that the devil will be as powerful and persuasive after the Millennium as he was before (Chapters 7 and 8). His motivation will also remain the same: to deceive men and lead them captive to his will (see Moses 4:4). His success will be great, for John describes those who follow him as being as numerous as the "sand of the sea." He will do all that he can to destroy the souls of men and thwart the Father's plan. To this end, he will gather his evil followers (described as armies) together as he did in the pre-existence and do battle against "the great God" (D&C 88:114).

While Satan gathers his forces, the Archangel Michael will also gather his armies together in preparation for battle. But this will not be a *war* in the sense of earthly wars—nor are these *armies* as we envision armies. This will not be a physical battle involving a force of arms. John's vision is symbolic. The conflict that will take place will be much like the premortal war in heaven where the angry disobedience of Lucifer and his followers was pitted against God and his plan of salvation (see Revelation 12:7). By the end of the little season, however, the plan will have reached its apex: the Saints of God will have been resurrected, and Michael will be gathering the righteous together to witness God's final and eternal expulsion of the wicked.

Both John the Revelator and Joseph Smith describe this climatic battle in abrupt terms. John states: "Fire came down from God out of heaven, and devoured them [the wicked]," and they were "cast into the lake of fire and brimstone . . . for ever and ever" (Revelation 20:9–10). Joseph calls Satan's armies the "hosts of hell" (D&C 88:113) and states: "And then cometh the battle of the great God; and the devil and his armies shall be cast away into their own place, that they shall not have power over the saints any more at all. For Michael shall fight their battles, and shall overcome him who seeketh the throne of him who sitteth upon the throne, even the Lamb" (D&C 88:114–115).

This final destruction of all wickedness is described by Joseph as "the glory of God, and the sanctified" (D&C 88:116). The devil and his followers will be cast down into a kingdom wherein there is *no* glory. They will live for eternity in this "outer darkness" where they will endure "everlasting punishment, which is eternal punishment," meaning "God's punishment" (D&C 19:3–12). They can never associate with the Father's glory again. The "end thereof, neither the place thereof, nor their torment, no man knows." And it is not revealed—nor will it ever be to any man— "except to them who are made partakers thereof" (D&C 76:44–46).

The final dismissal of Satan—he who would "ascend into heaven . . . [and] . . . exalt [his] throne above the stars of God" (Isaiah 14:13)—is succinctly described by Isaiah:

> Is this the man that made the earth to tremble, that did shake kingdoms;
>
> That made the world as a wilderness, and destroyed the cities thereof; that opened not the house of his prisoners?
>
> All the kings of the nations, even all of them, lie in glory, every one in his own house.
>
> But thou art cast out of thy grave like an abominable branch, and as the raiment of those that are slain, thrust through with a sword, that go down to the stones of the pit; as a carcase trodden under feet.

Thou shalt not be joined with them in burial, because thou hast destroyed thy land, and slain thy people: the seed of evildoers shall never be renowned.

Prepare slaughter for his children for the iniquity of their fathers; that they do not rise, nor possess the land, nor fill the face of the world with cities.

For I will rise up against them, saith the Lord of hosts, and cut off from Babylon the name, and remnant, and son, and nephew, saith the Lord (Isaiah 14:16–22).

The Resurrection

The body and the spirit make up the soul of man (see D&C 88:15). When we are born, the spirit and the body unite; at death, the spirit separates from the body and the body returns to the earth. Resurrection is the reuniting of body and spirit. With resurrection (the "redemption of the soul;" D&C 88:16), the reunited body and spirit will be "restored to its perfect frame" (Alma 11:44), "never to be divided" again (Alma 11:45). Alma describes this process as the restoration of the body to the spirit. He writes, "Yea, and every limb and joint shall be restored to its body; yea, even a hair of the head shall not be lost; but all things shall be restored to their proper and perfect frame" (Alma 40:23; D&C 29:25).

Because of the fall of Adam and Eve, all men and women born to this earth will eventually die. But through the death and resurrection of Christ, all mankind will be made alive again (see 1 Corinthians 15:22). Paul writes:

But now is Christ risen from the dead, and become the firstfruits of them that slept.

For since by man came death, by man came also the resurrection of the dead.

For as in Adam all die, even so in Christ shall all be made alive.

> But every man in his own order: Christ the firstfruits; afterward they that are Christ's at his coming.
>
> Then cometh the end, when he shall have delivered up the kingdom to God, even the Father; when he shall have put down all rule and all authority and power.
>
> For he must reign, till he hath put all enemies under his feet.
>
> *The last enemy that shall be destroyed is death.*
>
> . . . And when all things shall be subdued unto him, then shall the Son also himself be subject unto him that put all things under him, that God may be all in all (1 Corinthians 15:20–26, 28; emphasis added).

Before the final judgment is over, all men and women who have lived upon this earth—be they good or evil—will have been resurrected, and death will be destroyed thereby. Were it not so, the mission of Jesus Christ would be thwarted and the Father's plan of salvation defeated.

There are three resurrections of the just that are all considered part of the "first" resurrection.

1.   The first resurrection began with the resurrection of Jesus Christ and all the righteous who had died from the time of Adam up to the Savior's resurrection. This resurrection also includes certain righteous individuals (i.e., Peter, James, and Moroni) who died after Christ's resurrection because of the part they would play in the restoration of the gospel (see Alma 40:16–19).

2.   The second part of the first resurrection will occur at the Lord's Second Coming. This resurrection is symbolically described as beginning with the sounding of the "trump of God," which will awaken the Saints from death's slumber.[6] Michael (Adam), along with the angels of God, will gather the elect from the four winds (see Matthew 24:31), and it will be Michael who "plays" the trump and sounds the call to resurrection. "Then shall all the dead awake, for their graves shall be opened, and they shall come forth—yea, even all" (D&C 29:26).

3.   The third part of the first resurrection will continue intermittently throughout the Millennium (and perhaps the "little season") as the worthy Saints of that period reach the age of a "tree"
and are "changed [resurrected] in the twinkling of an eye" (D&C
101:31).

Only the righteous, those who have died in Christ, will be
blessed to come forth in the first resurrection (see D&C 29:13;
88:96–98). They are the "redeemed" of the Lord (see D&C 133:52)
who will "stand on the right hand of the Lamb" and be partakers
of his glory (see D&C 63:49; 133:53–56).

Isaiah foresaw the first resurrection, and in poetic prophesy
he declared: "Thy dead men shall live, together with my dead
body shall they arise. Awake and sing, ye that dwell in dust: for
thy dew is as the dew of herbs, and the earth shall cast out the
dead" (Isaiah 26:19). The souls he describes are those who will
inherit a celestial glory, those who receive the testimony of Jesus
Christ and keep his commandments. They are those who have
repented of their sins, have been baptized, have received the Holy
Ghost as their personal guide, and have been washed clean by
the blood of the Lord's Atonement. They are the men and women
who will be "sealed by the Holy Spirit of promise" to receive the
fulness of the Father's kingdom, and they will "dwell in the presence of God and his Christ forever and ever" (D&C 76:51–70;
88:17–28). All other men and women born to this earth will inherit a lesser glory—that of the terrestrial or telestial kingdoms—
according to the state of their righteousness. And some, who have
been wicked beyond redemption, will be cast into "outer darkness," where there is no glory at all.[7]

Thus, our faith, our knowledge, our works, and our repentance from sin will determine our reward.

The Final Judgment

Instead of calling this event the final judgment, it might be
more accurate to describe it as the time when all judgment will
become final, for as has been shown, judgment has been going on
in one form or another since the pre-existence, and it will continue to go on throughout the Millennium and the "little season."
Nevertheless, by the end of the little season, each soul born to

this earth will have appeared before the judgment seat of God to receive his or her just reward (see 2 Corinthians 5:10). Every man and woman will ultimately be judged according to his or her works, "whether they be good or whether they be evil" (Mosiah 3:24). They will be rewarded for their works—good for good and evil for evil—and both heaven and earth will bear witness to God's just and final judgment (see Psalm 50:4).

The final judgment is the time when the devil, his angels, and all who have chosen to follow him in this life will be cast forever into outer darkness (see Jude 1:6). Mosiah states that they will be "consigned to an awful view of their own guilt and abominations, which [will] cause them to shrink from the presence of the Lord into a state of misery and endless torment, from whence they can no more return . . . [because] they have drunk damnation to their own souls." As a result, they will receive no mercy from the Lord (see Mosiah 3:25–27).

Even the earth will receive a final judgment. It was initially created as part of the plan to give mankind a home, and when the plan has been completed the earth will receive its second and final transformation. It will "pass away so as by fire" (D&C 43:32), for by the end of the little season it will have fulfilled "the measure of its creation." It will be "crowned with glory, even with the presence of God the Father" (D&C 88:19), and it will become the celestial kingdom for those who are worthy to reside there. "For this intent was it made and created" (D&C 88:20).

The earth's final, glorified state is described by Joseph Smith in the Doctrine and Covenants:

"This earth, in its sanctified and immortal state, will be made like unto crystal and will be a Urim and Thummim to the inhabitants who dwell thereon, whereby all things pertaining to an inferior kingdom, or all kingdoms of a lower order, will be manifest to those who dwell on it; and this earth will be Christ's" (D&C 130:9).

> For all old things shall pass away, and all things
> shall become new, even the heaven and the earth,
> and all the fulness thereof, both men and beasts,
> the fowls of the air, and the fishes of the sea;

And not one hair, neither mote, shall be lost, for it
is the workmanship of mine hand (D&C 29:24–
25).

Marvelous things await the faithful followers of Jesus the
Messiah.

Conclusion

**"For as the light of the morning cometh out of
the east, and shineth even unto the west, and
covereth the whole earth, so shall also the
coming of the Son of Man be."**

Joseph Smith–Matthew 1:26

Ever since the Lord first appeared in the flesh, men and
women have looked for his Second Coming. In their yearning
for the choice lifestyle they believed the Second Coming would
provide, the Jews of Christ's time transposed the signs of his first
coming with those of his second, and when the blessings they
anticipated did not materialize, they rejected their Savior. Even
the Lord's Apostles could not forebear asking him when the Second Coming would be. However, only the Father knows when
the Lord will come again—and he is silent on this point. All we
have are the prophesied signs of Christ's Advent to make us vigilant, lest we be caught unawares when he arrives.

The exact *time* of the Savior's coming is not important, but
the *words* that prophesy of his coming are, for they will all be
fulfilled. "Heaven and earth shall pass away," he said, "but my
words shall not pass away" (Matthew 24:35). Every Second Coming prophecy recorded in scripture—during Old Testament times,

in the New Testament, or in the latter days—will come to pass. The description of these prophesied signs has been the purpose of this book, with the hope that mankind may better recognize and understand them when they occur.

The following eight facts consistently apply to Second Coming prophecies:

Fact Number One: The general signs that have been prophesied—wars, rumors of wars, earthquakes in diverse places, unusual weather patterns, etc.—were not given as *specific* indicators of when the Lord would come. Rather, they were given to make the believer constantly aware of the fact that the Savior *will* come. These general signs are timeless—each generation has had them and future generations will receive them. Why? To remind mankind of the need to be prepared to meet the Lord (Chapter 9).

Fact Number Two: Specific signs of the Savior's Second Coming identify specific events, and those pertaining to the latter days warn us that time is getting short. The believers who lived in the era following Christ's crucifixion witnessed the fulfillment of some of these specific signs; i.e., the destruction of Jerusalem and the razing of the temple of Herod. Their faith must have been bolstered when they saw these prophecies fulfilled. Later, the Great Apostasy and the Restoration occurred (both specific signs), and these led to the completion of the times of the Gentiles. From the time of the Savior's earthly mission forward there have been many specific, faith-promoting signs to mark the mileposts of his coming, and they will continue until the time of his Advent.

Fact Number Three: The tribe of Judah is part of the Lord's covenant people, and a close observation of its history and its prophesied future will reveal more signs of the Second Coming. It is the only known tribe of Israel which has continuously maintained its identity under the covenant of Abraham, and it will continue to retain this unique identity until the Lord comes again. Its success in maintaining this unity, however, has caused it (and the world's religions) to confuse its identity with that of the other tribes of Israel. The other eleven tribes are seldom considered. This has caused the world's religions to become confused when trying to unravel the meaning of the prophecies regarding Judah, the other eleven tribes, and Israel as a whole (Chapter 5).

Fact Number Four: One of the major signs of the Restoration and the Second Coming is the gathering of the righteous in the latter days. This sign is multifaceted: it involves the gathering of the tribe of Judah, the tribe of Joseph (both Ephraim and Manasseh), the nation of Israel as a whole, the ten lost tribes of Israel in particular, the Gentiles as a group, and the non-Gentile and non-Israel groups (generalized as the Arabs and people of African descent in this text). The doctrine of the gathering is one of the major evidences of the truthfulness of the restored gospel (Chapter 6).

Fact Number Five: The devil's influence and the establishment of his evil latter-day kingdom provide us with major signs of the Second Coming. The prophecies regarding these signs, however, tend to be *specifically general.* Why? Because while many of the prophecies describe specific events and identify specific entities, they are written symbolically. This makes them difficult to understand. Almost no other signs of the Second Coming are this difficult to specifically identify. Nonetheless, John the Revelator marveled when he witnessed Satan's influence (see Revelation 17:6–7), and Isaiah described the devil's intentions with contempt (see Isaiah 14:12–16). These prophetic comments make it clear that the prophecies concerning Lucifer are authentic (Chapters 7 and 8).

Fact Number Six: Three cities play a prominent part in the prophecies of the Second Coming: Jerusalem, Zion, and the City of Enoch.

Jerusalem, like the tribe of Judah, will play a major role in both the signs of the Second Coming and in the rule of Christ during the Millennium.

Zion was specifically identified by the Lord as being in Jackson County, Missouri, but because of severe persecution by the Missourians and disobedience by the Saints, the city was never established. Latter-day Saints look forward to the time when the Lord will establish this righteous city and allow it to fulfill its prophetic destiny—both at the Second Coming and during Christ's millennial reign.

The *City of Enoch* serves as an example of what can be accomplished by a righteous people. It will return to the earth at Christ's

Advent, and its inhabitants will participate in a joyous reunion of the righteous at the Second Coming (Chapter 13).

Fact Number Seven: A period of catastrophic devastation unparalleled in mankind's history will occur prior to the Second Coming. As terrible as these occurrences will be, however, most of mankind will not recognize them as signs of the Second Coming. They will consider them abnormalities that occur in an otherwise normal life cycle: "For as in the days that were before the flood," people will be "eating and drinking, marrying and giving in marriage," and will not pay attention to the signs until—as in the time of Noah—it is too late (Matthew 24:38). The wicked will be destroyed, and the earth itself will revolt and change its aspect in preparation for the Lord's Advent (Chapters 11 and 14).

Fact Number Eight: The plan of salvation decrees that the Savior come again to rule upon the earth, to judge all men, and to destroy evil forever. The plan also involves certain periods of time and entities that are so important that they merited discussion:

The Millennium: Christ will reign throughout the Millennium, and although he is the ultimate judge of all mankind, he will employ others to assist him in determining the eternal glory that each man and woman born to this earth will receive (Chapter 15).

The Little Season: At the beginning of the Millennium the devil and his angels will be restrained, unable to act upon mankind for a thousand years; thereafter, they will be loosed for a "little season" to pursue their evil course and ensnare all who will accept them. During this time, the devil and his disciples will gather together to do battle against righteousness. The righteous will also gather—to observe the final destruction and punishment of the wicked (Chapter 16).

The wicked: The wicked will be cast out into an eternal kingdom of darkness wherein the glory of the Father and that of the Light of the World, Jesus Christ, will never be seen. The literal battle that the devil and his kingdom will wage against Jerusalem at Armageddon, and the great ideological battle that will occur at the end of the "Little Season," are described in scripture as the battles and final destruction of Gog and Magog (Chapter 16).

The prophesied signs of the Second Coming have been given so that we might recognize the fact that the Savior *will* come in the not-too-distant future. The signs help us prepare, and they help us remain vigilant. The Savior does not want us caught with insufficient oil in our lamps. He gave us the parable of the ten virgins so that as members of the Church, we will clearly understand what can happen to us if our preparation is inadequate (see Matthew 25:1–13).[1] Remember, the five unprepared virgins had *some* oil! They were neither totally unprepared nor entirely unknowledgeable, and had the bridegroom come when *they* expected him, they would have participated in the joy of his kingdom. But the bridegroom tarried and only half of the virgins had sufficient oil to sustain them through the night. Does this literally mean that *only half of the Saints will endure to the end and be prepared to meet the Savior at his Second Coming*?

There are many reasons for unpreparedness. The Lord may come later than many people anticipate, causing them to falter and lose faith. Some will say that there will be no Second Coming, that there are no living prophets, that the scriptures are not true or are merely babblings of religious fanatics. Some will leave the strait and narrow path and follow after false Christs or false prophets, some will succumb to the ways of the world and allow their spiritual senses to become dulled to the truth, and still others will try to force the fulfillment of prophecy and will become disillusioned when the times they live in do not fit the signs of his coming. When the signs they anticipate are not fulfilled as they expect, they will become discouraged and fall by the wayside.

In these and many other ways, the oil that so many of us have so tediously acquired over the years will be wasted, used up, and when the cry is heard, "Behold, the bridegroom cometh; go ye out to meet him" (Matthew 25:6), we may or will have no reserves.

Waiting for the bridegroom requires faith, patience, and hard work. There is no question that recognizing the signs of the Savior's Second Coming can be very difficult—but the rewards are glorious! "The ransomed of the Lord shall return, and come to Zion with songs and everlasting joy upon their heads: they shall obtain joy and gladness, and sorrow and sighing shall flee away" (Isaiah 35:10). When that day comes we will greet the loved ones who parted the veil before us, we will fall upon each other's neck and weep for happiness, we will receive a *fulness* of joy, because we will live again, as Christ lives:

And love and life will be restored,
made perfect,
Free of pain,
Full of light,
Never to be parted again.[2]

How glorious is the Second Coming of Jesus the Messiah!

Notes

Introduction

1. Miracles p. 8.
2. Sermons p. 99.
3. Ed 2:28.

Chapter 1: "All These Are the Beginning of Sorrows"

1. Sermons p. 203.
2. MM 3:408.
3. For example, see Acts 5:36; 8:9; and 21:38, where individuals claimed authority that they did not have, and Revelation 2:2, 9, in which some claimed to be the Lord's Apostles when they were not, or "representative" Jews when they were not.
4. Josephus, Wars II:13:4–5; Antiquities XX:5; 8:10.
5. Jerusalem pp. 128–29.
6. Josephus, Wars, Preface, Books I–VII.
7. CC p. 259 et. seq.
8. Josephus, Wars V:4.
9. Josephus, Wars VI:3:4.
10. Ed 1:120.
11. Sermons p. 214.
12. Some remnants of the lost tribes are identified in the New Testament: Elizabeth, the mother of John the Baptist was from the tribe of Levi (see Luke 1:5); Anna the prophetess was from the tribe of Asher (see Luke 2:36); and Paul declared that he was from the tribe of Benjamin (see Philippians 3:5). There were undoubtedly others.
13. AGQ 1:142.

Chapter 2: The Great Apostasy

1. Miracles p. 131.
2. CC p. 577.
3. CHCC p. 27.
4. CHCC p. 43.
5. CHCC p. 39.
6. CHCC p. 40.
7. CHCC p. 44.

8. CHCC p. 51.

9. CHCC p. 50.

10. CC p. 664; CHCC p. 50.

11. CC p. 559.

12. CHCC p. 46.

13. CHCC p. 11.

14. CHCC p. 45.

15. "We believe in one God, the Father almighty, maker of all things visible and invisible; and in one Lord Jesus Christ, the Son of God, begotten from the Father, only-begotten, that is, from the substance of the Father, God from God, light from light, true God from true God, begotten not made, of one substance with the Father, through Whom all things came into being, things in heaven and things on earth, Who because of us men and because of our salvation, came down and became incarnate, becoming man, suffered and rose again on the third day, ascended into heaven, and will come to judge the living and the dead; And in the Holy Spirit.

But as for those who say, there was when He was not, and, before being born He was not, and that He came into existence out of nothing, or, who assert that the Son of God is of a different hypostasis or substance, or is created, or is subject to alteration or change—these the Catholic Church anathematizes" CE IV, p. 435.

16. "We believe in one God, the Father almighty, maker of heaven and earth, of all things visible and invisible; and in one Lord Jesus Christ, the only begotten Son of God, begotten from the Father before all ages, light from light, true God from true God, begotten not made, of one substance with the Father, through Whom all things came into existence; Who because of our salvation came down from heaven, and was incarnate from the Holy Spirit and the Virgin Mary and became man, and was crucified for us under Pontius Pilate, and suffered and was buried, and rose again on the third day according to the Scriptures, and ascended to heaven, and sits on the right hand of the Father, and will come again with glory to judge living and dead, of Whose kingdom there will be no end; and in the Holy Spirit, the Lord and life-giver, Who proceeds from the Father, Who with the Father and the Son is together worshipped and together glorified, Who spoke through the prophets; in one holy Catholic and apostolic Church. We confess one baptism to the remission of sins; we look forward to the resurrection of the dead, and the life of the world to come. Amen" CE IV, p. 435.

17. CC p. 595.

18. HC 2:193. For the complete charge to the restored Twelve, see HC 2:193–98.

Chapter 3: The Times of the Gentiles

1. See also Exodus 29:45; Leviticus 26:12; 2 Samuel 7:24; Ezekiel 14:11; Romans 9:4.

2. CHCC p. 168.

3. CHCC p. 168.
4. CHCC p. 11.
5. CHCC p. 223.
6. CHCC pp. 236, 238, 247.
7. Miracles pp. 45–49.

Chapter 4: The Restoration

1. HC 3:51.
2. The ten kingdoms and the approximate time of their organization after the fall of Rome are: Italy (496), France (752), England (830), Belgium (865), Holland (922), Austria (1158), Portugal (1138), Prussia (Germany) (1139), Spain (1471), and Greece (1828).
3. ER p. 197, wherein John A. Widtsoe states that every President of the Church is the seer "like as Moses."
4. Revelation 14:6–7; D&C 20:6–12; 133:36.
5. HC 1:75.
6. Parables p. 30.
7. 2 Nephi 30:8; 3 Nephi 25:5–6; D&C 2:1; 35:4; 113:6; 124:58; 128:17; 128:19–21; Joseph Smith–History 1.

Chapter 5: Judah

1. HC 4:456–57.
2. HC 4:459.
3. GM p. 23.
4. AIC p. 21.
5. GM p. 210; OJ pp. 17–18, 29–39.
6. GM p. 226.
7. Zechariah 10:6, 12; 1 Nephi 19:13–17; 2 Nephi 10:7–8; Ether 13:11–12; D&C 110:11.
8. GM p. 105.
9. HC 4:457.
10. GM p. 23.
11. JD 15:277; see also WW p. 509.
12. GM p. 214.
13. Jeremiah 31:31–34; 1 Nephi 10:14; 2 Nephi 6:11; 3 Nephi 20:29–31.
14. JD 18:111.
15. See also Deuteronomy 10:8; Malachi 3:3; 3 Nephi 24:3; D&C 84:31; 124:39; 128:24; HC 4:211.
16. Ezekiel 38:1–7, 9, 13; Joel 3:1–21; Zechariah 14:1–21; Revelation 11:1–13; D&C 45:26–27.
17. IDYK p. 197.
18. DNTC 3:509.

19. Torah p. 593.
20. See also JD 16:329 (Orson Pratt).
21. Isaiah 54:15–17; Jeremiah 30:3–9; Zechariah 14:3; 3 Nephi 22:12, 15–17; JD 15:277–78.
22. HC 4:457.
23. Torah p. 309.
24. Isaiah 55:3–4; Jeremiah 23:5–8; Ezekiel 37:24–28; Hosea 3:4–5; Zechariah 12:6–9.
25. Joel 3:14; D&C 45:48; 133:20; .
26. Zechariah 14:9; 2 Nephi 6:14–15; D&C 133:41–42; Charles W. Penrose, "The Second Advent," MS 21:582–83.
27. Hebrews 12:22; D&C 133:19–24.

Chapter 6: The Gathering

1. Torah p. 526.
2. Torah p. 431.
3. An example of this nondefinitive use of both the words *Jew* and *Gentile* is in the title page of the Book of Mormon where it states that it came forth "to the convincing of the Jew and Gentile that Jesus is the Christ." There are numerous such uses throughout all the scriptures.
4. HC 1:176 ftnt.
5. See also Isaiah 43:6; 49:12; Jeremiah 23:8; 31:8; Zechariah 10:10; Ether 13:11.
6. See also Isaiah 35:8–10; 51:11; Jeremiah 31:10–14; D&C 66:11.
7. See also Isaiah 35:1–2; 2 Nephi 30:6; 3 Nephi 21:22–25; D&C 3:20; 30:6; 109:65.
8. See also Isaiah 11:11; 1 Nephi 22:4; 2 Nephi 10:8, 20; 29:7.
9. HC 2:492.
10. HC 2:XXVII.
11. HC 6:12.
12. HC 2:254.
13. HC 1:315.
14. Isaiah 2:2–3; 10:20–22; 11:11, 13; 13:2–4; 14:1–3; 30:18–25; 33:17–24; 40:27–31; 43:5–7; 49; 52:2–3, 6–7; 62.
15. Jeremiah 3:17–18; 23:3–8; 31; 32:37–44; 50:4–6.
16. Ezekiel 11:16–20; 20:34–38; 34:11–19; 36:16–38; 37:1–14, 16–22.
17. Micah 2:12; 4:6–7; 5:3.
18. Joel 2:32; Zephaniah 3:14–21; Zechariah 8:4–7, 12–13; 10:6–12; 14:10–11.
19. 1 Nephi 15:14; 22:11–12; 3 Nephi 5:24–26; chapters 20–21.
20. See D&C Index, s.v. Gather, Gathering.

Chapter 7: The Devil and His Kingdom

1. See Moses 4; Genesis 3, while the devil was in the garden of Eden; the temptations of Moses, Moses 1:12–24; the temptations of Jesus, Matthew 4:1–11; Mark 1:12–13; Luke 4:1–13.
2. HC 1:5.
3. HC 1:82–83.
4. HC 1:175 ftnt; 2:352.
5. HC 1:182.
6. HC 3:LIX–LXII.
7. HC 3:68.
8. HC 1:109.
9. HC 2:140.
10. HC 2:139–141.
11. HC 3:178–179.
12. HC 1:203.
13. HC 3:391.
14. HC 3:392.
15. HC 2:352.
16. HC 4:608.
17. HC 1:146.
18. HC 5:36–40.
19. HC 5:24.
20. HC 4:358.
21. See Isaiah 24–27; Ezekiel 1; 9–10; 38; 40; Daniel 7–12; Zechariah 9–14.

Chapter 8: The Devil and His Kingdom-Continued

1. The *tefillin* are small boxes with leather straps to attach to hand and forehead. The box contains parchments of scripture. They are worn during morning worship, *The Torah* p. 1367.
2. CC pp. 63–64.
3. CC p. 388.
4. See Isaiah 62:5; Hosea 2:18-23; Matthew 9:15; 25:1; John 3:29; Revelation 19.
5. Isaiah 5:24–25; 13:14–22; 14:17–32; 18:4–6; 24:1–18; 65:1–16; 66:3–4, 15–18; D&C 112:24–26; Joseph Smith–Matthew 1:31.
6. Deuteronomy 32:21; 2 Nephi 15:25; Moses 6:27.
7. Psalm 72:4; Ezekiel 5:9–12; 38:22; Joel 1:19–20; 2:3; Zephaniah 1:2–3; Malachi 4:1; D&C 45:40–41; 97:25–26; 101:24.
8. Jeremiah 8:13; Zechariah 14:12; Matthew 3:12; 2 Nephi 26:6; D&C 29:3, 9, 21; 45:57; 63:34; 64:24; 88:94; 101:23–25, 66.

Chapter 9: Signs: Both General and Specific

1. Torah p. 61 emphasis added.
2. Torah p. 61.
3. Torah pp. 133–34.
4. Torah p. 135.
5. Parables pp. 121.
6. Such circumstances were prophesied by several other prophets as well with both specific and general reference as to upon whom it would occur. See Isaiah 18:6; Jeremiah 15:3; Ezekiel 39:17–20; Revelation 19:17–18.
7. HC 4:11.
8. Parables p. 101, 107.

Chapter 10: Signs: The Earth's Three Phases

1. See Judges 5:1–5 where Deborah and Barak used the phrase in their song of praise to God after their military victories and Moses 6:34 where Enoch was blessed with the power to cause mountains to flee before him.
2. Because many of the visions John saw were also seen in full or in part by other prophets, Revelation 7–22 should be read in conjunction with Isaiah 24–27; Daniel 7–12; and Zechariah 9–14 to get their perspective.
3. HC 4:414–15.
4. CC pp. 457–58.
5. *The National Geographic,* May 1986; June 1992 (map).
6. Torah p. 1538.
7. Other visions and scriptures also refer to these events. See Joel 3:12–14; D&C 76:107; 88:106; 133:46–51.
8. There are seven seals, two sets of seven angels and four angels of destruction in John's Revelation. First the seven seals are opened. After the seventh seal is opened the seven trumpet angels are released. The seventh trumpet angel releases the seven angels with vials. The sixth trumpet angel releases the four angels of destruction which give John the vision of the last great war.
9. Miracles p. 175.
10. WTB p. 33.
11. WTB p. 58.
12. WTB p. 105.
13. NBC Evening News 2/27/00.
14. Mission p. 179.
15. Isaiah 24:6; Nahum 1:5; 1 Nephi 22:15; D&C 29:9; 63:34; 64:24.
16. Mission p. 75.
17. DNTC 3:499.
18. Isaiah 10:16–19; Malachi 3:1–6; 4:1–6; 2 Thessalonians 1:7–8; D&C 133:41, 64.
19. Parables p. 150.

Chapter 11: Signs: Increased Devastations

1. Joel 1:19–20; D&C 45:40–41; 97:26.
2. Genesis 19:28; 1 Nephi 19:11; 3 Nephi 10:13; Mormon 8:29; D&C 87:6.
3. HC 3:390.
4. HC 3:391.
5. See Bible Dictionary p. 789.
6. HC 3:XLI.
7. HC 3:XVIII.
8. HC 3:LXIII.

Chapter 12: Six Signs: Beginning with the Church

1. Parables p. 150.
2. Parables p. 139.
3. HC 6:196.
4. Isaiah 13:10; Joel 2:10; 3:15; Acts 2:19–20; D&C 29:14; 34:9; 45:42; 88:87; Joseph Smith–Matthew 1:33.
5. Isaiah 24:23; D&C 133:49.
6. Isaiah 60:19–20; Revelation 21:23; 22:5.
7. Acts 2:19; Revelation 6:12; D&C 29:14; 34:9; 45:42.
8. D&C 88:87.
9. Joel 2:10.
10. Isaiah 13:10; D&C 133:49; Joseph Smith–Matthew 1:33.
11. Isaiah 24:23.
12. Revelation 6:13; D&C 29:14; 34:9; 45:42; Joseph Smith–Matthew 1:33.
13. Joel 2:10; 3:15; Revelation 8:12; D&C 34:9.
14. D&C 88:87.
15. HC 6:254.
16. HC 6:254.
17. HC 3:35.
18. HC 3:388.
19. HC 3:386–387.

Chapter 13: The Three Cities

1. HC 4:541.
2. HC 1:189.
3. HC 1:196.
4. HC 1:199.
5. HC 1:358–359.
6. HC 3:175.
7. HC 3:LXIII.

8.   Junius F. Wells, *Improvement Era,X* "A Prophecy and Its Fulfillment," November, 1902, p. 9.

9.   FM p. 14.

10.   HC 3:208.

11.   AC p. 360.

12.   AC p. 351.

13.   AC p. 342.

14.   AC p. 348.

15.   TPJS p. 17.

16.   HC 1:199.

17.   HC 1:359 et seq.

18.   HC 2:239.

19.   Jerusalem p. 9.

20.   Jerusalem p. 9.

21.   Jerusalem p. 13.

22.   Jerusalem p. 320. Orson Hyde's dedicatory prayer date inserted in italics.

23.   Jerusalem pp. 128–29.

Chapter 14: The Coming of the Lord

1.   Parables p. 139.

2.   David uses it when he says the Lord will make his enemies "as a fiery oven" in the time of his anger (Psalm 21:8–10), Nahum says the wicked will be "devoured as stubble" (Nahum 1:10), Nephi uses the descriptive words of Malachi and Nahum (see 1 Nephi 22:15,23), Isaiah warns earth's inhabitants that the Lord will burn them with "flames of fire" (Isaiah 24:6; 66:15–16), Joseph Smith recorded that those who tithe "shall not be burned" (D&C 64:23; emphasis added; see also Malachi 3:10), and the Lord also used the example in the terms of Malachi both to the Book of Mormon people (see 3 Nephi 25:1) and in the restoration warnings (see Malachi 4:1; D&C 64:24; Joseph Smith–History 1:37).

3.   Mill M p. 382.

4.   Revelation 21:8; D&C 29:28; 43:33; 63:54.

5.   Other descriptions of the wicked and warnings of their eventual destruction are couched in terms such as those who "watch for iniquity" and seek "opportunity" to do evil. They will be "brought to naught." "Calamity shall cover the mocker" and the "scorner [will] be consumed." All of these will be "hewn down and cast into the fire." (See Isaiah 29:20; D&C 45:50.)

6.   That the Lord in his wrath will take vengeance upon and destroy the wicked is found in many scriptures (see Revelation 6:16; D&C 1:9; 29:17; 43:26). The Lord spoke through Ezekiel to give a type and warning to future wickedness as he condemned the kingdom of Judah for their refusal to repent, thinking they could hide their evil (Ezekiel 21:31–32). And even the

writer of Proverbs, while praising the righteous, warns that mere "riches" will "profit not in the day of wrath" (see Proverbs 11:4–8).

7. The plagues of Egypt were: blood (see Exodus 7:19); frogs (see Exodus 8:2); lice (see Exodus 8:16, 18); flies (see Exodus 8:21); grievous murrain (see Exodus 9:3); boils and blains (see Exodus 9:9); hail (see Exodus 9:18); fire along the ground (see Exodus 9:23); locusts (see Exodus 10:14); thick darkness (see Exodus 10:22); and death of the firstborn both of man and beast (see Exodus 11:5).

8. Sermons p. 211.

9. CL p. 13–14.

10. CL p. 14.

11. HC 5:326.

12. CL p. 14.

13. *The Phoenix Gazette*, October 30, 1995, Paul Brinkley-Rogers. Page A1, "Children of Light Only 7 Left as Shaker-Like Commune Fades Away."

14. GRF: particularly chapter 14.

15. HC 2:182.

16. HC 5:336–37.

17. JD 14:5, January 1, 1871; JD 18:37, June 27, 1875; MS 51:595–96, July 29, 1889; CR p. 57, April 1898.

18. Deseret News, June 15, 1901.

19. JD 19:161.

20. Parables p. 150.

21. Joseph Smith stated that the "devil knows many signs, but does not know the sign of the Son of Man, or Jesus" (HC 4:608).

22. HC 5:337.

Chapter 15: Judgment

1. TPJS p. 365.

2. Alma 1:29; Helaman 6:17; 12:1–2; 4 Nephi 1:23. Generally assumed and proclaimed throughout *The Book of Mormon* record.

3. Helaman 13:20–21, 31–33; Mormon 1:18.

4. Farrar 2:80.

5. Ed 2:178–79.

6. Geikie 2:298.

7. Miracles p. 73.

8. See Matthew 7:1–5; Mark 2:1–12; John 5:1–14; 8:4–11.

9. HC 5:388.

10. HC 402–3; 5:389.

11. HC 6:363.

12. *The Random House Dictionary* (New York: Ballantine Books, 1978).

13. Parables p. 150.

14. Parables p. 101.

15. Sermons p. 145.

16. Mission p. 155.
17. Parables p. 30.
18. See also D&C 64:40; 107:72, 75.

Chapter 16: Millennial Peace, War, and Resurrection

1. DS 1:86.
2. DS 1:81.
3. The first mention of the name *Magog* is in Genesis. It is the name of the second son of Japheth (see Genesis 10:2). The first mention of *Gog* is in 1 Chronicles (1Chronicles 5:4). It is the name of the son of Shemaiah from the tribe of Reuben. These referenced names have nothing to do with the battles being described.
4. *Smith's Bible Dictionary* p. 375.
5. See Zephaniah 3:8–20; Zechariah 12–14;Revelation 16:16; D&C 29:21.
6. D&C 43:18; 45:45; 49:23.
7. See D&C 76:25–38, 43–49; 88:99–102.

Conclusion

1. Parables p. 150.
2. Excerpt from a poem by Gail Howick.

Subject Index

-A-

Aaronic Priesthood, restored by John the Baptist, 41

Abraham, Covenant of, chosen people part of, 24; explained, 23;, parts of, 24; Priesthood part of, 24; promised land part of, 24; reestablished, 41; responsibilities of accepting, 25; restored by Elias, 42; withdrawal of brings times of the Gentiles, 26

Adam-ondi-Ahman, council at prior to Second Coming, 176

Age of Enlightenment, brought about through Protestantism, 27

Angel, opening of the seventh seal by, 130; the seven with trumpets, 132; the seven with vials, 144

Apostasy, development approach of early brings, 19; good times sin of described, 28; lack of central authority brings, 18; sign of Second Coming, 17

Apostles, apostasy began during early ministry of, 17; disappearance of brought apostasy, 18; false in early church, 18; first signs regarding, 9; judgment of at Second Coming, 226; true church must be founded on, 21

Arabs, to be gathered, 68

Armageddon, first battle of Gog and Magog leads to, 235

Army, John describes the last great against Judah, 137

Ascension, first signs begin after, 10

Authority, lack of central brings apostasy, 18

-B-

Babylon, devil's kingdom as, 73; "Mystery," as used by John the Revelator, 82, 98

Balfour, James Arthur, initiates homeland moves for Judah, 48

Balfour Declaration, fulfills prophesy concerning Judah, 48

Beelzebub Argument, Protestantism similar alternative argument of, 27

Beast, the Antichrist, leader of the devil's latter-day kingdom, 81; seen by Daniel also, 84

Beast, image of the, 90; mark of, 92; the second, of Revelation representing the devil's false prophet, 89

Bible, Book of Mormon needed to confirm truths of, 39; used as excuse to reject Book of Mormon, 39

Blood, hail and fire mingled with, 133

Book of Mormon, Bible used as excuse to reject, 39; needed to confirm Bible truths, 39; restoration of foreseen by ancient prophets, 39; sign of beginning of restoration, 38; witness of divinity of Christ, 39

-C-

Calling and election, to damnation 220; to exaltation, 219

Calvin, John, architect of Protestantism, 31; religions from mixed blessing, 31

Chosen, anyone can become, 25; to be, is part of Covenant of Abraham, 24

Christ, Jesus, appears to Judah at Second Coming, 56; the Bridegroom cometh, 210; coming of, 199; date of coming prophesied by Father Miller, 207; is David that will lead Judah in last days, 55; delayeth his coming, 201; dressed in red at his coming, 212; latter-day prophets prophesy of time of his coming, 208; Sign of the Son of Man, 211; Transfiguration of compared to earth's Paradisiacal glory, 150; two major events of prophesied, 1; when will the Lord come?, 203; year of coming prophesied by Joseph Smith, 208

Children of Light await his coming, 207

Christianity, adopted paganism, 20; Constantine determined to unify early, 19; conversion stories of Constantine to, 19

Church, began predominately Jewish, 17; dissention in early, 17; development approach of early brings apostasy, 19; prophesied would fall away, 17

Church of Jesus Christ of Latter-day Saints, called out of the wilderness, 41; cleansing prior to Second Coming begins with, 166; members of commanded to gather, 65; true church must claim authority to gather Israel, 59

Cities, facts concerning, 245; three involved in the Second Coming, 181

Civil War, as beginning of wars and rumors of war, 158

Constantine, calls Council of Nicaea, 19; conversion of at death, 19; conversion stories of, 19; determined to unify Christianity, 19

Constantinople, Council of, called in 381 A.D., 20; Creed of, 20

Creed, of Constantinople, 20; of Nicaea, 20

-D-

Daniel, foresees restoration of gospel, 35; interprets Nebuchadnezzar's dream, 36; prophesies of end of Jerusalem and daily sacrifice, 13

Dark Ages, enlightenment creeps into, 27; Protestantism loosens grip of, 27

Darkness, plague of the fifth angel with a vial on the seat of the beast, 146

David, another to lead Judah, 55

Day, great and terrible of the Lord, 198

Devastations, facts about the signs of, 246; of the final cleansing of the earth, 154

Devil, Antichrist beast of latter-day kingdom, 83; calling and election to damnation, 220; counterfeit doctrines, 78; destruction of the righteous is intent of, 99; end of latter-day kingdom of described, 104; failed first estate, 75; fights for dominion of people, 22; final destruction of, 237; future of, 79; gathers his forces for battle of Gog and Magog, 235; John the Revelator describes terms of kingdom of, 81; Joseph Smith rarely taught on, 78; kingdom of not a particular church, 79; latter-day kingdom is economic, 94; past of described, 74; plague on the seat of the beast, 146; presence in the latter-days described, 76; rebelled against God, 75; second beast of his kingdom as seen by John the Revelator, 88; signs concerning, are specifically general, 244; signs of kingdom of, 73; was in preexistence with God, 74; what is the latter-day kingdom of?, 85; who is?, 73; woman represents kingdom of, 97

Dinoflagellate, as a plague on the fresh waters, 145

-E-

Earth, cleansing of, 132; desolating scourge used for cleansing of, 154; returns to its Paradisiacal glory, 149; three phases of, 127; tumults to, 128

Earthquakes, and the Mount of Olives, 56; plague of the seventh angel with a vial, 148

Economics, latter-day kingdom of the devil is based on, 94

Elias, restores Covenant of Abraham, 42

Elijah, restores sealing power, 42

Enoch, prophet, 183

Enoch, city of, sign concerning the Second Coming, 183

Ephraim, must be gathered, 65

Euphrates, plague of the sixth angel with a vial on, 147

-F-

False, Christs and prophets, 11, false prophet of devil's kingdom in the latter-days, 89

Fire, great mountain burning with, 134; used as description, 150

-G-

Gathering, allegory on, 60; Church members commanded to, 66; dedicatory prayer of Orson Hyde for Judah, 45; fact of sign concerning, 245; five groups must be, 63; of Gentiles (including Arabs and Blacks), 68; Golda Meir's comment on of Judah, 46; Isaiah prophesies of Judah, 47; of Judah begins, 45; sign of, 58; stakes in Church designated as places for, 68; true church must claim authority to, 59; twelve tribes to be, 59

General signs, reason for giving, 244

Generation, each try to fit signs in current events, 5

Gentiles, definition of, 60; did not influence apostasy on Western Hemisphere, 21; end of times of 31; gathering of, 68; restoration of gospel a marvelous work among, 38; spiritual darkness of prophesied of, 28; times of begin, 23; times of began when Covenant of Abraham withdrawn, 26; to be a scourge to descendants of Joseph, 30; warned to be righteous in America, 28

Gog and Magog, battles of described, 234; first battle of leads to Armageddon, 235

Good times sin, described, 28

Gospel, devil's counterfeit doctrines of, 78; John the Revelator sees restoration of, 37; restoration of fulfilled times of Gentiles, 31; restoration of predicted by Nebuchadnezzar's dream, 37; restored, 42

Grass, destroyed by angel with
     trumpet, 133
Great and Abominable Church,
     not a actual church, 79;
     represented as a woman by
     John the Revelator, 97

-H-

Hailstorm, plague of, 160; used by
     Lord for destruction, 160;
     weight of hail described, 161;
Heavens, signs of the Second
     Coming in, 173; third part
     affected by angel with
     trumpet, 135
Hitler, Third Reich destruction
     predicted by Isaiah, 49
Holy Roman Empire, controls
     spirituality, 26; rises from
     ashes of fall of Rome, 26
Hyde, Orson, dedicates Palestine
     for return of Judah, 45; prayer
     on Mount of Olives, 45

-I-

Indulgences, cult of sanctioned in
     apostasy, 27
Isaiah, foresaw apostasy of Israel,
     22; prophesies of gathering of
     Judah, 50
Israel, acceptance of gospel makes
     part of, 25; scattering began in
     721 B.C., 14; Jews incorrectly
     identified as entire tribes of,
     59; prophesied scattering of,
     15; State of created by UN, 48

-J-

Jerusalem, becomes part of State of
     Israel, 49; city of as sign of
     Second Coming, 192; first
     prophesies of destruction of,
     12; history of, 192; Isaiah's

description of glorified, 196;
     to be a "burdensome stone for
     all people," 15; to be trodden
     down by Gentiles, 30; temple
     to be built in, 51; to fall again
     by war, 52; two prophets to be
     raised up in, 52
Judah, another David to lead, 55;
     confusion of signs concerning,
     244; diaspora of ended with
     restoration, 45; future signs to,
     50; Golda Meir's comment on
     gathering of, 46; Hitler's
     Third Reich holds Judah as
     "prey" of the mighty, 49; keys
     to gather restored, 45; Lord
     appears to at Second Coming,
     56; Orson Hyde dedicates
     Palestine for return of, 45;
     promised land restored to, 57;
     prophesies concerning, 44;
     scattered by Rome, 44; signs
     of that have been fulfilled, 45;
     State of Israel created as
     homeland, 48; substituted for
     Israel in gathering scriptures,
     59; to be spiritually enlight-
     ened, 51; two prophets to be
     raised up to, 53; USSR holds
     Judah as "prey" of the mighty,
     49
Judgment, by Apostles at Second
     Coming, 226; by the Bishop,
     228; books of, 221; calling and
     election, 219; at death, 224;
     delegated, 226; during the
     Little Season, 237; final, 240;
     by the Elders, 228; on the
     earth, 218; faith determines,
     222; Millennial, 230; by
     Nephite disciples, 227; in the
     preexistence, 216; recom-
     pensed to everyone in kind,
     222; at the Second Coming,
     225

-K-

Keys, of gospel restored, 42

-L-

Laborers, the last as a sign, 172
Lamanites, must be gathered, 64; to be scattered by Gentiles, 28
Land, promised, America is 68; part of Covenant of Abraham, 24; established in restoration, 41; State of Israel is Judah's, 63
Latter-days, begin, 35
Little Season, of judgement and war, 234
Lost ten tribes, information on, 63; must be gathered, 63; who are they, 59
Luther, Martin, religions from mixed blessing, 27; revolts against Holy Roman Empire, 27

-M-

Mankind, effects of the signs on, 121
Mark, as used by John the Revelator, 82; as worn by the Jews, 93; of the beast, 92; of God, 93
Mathias, called to replace Judas Iscariot, 21
Meir, Golda, comment on gathering of Judah, 46
Melchizedek Priesthood, restored, 41
Millennium, judgment during, 230; knowledge expanded in, 231; pure language in, 231; Satan cannot tempt during, 231; Zion and Jerusalem world capitals during, 232
Missouri, Independence, city of Zion, 67, 161; punishment for destroying Zion, 189
Moroni, appears to Joseph Smith, 39

Moses, restores keys of gathering, 42
Moon, signs concerning prior to Second Coming, 135, 174
Mount of Olives, earthquakes and, 56; Orson Hydes' prayer on, 45
Mountain, burning with fire, 134
Mystery Babylon, representative of the devil's latter-day kingdom, 97

-N-

Nations, distress of described by Isaiah, 162; signs and destruction of prior to Second Coming, 161; uses to punish Israel, 162; general sign of Second Coming, 163
Nebuchadnezzar, dream of interpreted by Daniel, 35
Nicaea, Council of, Constantine calls to unify Christianity, 19; Creed of, 20
Noah, coming like as in the days of, 3, 115

-O-

Olives, Mount of, earthquakes and, 56; Orson Hydes' prayer on, 45
One hundred and forty-four thousand, knowledge about, 171; selected from each tribe of Israel, 170; sign of, 170

-P-

Paganism, early Christianity adopted, 20
Palestine, Israel created from, 48; to become productive, 49; UN votes to partition, 48
Paradisiacal Glory, as a burning, 149; earth to return to, 150; what is?, 149

Paul, Apostolic call of, 21

Perfect, to be part of Covenant of Abraham, 25

Plagues, of the seven angels with vials, 144; on the fresh waters, 145; noisome and grievous sores, 144; on the seas, 144

Pope, developed as supreme authority of Western Christendom, 20

Priesthood, part of Covenant of Abraham, 24; restored by John the Baptist, 41

Prophesies, of Columbus fulfilled, 27; of false Christs and prophets, 11; of Judah, 44; of Puritans fulfilled, 27; of scattering of Israel, 13; of Second Coming begin, 9; of United States of America fulfilled, 27; of wars, 11

Prophets, raised up to Judah, 52; devil's latter-day false, 89

Protestantism, brings Age of Enlightenment, 27; divides into various religions, 27; John Calvin architect of, 27; loosens grip on Dark Ages, 27

-R-

Rainbow, sign of prior to Second Coming, 175

Red, color of Christ's vesture at his coming, 212

Red Tides, as a plague of the third angel with a vial, 145

Restoration, begins, 38; Book of Mormon sign of beginning of, 40; foreseen by Daniel, 37; fulfilled the times of the Gentiles, 31; John the Revelator sees, 37; prophesied of, 17

Resurrection, discussion of first, 225

Revelation, book of, definations of terms used by John in, 81

Righteous, destruction of intent of the devil, 99

Rome, becomes center of Christianity, 20; fall of brings intellectual darkness, 26; persecution on early church, 19

-S-

Sacrifice, daily prophesied to end, 12; to be restored to Judah, 51

Scattering, of Israel prophesied of, 14; of Judah, 14; remnant of Joseph to Western Hemisphere, 15

Scourge, desolating used for cleansing of the earth, 154

Second Coming, all signs concerning will occur, 247; eight facts of the signs of, 244; first signs of, 9; Lord appears to Judah at, 56

Sign of the Son of Man, discussed, 211; Jews wanted at first coming, 2

Signs, Adam-ondi-Ahman, 176; as in the days of Noah, 136; beginning of, 9; beginning with the Church, 165; changing of times and seasons, 124; City of Enoch, 183; City of Jerusalem, 192; City of Zion, 186; cleansing of the earth, 129; concerning Judah (see Judah); desolating scourge, 154; devastations as cleansings, 154; dressed in red, 212; earthquake by the seventh angel with a vial, 148; earth's three phases, 127; effects of on mankind, 121; on the Euphrates river, 147; facts that consistently apply to, 244; first of Second Coming, 9; general and specific, 113; good times sin, 28, 116; of the great Apostasy, 16; the great

and terrible day of the Lord,
198; great heat, 150; hailstorm
plague, 160; in the heavens,
173; John describes the last
great army against Judah, 52,
138; lack of faith problem of
the last days, 202; last great
war, 137; the Lord delayeth
his coming, 201; last laborers,
172; on the nations, 161; one
hundred and forty-four
thousand, 170; the rainbow,
175; on the seat of the beast,
146; seven angels with vials
full of plagues, 144; the seven
trumpet angels, 132; the three
cities of the Second Coming,
181; temple to be built in
Zion; 191; tumults to the
earth, 128; wars and rumors
of, 157

Sin, good times, described, 28, 116

Smith, Joseph, compared to
Moses, 38; first vision of 38;
prophesied of, 38; prophesied
the year of the Lord's coming,
208; rarely taught on Devil,
78; receives keys to gather
Israel, 42; vision of Moroni,
39; work of restoration begins
with birth of, 38

Specific signs, reason for giving,
244

Stars, signs concerning prior to
Second Coming, 174

Sun, plague of the fourth angel
with a vial on, 146; signs in
prior to Second Coming, 135,
174

-T-

Tefillin, wearing of the law, 93

Temple, of destruction of in
Jerusalem, 12; sacrifice to
occur again in Jerusalem, 52;
Wilford Woodruff predicts

construction of in Jerusalem,
51; to be erected in Zion, 191

Ten Lost Tribes, information on,
63; must be gathered, 63; who
are they, 59

Time, as used by John the Revelator, 81; exact of Lord's coming
unimportant, 243; when will
the Lord come, 203

Times and seasons, sign of
changing of, 124

Trees, destroyed by angel with
trumpet, 133

Tumults, that will occur to the
earth, 128

-U-

United Nations, votes to partition
Palestine, 48

USSR, destruction of predicted by
Isaiah, 49

-V-

Volcanos, a mountain burning
with fire seen by John the
Revelator, 134

-W-

War, battles of Gog and Magog,
234; Civil War beginning of in
latter-day, 158; during the
Little Season, 234; first
prophesies of, 11; four angels
describe last great to John the
Revelator, 137; and rumors of,
157

Water, angels with trumpets
plague, 134, 145; dinoflagellate as a plague on, 145; fresh
waters turn as to blood, 145;
plague as the blood of a dead
man, 144

Western Hemisphere, apostasy of
people of, 21; promised land

of tribe of Joseph, 24; remnant
of Joseph scattered to, 15
Wickedness, final destruction of
all, 237
Woman, described as the devil's
"mother of harlots," 99;
represents latter-day kingdom
of devil as seen by John the
Revelator, 97
Woodruff, Wilford, predicts Judah
will rebuild temple, 51
Wormwood, sign seen by John the
Revelator, 135; a bitter herb,
135
Worship, as used by John the
Revelator, 82

-Z-

Zion, established in Independence, Missouri, 67, 161; is
promised land, 41; name used
to identify many things, 182
Zion, city of, also called the New
Jerusalem, 186; role of in
Second Coming, 186; Sidney
Rigdon dedicates location of,
188; temple in, 191; where
established, 186

Scripture Index

Verse references marked (IV) are from the Inspired Version of the Bible. Verse references marked (JST) are from the Joseph Smith Translation from the King James version of the Bible.

Many individual verses are treated in this work in context of the chapter in which they reside and are therefore not specifically listed here. When researching a specific verse that is not contained in this index consider the chapter reference instead.

OLD TESTAMENT

Genesis

1:14	124
3	253n1
3:18	231
4:11–15	231
5:18–24	183
6:11	117
7:85 (IV)	60
9:11–16	175
10:1	60
10:2	60, 258n3
10:3–5	60
10:25	152
17:1	13, 23, 25
17:8	24
17:21	25
19:12–15	172
19:24	90, 152
19:28	255n2
32:28	25

Exodus

6:7–8	25
7:15–18	134
7:19	134, 257n7
7:20–21	134
8:2, 16, 18, 21	257n7
9:3, 9, 18	257n7
9:23	90, 257n7
10:14	257n7
10:22	146, 257n7
10:23	146
11:5	257n7
13:9	93
14:5	201
14:10–12	201
14:13	201
19:5	58, 162
19:6	162
24:17	150
29:45	250n1
40:34–35	141

Leviticus

2:13	169
13:42	144
26:12	250n1

Numbers

18:19	169

Deuteronomy

4:20	25
4:27	14
4:29–31	69
4:48	181
6:8	93
10:8	251n15
17:6	39
29:18	135
32:21	253n6

Joshua

10:11	161

Judges

5:1–5	254n1

2 Samuel

5:7	181
7:24	250n1

1 Kings

11:31	13
11:36	14
12:17	14
12:21–23	14
18:38	90

2 Kings

17:6	59
18:11–12	59
23:5	98

1 Chronicles

1:19	152
5:4	258n3

2 Chronicles

13:5	169

Nehemiah

1:9	61

Esther

2:5	59

Job

2:7	144
41:31	150

Psalms

21:8–10	256n2
44:4	56
50:4	241
72:4	253n7
77:18	128
122:1–9	57

Proverbs

11:4–8	256–7n6
22:6	218
23:7	222

Ecclesiastes

3:1–8	124
5:10	119

Isaiah

1:26–27	196
2:2	57, 100, 252n14
2:3	57, 100, 190, 196, 232, 252n14
2:4	232

2:5	5	19:20, 23–24	164
2:21	91	20–22	162
2:23	92	22:12	117
4:1–4	191, 197	22:13	28, 117
5:3–19	22	22:14	117
5:20	26, 91	23	162
5:24–25	253n5	24	253n21, 254n2
5:26	39	24:1	123, 128, 253n5
10:16–19	254n18	24:2	123, 170, 253n5
10:20–22	252n14	24:3–4	253n5
11:1	55	24:5	22, 26, 128, 253n5
11:6–9	231	24:6	127, 149, 253n5,
11:10	56		254n15, 256n2
11:11	68, 252n8, 252n14	24:7–9	253n5
11:12	39, 45	24:10	104, 253n5
11:13	57, 252n14	24:11–13	253n5
11:14–15	57	24:14–18	128, 253n5
11:16	64	24:19–20	128
13	162	24:21–22	224
13:2–4	252n14	24:23	255n5, 255n11
13:5	64	25–26	253n21, 254n2
13:6–9	200	26:19	240
13:10	174, 255n4, 255n10	27	253n21, 254n2
13:11–12	200	27:1	107
13:13	129	28:7	167, 168
13:14–18	253n5	28:8	168
13:19	71, 253n5	28:18	157
13:20–22	253n5	28:20	221
14	162	29	30
14:1–3	252n14	29:4–8	40, (IV) 40
14:12	74, 245	29:9–10	28, 40, (IV) 40
14:13	74–5, 237, 245	29:11–12	40, (IV.) 40, (JST) 40
14:14	74–5, 245	29:13	(IV) 40, (JST) 40, 42
14:15	74, 245	29:14	30, 33, (JST) 40, 42
14:16	74, 238, 245	29:15–16	(JST) 40
14:17–22	238, 253n5	29:17	(JST) 40, 50
14:23–32	253n5	29:18–19	(JST) 40
15–17	162	29:20	(JST) 40, 107, 256n5
18	42, 65, 68, 162	30:2–7	164
18:4–5	253n5	30:10	22
18:6	253n5, 254n6	30:18–25	252n14
19	162, 164	30:27	150

31	164	57:20–21	108
31:1–5	164	59:18	224
32:5–6	226, 232	60:1	33
33:17–24	252n14	60:2	26
33:20	191, 196	60:3	26
33:21–24	191	60:8	64
34:4	149, 173	60:9	50, 64
35:1–2	50, 231, 252n7	60:10–12	64
35:3–6	214	60:13	51
35:7	214, 231	60:18	197
35:8–9	64, 252n6	60:19–20	174, 197, 255n6
35:10	64, 68, 247, 252n6	60:21	197
40:1–2	51	62	252n14
40:4	129, 152	62:1–4	196
40:5	1, 211	62:5	49, 196, 253n4
40:9	48	62:6–7	49, 196
40:15–17	212	62:8–11	49
40:27–31	252n14	62:12	49, 196
43:1	58	63:1–3	213
43:5	252n14	64:1	129, 173
43:6	252n5, 252n14	65:1–16	253n5
43:7	252n14	65:17–18	152, 233
43:15	56, 58	65:19	232, 233
43:49	252n14	65:20	152, 230, 233
47:1	98	65:21–22	152, 232, 233
48:4–5	44	65: 23–25	152, 233
49:4–5	47	66:3–4	253n5
49:6	47, 60	66:8	181
49:7–11	47	66:15–16	253n5, 256n2
49:12	47, 252n5	66:17–18	253n5
49:13–16	47		
49:17–20, 22–25	48		
49:26	48, 49		
51:11	252n6		
51:18–20	54		
52:2–3	252n14		
52:6–7	252n14		
54:10	152		
54:15–17	252n21		
55	42		
55:3–4	252n24		
56:10–11	169		
57:3–13	108		

Jeremiah

1:5	217
3:17	252n15
3:18	64, 252n15
5:9	102
5:28	102
5:31	102
6:13	102
7:15–16	102
8:13	253n8
9:16	14

15:3	254n6
16:14–15	63, 65, 68, 70
16:16	65, 68, 70
23:3–4	252n15
23:5–6	252n24, 252n15
23:7	70, 252n24, 252n15
23:8	70, 252n5, 252n15, 252n24
23:17	28
23:21	11
28	11
30:3–8	252n21
30:9	55, 252n21
31	252n15
31:8	252n5
31:10–14	252n6
31:31–33	41, 251n13
31:34	251n13
32:37–44	252n15
37:5	164
37:7	164
50:4–6	252n15

Lamentations

3:25–26	123

Ezekiel

1	253n21
5:9–12	253n7
9	253n21
9:4–6	94
10	253n21
11:16–20	252n16
12:11–13	44
12:14–16	15, 44
13:13	160
14:11	250n1
16:49	118
20:34	68, 252n16
20:35–36	252n16
20:37	68, 252n16
20:38	252n16

21:31–32	256n6
28:13–19	74
33:12	165
34:11–19	252n16
34:23–24	55
36:16–33	252n16
36:34–35	50, 252n16
36:36–38	252n16
37:1–14	252n16
37:16–20	252n16
37:21	58, 252n16
37:22	252n16
37:24–28	252n24
38	253n21
38:1	251n16
38:2	235, 251n16
38:3–5	251n16
38:6	235, 251n16
38:7, 9, 13	251n16
38:15, 16	235
38:19	160, 161
38:20–21	160
38:22	160, 253n7
38:39	148
39:3, 6	235
39:8–10	55
39:17–20	254n6
40	51, 253n21
47:1	231
43:2	129, 231
43:3	231
45:4–8	57, 231
47:9–12	231

Daniel

11:1–30	203
11:31	12, 195, 203
11:32–34	203
11:35–45	204
12	205
12:1–4	204
12:6–7	23, 204

12:8–10	204
12:11	12, 204, (JST) 204
12:12–13	205
2	37, 42, 68
2:1	36
2:2	36, 98
2:3–9, 24	36
2:31–33	36
2:34–35	37
2:38, 41	36
2:42	101
2:43	36, 101
2:44	37
3:23–25	150
7	84, 101, 104, 253n21, 254n2
7:8	85
7:9	176
7:10	176, 177
7:11–14	176
7:22	177
8–9	253n21, 254n2
9:27	12, 13, 44
10–12	253n21, 254n2

Hosea

1:7	51
1:10–11	69
2:18–23	41, 253n4
3:4–5	252n24
6	208

Joel

1:19–20	253n7, 255n1
2:1	198
2:3	253n7
2:9	128
2:10	128, 173, 255n4, 255n9, 255n13
2:11	198
2:30	173
2:32	196, 252n18

3:1–8	52, 251n16
3:9	159, 251n16
3:10	159, 232, 251n16
3:11	159, 251n16
3:12–13	159, 251n16, 254n7
3:14	159, 251n16, 252n25, 254n7
3:15	251n16, 255n4, 255n13
3:16	173, 190, 251n16
3:17–19	251n16
3:20–21	196, 251n16

Amos

8:11–12	22
9:8–9	13
9:11–13	69
9:14–15	50, 69

Micah

2:12	252n17
3:6	26
4:2	190, 196
4:3–5	232
4:6–7	252n17
5:3	252n17
6:2	167
6:8	167

Nahum

1:3	107
1:5	254n15
1:10	256n2

Zephaniah

1:2–3	199, 253n7
1:4–18	199
2:8	199
3:8	200, 258n5
3:9	231, 258n5
3:10–13	258n5
3:14–20	252n18, 258n5

3:21	252n18

Zechariah

1:16	51
2:6	64
2:8	15
2:12	49
4:11–14	54
6:13–15	51
8:1–3	197
8:4–6	197, 252n18
8:7	51, 197, 252n18
8:8	51, 197
8:9	51
8:12–13	252n18
8:23	51
9	253n21, 254n2
9:1–8	162, 164
9:9	56
10	253n21, 254n2
10:6	65, 251n7, 252n18
10:7–9	65, 252n18
10:10	65, 252n5, 252n18
10:11	65, 252n18
10:12	65, 251n7, 252n18
11	253n21, 254n2
12–14	253n21, 254n2, 258n5

12:2	15
12:3	15, 160
12:6	49, 252n24
12:7	252n24
12:8	56, 252n24
12:9	252n24
12:10	56
13:1–5	42
13:6	56
14:1–2	251n16
14:3	251n16, 252n21
14:4–5	56, 251n16
14:6–7	251n16
14:8	214, 251n16
14:9	214, 251n16, 252n26
14:10–11	251n16, 252n18
14:12	122, 251n16, 253n8
14:13–21	251n16

Malachi

3:1–2	254n18
3:3	251n15, 254n18
3:4–6	254n18
3:10	256n2
3:16	221
4:1	253n7, 254n18, 256n2
4:2–4	254n18
4:5–6	42, 254n18

NEW TESTAMENT

Matthew

1:26	(JST) 212
3:12	253n8
4:1–11	253n1
5:5	149
5:13	169
5:45	123
5:48	25
6:20	119
6:21	119, 121

6:24	120
7:1–5	257n8
9:15	253n4
13:24–30	41, 63, 225
13:37	41
13:38	41, 107
13:39–43	41
15:24	16
16:2–3	125
17:2	150
19:28	228

22:1–14	199
23	9, 205
23:27–28	167
23:37	12, 44
23:38	12
24	3, 204, 205
24:1	195
24:2	9, 12, 195
24:3	10, 195, 205
24:4	10, 11, 113, 212
24:5	11
24:6	11, 157
24:7	157
24:8	4, 10, 157
24:9–10	10
24:11	11
24:14	42
24:15	12, 44
24:16–23	199
24:24	11
24:27	212
24:29	211
24:30	211, 212
24:31	65, 239
24:32–33	114
24:35	231, 243
24:36	209
24:37	115
24:38	115, 202, 246
24:39	202
24:40–41	3
24:42	3, 210
24:43–44	210
24:45	116
24:48	116, 203
24:48	210
24:49–51	116, 210
25:1	165, 247, 253n4
25:2–13	165, 247
25:34–46	224
27:45	146
28:19	10, 16, 172
28:20	16, 172

Mark

1:12–13	253n1
2:1–12	257n8
12:42–44	221
13:2	12
13:8	128
13:12	122
13:19–20	123
13:24–26	174
13:28–29	114
13:32	209
16:15	16
16:16	16, 25

Luke

1:5	249n12
2:36	249n12
3:37	183
4:1–13	253n1
12:16–19	118
12:20	118, 119
13:1–5	219
16:20	144
17:20	205
17:28–29	116
19	12
19:41	12
19:43	12
21:6	12
21:9	160
21:10	161
21:11	128, 174
21:24	23, 30
21:25	161
21:26	121, 174
21:29–30	114
21:31	5, 114
21:34–36	120
22:30	228
24:47	16

John

3:29	253n4
5:1–14	257n8
5:22	216
8:4–11	257n8
8:12	147
9	219
9:1–3	219
12:14–15	56
15:20	11
16:2	10
17:12	227
19:37	56

Acts

1:9–11	203
1:21	227
1:23	21, 227
1:24–26	21
2:19	173, 255n4, 255n7
2:20	255n4
2:41	16
3:19–21	37
3:21	17
5:36	249n3
8:9	249n3
10	17
12:2	18
12:21–24	157
13:38–39	18
18:6	17
21:38	249n3

Romans

8:14–17	26
9:4	250n1
11:16–24	69
11:25	30, 69
11:26	69
13:14	121

1 Corinthians

4:5	226
11:19–22	18
15:5–8	21
15:20–21	239
15:22	238, 239
15:23–26, 28	239

2 Corinthians

5:10	241
11:14–15	73

Galatians

2:2	18
2:16	18
2:21	18
4:4–7	26
5:1	18

Ephesians

1:10	35
2:12	162
2:20	21
4:11–12	16

Philippians

3:5	249n12
3:8–9	18

Colossians

2:8	79

1 Thessalonians

4:16–18	206
5:1–2	206

2 Thessalonians

1:7–8	254n18

2:1	37, 195, 206
2:2	27, 37, 195, 206
2:3	27, 37, 83, 195, 206
2:4	83, 92
2:5–8	83
2:9–10	17, 83, 91
2:11	17, 83
2:12	91
3:5	210
3:11	206

1 Timothy

| 6:9–10 | 114 |
| 6:20 | 79, 125 |

2 Timothy

2:18	18
3:1–7	79
4:3–4	20, 113

Hebrews

| 11:5 | 183 |
| 12:22 | 252n27 |

James

| 2:26 | 222 |

1 Peter

1:13	179
2:9	162
3:18–19	225
3:20	224, 225

2 Peter

1:10	220
1:19	220
3:3–4	202
3:9	203
3:10	149, 203

| 3:11–12 | 149 |

1 John

| 3:20 | 229 |

Jude

| 1:6 | 241 |
| 1:14–15 | 183, 225 |

Revelation

1:7	56, 212
1:15	129
2	87
2:2, 9	18, 249n3
2:17	232
3	87
4:1	137
4:4	140
4:7	141
5:5	55
6:4	158
6:5–6	155
6:12	255n7
6:13	255n12
6:14	149, 152, 174
6:15	122
6:16	122, 256n6
7	254n2
7:1–3	129, 137
7:4	130, 170
7:5–17	130
8	130, 254n2
8:3–5	132
8:7	133
8:8–11	133, 144
8:12	133, 146, 255n13
8:13	133, 135
9	133, 135, 137, 254n2
9:1	75, 76, 136
9:2–3	76, 136
9:4	76, 93, 136, 170

9:5	76, 81, 93, 136	13:16	88, 220
9:6–11	76, 136	13:17	88, 94, 220
9:12–13	136	13:18	88, 220
9:14	130, 136	14	140, 254n2
9:15	136, 137	14:2	129
9:16	52, 136	14:4–5	172
9:17–19	136	14:6	37, 39
9:20–21	136, 138	14:6–7	208, 251n4
10	133, 254n2	14:8	71, 107
10:9–10	70	14:9–11	108
11	54, 56, 85, 141, 254n2	14:13–16	225
11:1–2	52, 138, 251n16	14:15–20	141
11:3	52, 55, 85, 138, 251n16	15	141, 254n2
11:4	52, 138, 251n16	15:2	109, 141
11:5–6	52, 55, 138, 251n16	15:3–5	141
11:7–8	52, 138, 251n16	16	14–1, 143, 147, 254n2
11:9–12	52, 55, 138, 251n16	16:2	107, 155
11:13	56, 139, 251n16	16:3	145, 231
11:14	139	16:4	231
11:15	139, 140	16:5	145, 231
11:17–18	139, 140	16:12–13	52
11:19	139, 140–1, 160, 174	16:14	52, 147
12	81, 140, 254n2	16:15	52
12:1	97	16:16	52, 258n5
12:3–4	75	16:17	148
12:5	37, 75, (JST) 101	16:18	56, 152, 160, 174
12:6	37, 41, 75, 101	16:19	160
12:7	75, (JST) 81, 236	16:20	152, 160
12:8–9	75	16:21	149, 160, 161
12:12–17	22	17	81, 95, 100, 103, 254n2
13	140, 147, 254n2	17:1	79, 97
13:1	79, 81, 83, (JST) 83, 138	17:4	97
13:2	79, 84, 138	17:5	74, 79, 97
13:3–4	79,138	17:6	79, 99, 245
13:5	85, 79, 138	17:7	100, 245
13:6	79, 85	17:8–9	100
13:7–8	79, 86	17:10–11	101
13:9	79, 87	17:12	97, 101
13:10	79, 87	17:13	97
13:11–12	88, 89	17:14	109
13:13	88	17:15	103
13:14	88, 90	17:16	104, 137
13:15	88	17:17	107

17:18	103	20:7–8	234, 236
18	104, 254n2	20:9–10	234, 236, 237
18:2	109	20:12	221
18:4, 7, 9–10	108	21	70, 203, 254n2
18:11	108, 147	21:1	152
18:12–13	108	21:2	185
18:14, 16–19	109	21:4	152, 231
18:20–21, 22	109	21:8	256n4
18:24	107	21:10–14	185
19	203, 253n4, 254n2	21:23	185, 255n6
19:11–16	213	21:25–27	185
19:17–18	254n6	22	203, 254n2
20	203, 254n2	22:3	231
20:1	108	22:5	185, 255n6
20:2–3	108, 232	22:14	181
		22:16	56

BOOK OF MORMON

1 Nephi

		22:7–8	38
		22:11–12	252n19
1:4	173	22:15	109, 254n15, 256n2
2:20	24	22:16–18	109
5:14	59	22:22	122
10:12	15	22:23	256n2
10:14	251n13	22:25	65
12:7–10	228		
13:6	79		
13:12–13, 16–19	27		
13:20–29, 34–35	39		
13:36–37	39, 182		
13:38–41	39		
14:10	79		
14:15	161		
15:14	65, 252n19		
15:16	64		
15:20	48		
15:32–36	108		
19:11	255n2		
19:13–14	15, 251n7		
19:15–17	251n7		
22:4	252n8		

2 Nephi

3	38
3:12	39
6:11	251n13
6:14–15	252n26
10:7	251n7
10:8	251n7, 252n8
10:20	252n8
15:25	253n6
23:11	200
25:23	229
26:6	253n8
26:15–16	40
27:1	28

27:5	28
27:6–29	30, 40
27:30–35	30
28:8–9	103, 120
28:14	123
28:20	92, 103
28:21	92, 103, 182
28:22	103
28:29	39
29:1–2	40
29:3	39, 40
29:4–6	40
29:7	40, 54, 59, 252n8
29:12	54
29:13	54, 59, 63
30:1–2	25, 60
30:3	65
30:4	59, 65
30:5	65
30:6	65, 252n7
30:7	51
30:8	251n7
30:10–11	122
30:12–16	234
30:17	231, 234
30:18	234

Jacob

5	60
5:4–22, 25–28	61
5:29, 38–70	62
5:71–74	62, 173
5:75	63, 173
5:76–77	63

Enos

1:13–16	40

Words of Mormon

1:15	11

Mosiah

3:24–27	107, 241
12:6	160
16:2	107

Alma

1:29	257n2
9:16–17	65
9:28	224
10:3	14
11:44–45	238
40:16	225, 239
40:17–19	239
40:23	238
41:2–5	224

Helaman

5:23–24	150
6:17	257n2
12:1–2	257n2
13	159
13:20–21, 31–33	257n3
14	159
14:4	201
14:20	202
15	159
15:11–16	64

3 Nephi

1:5–6, 9	202
2:1	202
5:21–23	65
5:24–26	65, 252n19
8	21, 202
8:4	202
8:19	147
9–10	202
10:13	255n2
16:1–3	69
16:4	54, 69

16:7, 10	69
17:4	59, 63
20	65
20:13–14	24
20:22	190
20:28	28, 30
20:29	49, 57, 251n13
20:30–31	251n13
20:33	49
20:34	49, 57
20:35–46	57
21	41, 65
21:1–9	38
21:22–23	190, 252n7
21:24–25	252n7
21:26	59, 63, 64
22:12, 15–17	252n21
23:4	41
24:3	251n15
25:1	256n2
25:5–6	251n7
26:3	149, 174
29:8	51

4 Nephi

1:23	257n2
1:24, 26	21
1:38, 45	22

Mormon

1:18	257n3
3:19	228
5:12–15	40, 51, 65
5:23	149
5:24	28
7:1–10	65
8:14–15	41
8:21	190
8:26–28	40
8:29	255n2
8:29–31	40

Ether

13:3	182, 185
13:4	57, 185, 186
13:5–6	57, 186
13:5–8	57
13:9	57, 197
13:10	57, 182
13:11	57, 197, 251n7, 252n5
13:12	251n7

Moroni

7:17	73
10:27	40

DOCTRINE AND COVENANTS

1:2–3	111	6:28	39
1:4	172	6:33	224
1:9	107, 256n6	13	31, 41, 42
1:10	167, 222	13:1	52
1:11	172	18:26	69
1:35	158	19:3–12	237
2:1	251n7	20:6–12	251n4
3:20	252n7	27:13	173
4:3	173	28:9	186
5:19	154	29	155
6:7	94	29:3	253n8

29:7	66, 123, 231	43:29	209
29:8	66	43:32	241
29:9	127, 199, 253n8, 254n15	43:33	256n4
29:12	212, 227	45:12	185
29:13	128, 214, 240	45:24–25	35
29:14	121, 155, 255n4, 255n7, 255n12	45:26	35, 121, 157, 159, 203, 251n16
29:15	155, 173	45:27	35, 121, 251n16
29:16	121, 155, 161	45:28	30, 35
29:17	155, 256n6	45:29	35
29:18–20	122, 155	45:30	30, 35
29:21	107, 155, 253n8, 258n5	45:31	121, 154
		45:33	128
29:24	242	45:39	126
29:25	238, 242	45:40	113–4, 173, 253n7, 255n1
29:26	239		
29:28	256n4	45:41	115, 253n7, 255n1
29:29	75	45:42	115, 255n4, 255n7, 255n12
30:6	252n7		
32	64	45:43	115
33:3	172	45:44	115, 212
33:5	41	45:45	115, 258n6
33:17	165, 211	45:47	115
34:7	209, 212	45:48	115, 128, 252n25
34:8	161	45:49	115
34:9	255n4, 255n7, 255n12, 255n13	45:50	115, 125, 256n5
		45:51	115
35:4	251n7	45:52	57, 115
37:3	66	45:53	57
38:4	185	45:55	115
38:12	132	45:56	153, 165, 210
38:18–20	41	45:57	153, 165–6, 200, 211, 253n8
38:21	231		
38:29	159	45:58	153, 165
42:8	186	45:59	153, 165, 214
42:9	66, 186	45:63	158
42:35	186	45:64–65	67
42:36	187	45:66	67, 186, 187
42:58	25	45:67	186, 187
42:62	187	45:68	161
43:18	128, 173, 258n6	45:69	161, 187
43:26	256n6	45:70–71	187
43:28–30	173	48:5	41, 187

49:7	209	76:39	217
49:22	212	76:43	108, 217, 258n7
49:23	129, 211, 212, 258n6	76:44–46	108, 237, 217, 258n7
49:24	65		
50:5	5	76:47–49	108, 217, 258n7
52:1	187	76:51–70	240
52:2	41, 67, 187	76:107	254n7
52:3	67, 187	77	171
52:5	41	77:7	155, 158
52:42	41, 67, 187	77:8	130
52:43	187	77:11	171
56:20	153	77:14	70
57:1	41, 67, 188	82:3	170
57:2	41, 67, 162, 181, 188	84:2	41, 182, 188
57:3	41, 67, 162, 188, 191	84:3–4	188
58:16–18	228	84:31	251n15
58:26–29	166	84:98	232
58:57	188	84:99–102	215
59:2	153	84:118	128, 173
61:14	145, 231	85:9	221
61:15	145	86:1–7, 9	41
61:18–19	145	87:1–4	158, 159
61:39	3, 210	87:6	160, 190, 201, 255n2
63	150, 159	88:15–16	238
63:20	153	88:17–18	240
63:21	150	88:19–20	240, 241
63:32	107	88:21–28	240
63:33	121	88:81–82	25
63:34	121, 253n8, 254n15	88:87	128, 255n4, 255n8, 255n14
63:49	230, 240		
63:50–51	230	88:89	128
63:54	211, 256n4	88:90	128, 174
64:23	256n2	88:91	121
64:24	200, 253n8, 254n15, 256n2	88:92–93	211
		88:94	107, 253n8
64:30	182	88:95	132, 173
64:40	258n18	88:96–98	240
64:43	161	88:99–102	258n7
65:2	42	88:106	254n7
66:11	252n6	88:110	230, 235
68:11	111	88:111–112	234
75:19–22	229	88:113	234, 237
76:25–38	108, 217, 258n7	88:114	234, 236, 237

88:115–116	234, 237	115:18	68
90:8	69	116	176, 230
95:17	176	121:12	125
97:19	182	121:13–14	121
97:21	182	121:34–35	103
97:22	154, 200	121:36–39	168
97:25	182, 253n7	121:41–45	170
97:26	182, 253n7, 255n1	123:7	127
101:2	162	124:39	251n15
101:21	68	124:49–52	189
101:23	200, 253n8	124:58	251n7
101:24	152, 200, 253n7, 253n8	128:17, 19–21	251n7
		128:24	251n15
101:25	152, 200, 253n8	130:1	214
101:26–27	152, 231	130:9	241
101:28	152, 231, 232	130:10–11	232
101:29	152, 231	130:12–13	159
101:30	152, 226, 231	130:14	207
101:31	152, 226, 230, 240	130:15	207, 209
101: 32–34	152, 231	130:16–17	207
101:44–62	63	130:22	214
101:65	107	131:5–6	220
101:66	107, 253n8	133:3	201
103:4	162	133:7–8	65
105:9	68, 162	133:9	182
105:32	182	133:10–11	209
107	31	133:13	57
107:48	183	133:14	74
107:53–57	176	133:18	171, 173
107:72, 75	258n18	133:19	252n27
109:30	161	133:20	252n25, 252,27
109:39	68	133:21	231, 252n27
109:64	51	133:22	129, 148, 252n27
109:65	252n7	133:23	148, 152, 252n27
109:74	129	133:24	57, 148, 150, 152, 191, 197, 252n27
110:3	129		
110:11	45, 63, 65, 251n7	133:25	191, 214
110:12	41	133:26	63, 191
110:15	42	133:27–28	64, 191
112:24	253n5	133:29	191, 231
112:25–26	166, 253n5	133:30–31	191
113:1–2	55	133:32	64, 191
113:6	56, 251n7	133:33	64

133:35	51	133:49	42, 174, 214, 254n7, 255n5, 255n10
133:36	39, 251n4	133:50	42, 214, 254n7
133:37	39, 42	133:51	42, 200, 214, 254n7
133:38–39	42	133:52–55	42, 240
133:40	42, 152	133:56	42, 191, 225, 240
133:41	42, 150, 252n26, 254n18	133:57–62	42, 225
133:42	42, 252n26	133:63	42, 200, 25
133:43	42	133:64	42, 200, 225, 254n18
133:44	42, 152	133:65–67	42, 200, 225
133:45	42	133:68	42, 145, 200, 225
133:46–48	42, 214, 254n7	133:69–74	42, 200, 225
		136:10, 18	68
		137:2–3	150
		138	225

THE PEARL OF GREAT PRICE

Moses

1:12–24	253n1
1:39	13
4	253n1
4:4	75, 236
6:5–8	221
6:21	183
6:25–26	184
6:27	253n6
6:31–32	184
6:34	254n1
6:37–38	184
7:4, 13–14	184
7:18	182
7:19	181, 184
7:21	184
7:27	185
7:48	127, 128, 184
7:62	69, 190
7:65	203
7:66	122
7:67	184
8:12	60
8:17–30	172

Abraham

1:3–4	24
2:11	24, 25
3:11	217
3:22–23	75, 217
3:24	217
3:25	25, 216, 217
3:26	75, 217
3:27–28	217

Joseph Smith–Matthew

1:4	7
1:18	9
1:22	94, 124, 221
1:26	243
1:30	122
1:31	42, 253n5
1:33	255n4, 255n10, 255n12
1:36	174
1:37	70
1:39	124, 155

Joseph Smith–History

1	38, 251n7
1:15–17	77
1:30–36	39
1:37	39, 199, 256n2
1:38–39	39
1:40	39, 45
1:41–44	39
1:45	39, 155
1:46–54	39
1:72	41

Articles of Faith

1:3	229
1:10	64, 182, 186, 191, 230